COGNITIVE SCIENCE
FOUNDATIONS OF INSTRUCTION

COGNITIVE SCIENCE FOUNDATIONS OF INSTRUCTION

Edited by

Mitchell Rabinowitz
Fordham University

LAWRENCE ERLBAUM ASSOCIATES, PUBLISHERS
1993   Hillsdale, New Jersey   Hove and London

Lawrence Erlbaum Associates, Inc., Publishers
365 Broadway
Hillsdale, New Jersey 07642

Library of Congress Cataloging-in-Publication Data

Cognitive science foundations of instruction / edited by Mitchell
  Rabinowitz.
      p. cm.
    Includes bibliographical references and indexes.
    ISBN 0-8058-1279-2 (alk. paper)
    1. Learning, Psychology of. 2. Teaching. 3. Cognitive science.
  4. Educational psychology. I. Rabinowitz, Mitchell.
  LB1060.C65 1993
  370.15′23—dc20   92–39390
                                                             CIP

Books published by Lawrence Erlbaum Associates are printed on acid-free paper, and their
bindings are chosen for strength and durability.

Printed in the United States of America

10 9 8 7 6 5 4 3 2 1

Contents

Preface

Fordham University offers a wonderful educational opportunity that I have not experienced at any other university or college. This opportunity is referred to as an "Institute." Institutes are topical seminars that are offered as minicourses. They are open for enrollment to graduate students for course credit and are also open to the academic community or general public on an auditing basis. What makes Institutes different from the ordinary graduate courses, from the instructor's perspective, is that all revenues from the class (tuition, auditing fees) go into a budget that serves as an operating budget for the Institute. This budget is primarily used to bring in "experts" on a given topic to talk about their work. Of course, income from the Institute has to be able to cover the expenses (plus cover overhead costs to the University). However, the availability of an operating budget provides the instructor with an opportunity to develop an instructional context where students actually get to see, hear, and talk to the people they would normally only read about during the course.

Most of the chapters in this book were derived from the talks the authors presented at the Institute of Applied Cognition. The Institute was developed because, at Fordham, we were in the process of developing an "applied cognition" graduate program within the field of educational psychology. The purpose of the Institute was to present to students and others an overview of research that might be considered to be "applied cognition."

The chapters within this book present and discuss current research that makes the connection between cognitive theory and instructional application. Two general issues are addressed. The first set of chapters is oriented towards specifying the relation between cognitive theory and the actual development and evaluation of instruction. The second set deals with the questions involved in understanding and assessing cognitive skills.

The outstanding features of these chapters are that they all present an in-depth discussion of the theoretical issues underlying instructional decisions. Many of the chapters present specific implementations that provide examples of concrete applications of theory. In addition, the settings in which these examples are implemented span a broad range of instructional areas and environments illustrating the generality and transferability of the application of theory to practice. The chapters serve as a presentation of current research for those who are interested in staying current with the field. The chapters, however, are also written so that they can serve as an introduction to the type of research and the issues involved while attempting to apply cognitive theory to instructional issues and, consequently, are suitable for interested students.

Bringing this book together for publication required a lot of help from a number of individuals. I would like to thank Max Weiner, Tony Cancelli, and John Houtz for their advice and support while I was designing and running the Institute on Applied Cognition. Thanks also goes to Carolyn Hedley who encouraged me to take the talks and develop an edited book. I would also like to thank Albert Alford who worked with me to compile the two indexes. I would particularly like to thank Larry Erlbaum, who gave his time and advice, while I was working through issues regarding possible publishers. Thanks also goes to the staff at Lawrence Erlbaum Associates who made the process of putting together a book an easy and enjoyable one. Finally, I would like to thank RBW, ASM, and MDR, just because.

Mitchell Rabinowitz

List of Contributors

Stephen J. Ceci, Human Development and Family Services, Cornell University, Ithaca, NY 14853.

Daniel Cervone, Department of Psychology, University of Illinois at Chicago, Box 4348, Chicago, IL 60680.

The Cognition and Technology Group at Vanderbilt, John D. Bransford, Learning Technology Center, Box 45, Peabody College, Vanderbilt University, Nashville, TN 37203.

Arthur S. Elstein, Department of Medical Education, 808 South Wood Street, 9th floor, University of Illinois at Chicago, Chicago, IL 60612.

Gareth Gabrys, Learning Research and Development Center, University of Pittsburgh, 3939 O'Hara Street, Pittsburgh, PA 15260.

Arthur C. Graesser, Department of Psychology, Memphis State University, Memphis, TN 38152.

Robert R. Hoffman, Department of Psychology, Adelphi University, Garden City, NY 11530.

John Huber, Department of Psychology, Memphis State University, Memphis, TN 38152.

Gary A. Klein, Klein Associates, Inc., 582 E. Dayton-Yellow Springs Rd., Fairborn, OH 45324.

Alan Lesgold, Learning Research and Development Center, University of Pittsburgh, 3939 O'Hara Street, Pittsburgh, PA 15260.

Barbara Means, SRI International, 333 Ravenswood Ave., Menlo Park, CA 94025.

Natalie K. Person, Department of Psychology, Memphis State University, Memphis, TN 38152.

Mitchell Rabinowitz, Graduate School of Education, Fordham University, 113 W. 60th Street, New York, NY 10023.

William D. Rohwer, Jr., School of Education, University of California, Berkeley, CA 94720.

Anna I. Ruiz, Human Development and Family Services, Cornell University, Ithaca, NY 14853.

John W. Thomas, School of Education, University of California, Berkeley, CA 94720.

Arlene Weiner, Learning Research and Development Center, University of Pittsburgh, 3939 O'Hara Street, Pittsburgh, PA 15260.

1 Proficient Autonomous Learning: Problems and Prospects

John W. Thomas
William D. Rohwer, Jr.
University of California, Berkeley

Current portrayals of productive outcomes of learning often contrast sharply with actual outcomes of learning. Cognitive science approaches to education, for example, have described productive learning outcomes as consisting of knowledge structures, including embedded skills, that are organized around the central principles of a specific domain. These structures furnish experts in a domain with powerful resources for representing and solving a wide range of problems, whether classic or novel.

In contrast, descriptions of the capabilities of high school and college graduates portray students whose learning outcomes equip them, at best, to solve only stylized textbook problems (Schoenfeld, 1985). Confronted with problems cloaked in the garb of the real world, these students evidently lack the resources to frame the problems with reference to principled knowledge structures, and thus to solve them on their own. Their learning, then, has not resulted in the construction of productive knowledge structures.

In addition to identifying the character of productive outcomes of learning, cognitive scientists have also furnished analyses of the sources of dysfunctional learning outcomes. Schoenfeld, for example, has argued that the construction of powerful knowledge structures in the domain of mathematics requires the kind of learning that results from participation in courses that embody a culture of mathematical inquiry. In contrast to such minicultures of mathematical inquiry, Schoenfeld's observations revealed that actual mathematics courses embody instead a culture that induces students to believe that mathematics is useful in finding single right answers to stylized textbook problems, but not for mapping real-world problems into a system that offers powerful solutions. Similarly,

Bereiter (1990) described the "schoolwork module" that operates in secondary school settings. According to this module, responsibility for learning is vested in the teacher; the role of the student is to carry out assigned work. Bereiter (1990) stated: "Fully situated in the school environment, the schoolwork module tends to prevent the activation of modules adapted to larger contexts of learning and makes it likely that what is learned will be too closely tied to characteristics of the school environment to transfer beyond it" (p. 619).

These analyses suggest that the proper outcomes of learning are not only domain specific; they are course specific as well. The proposition is that learning outcomes associated with academic courses vary with the manner in which those courses are conducted as well as with the subject matter addressed. In our research we have undertaken to verify this proposition and related ones as well.

Recent research on studying reveals that an understanding of its character and effects requires attention to the concurrent influence of several factors. These factors include entering characteristics of students, the cognitive and self-management activities that students engage in while studying, the proximate aspects of the study task, including materials and directions, and the more distal aspects of the setting, including the nature of the criterion and other features of the course of instruction (Brown, Bransford, Ferrara, & Campione, 1983; Entwistle, 1987; Thomas & Rohwer, 1986).

Studying involves learning that is isolated, effortful, often ill defined, and largely under a learner's direction and control. Students engaged in academic studying must process the to-be-learned material on their own. Often, they must play the role of the teacher, selecting material to study, reminding themselves of the criterial task, developing integrative study aids, and providing rewards. Moreover, students are largely responsible for carrying out task management activities as well, allocating study time, initiating study sessions, monitoring progress, evaluating readiness, and so forth. For these reasons, we refer to academic studying as *autonomous learning,* to distinguish it from the kind of studying in which direction and control are largely vested in an instructor or supervisor.

In the four sections of this chapter we describe prospects and problems associated with the development of autonomous learning proficiency. First, we set forth heuristic models of the cognitive and noncognitive components that autonomous learning comprises. Second, we discuss some of the educational policies and practices that stand in the way of improving autonomous learning proficiency. Finally, we present a projection of the characteristics of courses that act to promote or impede students' engagement in autonomous learning and the development of autonomous learning proficiency.

COMPONENTS OF AUTONOMOUS LEARNING PROFICIENCY

Two major approaches have been followed in attempting to define the components of proficiency in autonomous learning. When such learning is equated with studying, the traditional approach has been psychometric, through the use of factor analytic and correlational methods. A second means of establishing the component aspects of autonomous learning has been to compare examples of proficient and less than proficient studying, either through comparing the behaviors of experts and novices or through comparing the performance of trained and untrained students.

The psychometric approach has largely relied on the administration of questionnaires designed to assess students' styles of or approaches to learning (Biggs, 1978; Entwistle, 1988; Goldman & Warren, 1973; Pask, 1976; Schmeck & Grove, 1979), or more recently, their study strategies (Weinstein, Zimmerman, & Palmer, 1988) or study activities (Christopoulos, Rohwer, & Thomas, 1987). Particular study factors or scales are then defined and the relationship of these factors or scales to other personological variables or to outcome measures are examined. The strength of this approach is its potential for revealing relationships among a wide variety of psychological constructs. Biggs and Entwistle, for example, described three kinds of students, each having distinct approaches to studying and motivational characteristics.

Unfortunately, the psychometric approach has not been entirely satisfactory for providing a foundation for a psychology of studying (Rohwer, 1984). Most of the inventories upon which these investigations are based have low subscale reliability, have not been validated as diagnostic tools, have been administered without reference to particular subject matter domains, contexts, or course demands, and have questionable validity, in part because they are easy to fake (Rohwer, 1984; Weinstein et al., 1988). In addition, these instruments have not yielded information on the developmental or hierarchical relationships among particular study activities.

The expert–novice approach has revealed that successful students seem to differ from their less successful peers on the basis of the number and nature of strategies they bring to bear on a task (Paris, Lipson, & Wixson, 1983) and on the basis of their facility at selecting and monitoring strategies in task-appropriate ways (Pressley, Borkowski, & O'Sullivan, 1985; Rigney, Munro, & Crook, 1979; Smith, 1967). Three general classes of study activities have been singled out as the hallmark of the successful or expert learner: selective allocation activities, generative integrative processing activities, and cognitive monitoring activities (Rohwer & Thomas, 1987).

Selective allocation activities include the ability to encode idea units of high structural importance in a text (Einstein, Morris, & Smith, 1985; Meyer, Brandt,

& Bluth, 1980), to ask appropriate questions (Bransford, Nitsch, & Franks, 1977), and to establish, in detective-like fashion, what has to be done to satisfy criterion requirements (Armbruster & Anderson, 1981; Bransford, Stein, Shelton, & Owings, 1981).

Engagement in generative processing activities during studying, which includes the transformation (Brooks & Dansereau, 1983), reorganization (Day, 1986), and elaboration (Mayer, 1987) of learning material, has been consistently associated with performance benefits in laboratory studies. Likewise, expert as opposed to novice learners tend to ask themselves questions concerning the significance of to-be-learned information (Brown et al., 1983), to relate new information to previous knowledge (Bransford et al., 1981), to engage in deep-level processing (Fransson, 1977), and to reorganize and recontextualize knowledge (Bransford et al., 1977).

Successful students are also distinguished by the extent to which they monitor during learning and problem solving. Successful students tend to monitor their comprehension (Bransford et al., 1981; Brown, Armbruster, & Baker, 1986; Markham, 1979), the state of their memory (Flavell & Wellman, 1977), the adequacy of their strategy selection (Brown, Campione, & Barclay, 1979; Brown, Campione, & Day, 1981), and the effectiveness of their memory-enhancement activities and other strategies (Bates, 1979; Pressley et al., 1985). In addition, evidence from both studies of experts and from an examination of successful versus unsuccessful training studies points to the importance of effort management activities, activities engaged in to control emotion, to plan and manage time, and to develop and maintain a positive emotional state for learning (Culler & Holahan, 1980; Dansereau, 1985; Glaser, in press; Goldman & Warren, 1973; Paris et al., 1983).

These expert–novice investigations have served to establish the endpoints of the study-ability spectrum and have provided valuable clues to the progression from one end to the other. Needed now are models that specify the levels that intervene between the extremes. Such specification of progressive developmental levels is necessary for the accurate assessment of the study abilities of students who are in transit from novice to expert—the vast majority of students—and for understanding how they make this transition. Hierarchical conceptions have been used in other problem areas to explicate similar issues (e.g., the Structure of Learning Outcomes [SOLO] taxonomy to account for degrees of comprehension, Biggs & Collis, 1982; levels of text processing, Svensson, 1977; and levels of approaches to text, Marton & Saljo, 1984).

Extant approaches to the classification of and research on study activities, as well as our own experience in the measurement of study activities, has led us to distinguish two general classes of study activities, each of which is hypothesized to consist of progressive developmental levels. The first of these classes subsumes the cognitive activities students engage in during learning. The second subsumes the effort management activities that students follow in controlling the onset, duration, maintenance, and intensity of their cognitive activities. In addition, we recognize that the coordination of activities in these two general classes may entail overall executive planning and control functions, perhaps including provision for the role of metacognitive knowledge. For present purposes, however, delineation and assessment of these executive functions is premature. Thus, we have developed, for each of the general classes of study activities, a model of its constituents and of the relationships among these constituents.

Cognitive Study Activities

The model of cognitive activities, shown schematically in Fig. 1.1, includes four principal levels of cognitive processing: Basic Encoding activities, Selection activities, Integration activities, and Extension activities. Further, each of these four levels consists of two kinds of activities: monitoring activities and information-processing activities. Monitoring activities serve to manage and

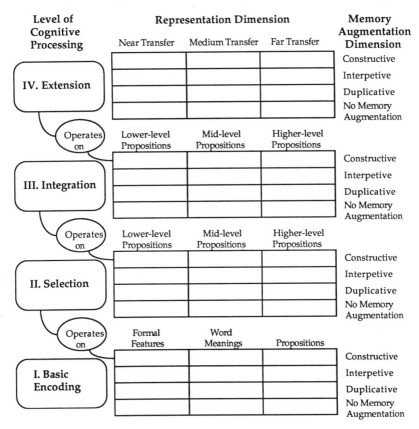

FIG. 1.1.   Hierarchy of cognitive study activities.

evaluate the conduct of the information processing that occurs during learning and have been described as central to the development of proficiency at encoding, selection, and higher level processing activities (Brown et al., 1983; Pressley & Ghatala, 1990).

The four processing levels are ordered hierarchically in two senses. First, activities at a higher level presuppose and operate on the cognitive representations that result from activities carried out at the next lower level. For example, absent the output of Basic Encoding activities, there would be no representations on which Selection activities could operate. Whereas the primacy of the Basic Encoding level seems true by definition, the ordering of the rest of the hierarchy is hypothetical in that it requires empirical confirmation.

The second sense in which the levels are ordered hierarchically is developmental; that is, the older the students or the more expert the students, in the sense of being proficient at learning autonomously, the greater the likelihood they will engage in higher level activities. This developmental ordering stems from empirical evidence already available concerning each of the levels. It has been shown that older or more expert students are more likely than younger or less expert students to engage in (a) Basic Encoding activities that involve comprehension enhancement (e.g., Bransford et al., 1981; Franks et al., 1982), (b) Selection activities (e.g., Brown et al., 1983; Meyer, 1984), (c) Memory Augmentation activities (e.g., Brown & Campione, 1978; Rohwer, 1980), (c) Integration activities (e.g., Bransford et al., 1981), and (d) Extension activities (e.g., Mayer, 1987). We hypothesize, however, that this generalization will depend on the criterion task; that is, the hypothesized ordering, of activity level as a function of age, for example, may be manifest only when criterion performance tasks demand access to the kinds of representations that result from engagement in higher level activities.

In addition to the activities designated by the various levels of the hierarchy, each of the sublevels of monitoring activities are held to be related hierarchically as well. For example, engagement in Selection Monitoring activities presupposes and operates on the results of engagement in Selection activities. Moreover, previous research indicates that the monitoring activities at each level are developmentally more advanced than the associated study activities themselves (e.g., Brown, Smiley, & Lawton, 1978).

As shown in Fig. 1.1, within the principal levels, two dimensions are distinguished. The first dimension on which the major processing levels can vary is in terms of the cognitive *representation* being processed. For example, integrative processing can be carried out at the level of words or phrases ("lower level propositions"), of simple propositions connecting concepts presented in adjacent sentences ("midlevel propositions"), or of complex themes and underlying principles that span paragraphs or content presentations ("high-level propositions"). Second, the levels can be ordered with respect to the presence and type of *Memory Augmentation* activity performed as an adjunct to processing. As memory augmentation activities are not obligatory, they may be absent or they may take one of three forms that presumably affect the retrievability of the material being processed: constructive processing, interpretive processing, or duplicative processing.

These within-level types, like the levels themselves, are held to be ordered, but this ordering is not necessarily hierarchical. Instead, these types are ordered with respect to representational richness and retrievability. Constructive memory augmentation processing of higher level propositions, for example, results in richer and more retrievable representations than duplicative processing of lower level propositions. Moreover, the most advanced kind of processing at the selection level (e.g., constructive) can produce, as indicated schematically in Fig. 1.1, richer and more retrievable representations, in principle, than the least advanced kind of processing at the next higher level (e.g., integrative processing of lower level propositions).

In addition to being ordered with respect to representational richness, and the constructiveness of memory augmentation activities, the available evidence suggests that in at least some instances these within-level types may also be ordered developmentally. For example, as students mature and become more accomplished, they move from reproducing subsets of lower level information through the selection of higher level propositions. Moreover, they become more apt to paraphrase and transform such selections in the process (Brown et al., 1978; Meyer, 1984). Similarly, basic research on memory development has shown that across the period of adolescence students move increasingly away from duplicative memory augmentation activities and toward constructive ones and from a focus on lower level to higher level propositions (Brown, Campione, & Barclay, 1979; Rohwer, 1980).

Despite these forms of potential ordering among the various within-level types, the relative productivity of these types, according to the present guiding conceptualization, depends critically on the character of course features, especially the demand features of criterion performance tests. For example, consider a multiple-choice recognition test in which the target and distractor response alternatives differ only in terms of formal features (e.g., spelling). With reference to such a test, Encoding or Selection activities that emphasize formal features might well be more productive than the richer representations that would presumably result from more integrative activities applied to higher level propositions. Indeed, experimental research has shown that inducing students to construct connections between new information and prior knowledge diminishes their performance on items requiring the reproduction of factual information (Barnett, Di Vesta, & Rogozinski, 1981).

Thus, two general hypotheses stem from the present hierarchical cognitive model. First, with reference to the principal levels of the model, the hypothesis is that the higher the level of activities students engage in the higher will be their achievement, provided that the achievement criterion is sensitive to the representations produced by those activities. Second, with reference to activity and information types within levels, the hypothesis is that the greater the congruence between test demands and the character of the representations produced by the activities the higher the achievement.

Domain Specific Variations in Cognitive Study Activities. To this point the cognitive-processing model has been characterized as if it applies uniformly across subject matter domains. This characterization may well hold for the basic encoding and selection levels, for it is plausible that such activities would obtain across domains. Even within these levels, however, the objects represented mentally would vary from domain to domain. Whereas declarative propositions might form the bulk of mental representations in history, for example, procedural propositions might be expected to be more dominant in mathematics or the sciences. Similarly, domain to domain variations would be expected in the nature of the objects of integration and extension activities, as these forms of processing would result in structures of declarative knowledge in some domains and structures of problem-solving knowledge in others.

Effort Management Activities

In contrast to the Cognitive hierarchy, the activities identified in the Effort Management Hierarchy, depicted in Fig. 1.2, have as their focus the student's general level of functioning or the climate for learning these activities create, rather than the kind of information processing performed. This distinction between cognitive and effort-related activities is similar to that offered by Dansereau (1985) in his distinction between primary and support activities and that of Paris et al. (1983) in their distinction between "skill" and "will."

Four levels of the Effort Management Hierarchy are proposed: Effort Monitoring Activities, Self-regulation Activities, Effort Planning Activities, and Effort Evaluation Activities. Note that unlike the cognitive hierarchy, monitoring is both a basic class of activity, the prerequisite for self-management to occur, and the adjunct of more complex self-management activities. Whereas the principle underlying the cognitive hierarchy is presumed to be the nature, source, and richness of cognitive representations, the organizing principle associated with the effort management hierarchy is hypothesized to be self-knowledge of (a) the connection between effort and achievement, (b) sources of effort interference, and (c) the value of strategic activities aimed at controlling effort and reducing interference.

As shown in Fig. 1.2, within each level of the hierarchy, two dimensions are distinguished. The horizontal dimension describes types of effort management activities. Although there is expected to be considerable overlap among these types, we distinguish between management activities focused on: Concentration, Time, and Learning Effectiveness. Concentration Management activities can be

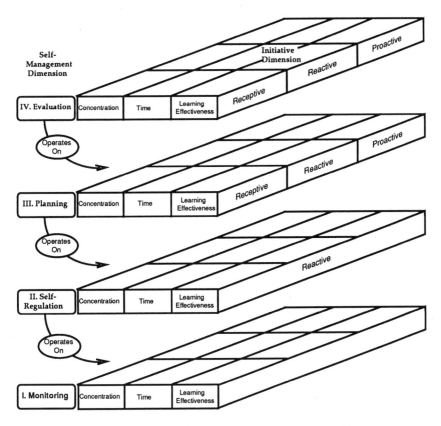

FIG. 1.2.   Hierarchy of effort-management study activities.

further divided into activities focused on Distraction Resistance and Diligence (getting started, persisting, returning to the task). Time Management activities can be subdivided into Time Allocation and Scheduling. Finally, managing Learning Effectiveness can be subdivided into considerations of Mastery (i.e., whether or not study activities have affected understanding, test readiness, or competence) and Test Relevance (i.e., the extent to which study activities have been focused on appropriate content or material).

The second dimension of the hierarchy refers to the source and degree of Initiative for engaging in a particular activity. Sources of initiative can involve following a procedure prescribed by others (receptive), responding to prompts from the environment or from others (reactive), or following an internal, self-initiated idea (proactive). It is anticipated that students who elect to set goals for themselves, prepare a study schedule, or prepare study aids exhibit more self-directed initiative than students whose study activities are largely prompted by external events.

The proposed levels of effort management activities are intended to form a hierarchy of activities ranging from awareness to more proficient autonomous learning performance characterized by planning and evaluation activities. These levels are hypothesized to be hierarchical in the senses of both development and proficiency. The hierarchy may be developmental in the sense that the capability to plan and schedule study time, for example, is expected to develop later than the capability to regulate study time during a study session that, in turn, is expected to require the development of an awareness of time and its relationship to learning. The hierarchy may also describe the development of learning proficiency, at least in some domains. Evidence for the existence of a hierarchy of effort management activities is, however, mostly speculative at this point (e.g., Zimmerman, 1990). Activities associated with the different levels of the effort management hierarchy follow.

Effort Monitoring Activities consist of three general types: self-assessment of the degree to which the student is engaged with and concentrated on the study task, the sufficiency of time devoted to studying, and the extent to which the engaged effort is productive, with respect to learning or task mastery. The self-knowledge that arises from such assessment provides the basis on which action can be taken to improve the regulation of concentration, time management, and learning effectiveness considerations in subsequent study episodes.

Self-regulation Strategies can be engaged in order to cope with the kinds of internal distractions to concentration that Covington (1986) referred to as negative affect and defensive posturing, or they can be employed in order to deal with potential or actual external distractions (cf. Corno, 1986; Dansereau, 1985). Self-regulatory time management strategies are those that are engaged in during a study episode in order to cope with estimations of time difficulties, principally, insufficient time available to complete study objectives, and can include modification of pace or of content coverage (Pressley & Ghatala, 1990). Self-regulation activities focused on learning effectiveness refer to sequences of monitoring and repair activities in which the student evaluates and alters other study activities in order to seek mastery of the subject matter. The term self-regulation is used here in a narrow sense (cf. Corno, 1986) to refer to the presence of "on-task" effort monitoring and correction.

The regulation of concentration, time, and learning effectiveness while studying can lead to more advanced knowledge concerning volitional, environmental, and strategic factors presumed to affect the productivity of future study episodes. This self-knowledge can lead, according to the hypotheses behind the hierarchy, to the development of Effort Planning Strategies: activities that students might engage in to plan, in advance, their effort on a single study task or across multiple tasks. According to Corno (1987), effort planners "direct the educational experience" to insure learning (p. 249). Effort-planning activities are conceptually distinct from self-regulation activities because their onset occurs before, sometimes well before, a study episode. These activities may resume again after a study episode ends in response to the results of monitoring the effectiveness of that episode. Effort-planning activities involve acting on one's knowledge of self and of the requirements of the task at hand in order to design and carry out an optimal study episode. Thus, effort-planning activities are hypothesized to be hierarchically distinct from self-regulation activities in that their acquisition is presumed to depend on the prior acquisition and use of self-regulation activities.

Finally, Effort Evaluation Activities assume prior acquisition of knowledge concerning the ingredients of a successful study plan. Students who engage in effort evaluation are those who have learned, from past study–test events, those concentration and time management activities and self-checking tactics that result in maximum test readiness and achievement. Although, it is conceivable that students might evaluate their plans with respect to concentration and time management (e.g., making judgments about the adequacy of a study environment or schedule), we expect that evaluation efforts will more typically be focused on learning effectiveness. Such evaluations are assumed to be a means by which students substitute one information-processing strategy for another.

Domain Specific Variations in Effort Management Activities.   Variations across domains in demands for different types and levels of effort management activities may take several forms. First, domains differ in the extent to which mastery of the subject matter depends on the completion of large-scale assignments and projects. Acquiring proficiency in computer programming, for example, seems to require the ability and disposition to put large blocks of time into the completion of coursework, to establish procedures for obtaining guidance, and to cooperate with others in order to gain access to materials and equipment. In other domains in which the essential tasks consist of little more than reading and listening, knowledge regarding the importance of time and concentrated effort might not develop as readily as it would in domains characterized by extended tasks. Second, domains differ to the extent that being knowledgeable in the domain requires the mastery of procedures and operational skills. Attaining competence in the domain of medicine or trial law, for example, would seem to place greater demands on the ability to evaluate one's progress in the mastery of skills (i.e., planning study–test episodes, monitoring, self-regulation, evaluation of learning effectiveness) than would be true in domains in which intellectual skills alone are the mark of expertise.

COURSE-SPECIFIC IMPEDIMENTS TO ENGAGEMENT IN AUTONOMOUS LEARNING

In the broadest sense, the capabilities depicted in Fig. 1.1 and 1.2 are presumed to develop naturally as human beings engage with one another in the activities that constitute their individual and social lives in communities of practice (cf. Lave, 1988). The specific contexts of these activities, however, may have features that either prompt or impede engagement in the autonomous learning activities that underlie these capabilities. Similarly, formal courses, whether in schools or workplaces, may have characteristics that elicit or inhibit students' autonomous learning capabilities. These features of courses may influence not only students' engagement in particular cognitive and effort management activities but the extent to which they continue to develop, master, and refine these activities as well.

Our attention to this relationship between features of courses and students' study activities and to conditions that limit students' development of proficiency at autonomous learning began with a survey of students' study activities that we conducted during the 1985–1986 school year (Thomas & Rohwer, 1987). In this investigation, we observed typical teaching episodes and teacher-led reviews in a number of junior high school, high school, and college social studies courses. We also collected all materials, including tests, associated with a particular marking period in these courses. Our principal goals for the investigation were to (a) describe students' study activities and their development across the period of adolescence, and (b) investigate certain hypotheses concerning the influence of course characteristics on students' study activities. With respect to this latter goal, we relied initially on what was known about the relationship between task conditions and learning activities from laboratory studies. Accordingly, we gave special attention to features such as information load, text difficulty, retention interval, and the nature of the criterion measure (e.g., Anderson & Armbruster, 1984; Brown, 1978; Cronbach & Snow, 1977; d'Ydewalle, Swerts, & DeCorte, 1983).

In the course of conducting this investigation, some of the interim data from classroom observations and analyses of course documents were quite surprising. Although previous surveys had led us to expect differences between courses (e.g., between secondary school and college) in the amount and difficulty of information students were called upon to process and retain, we were not prepared, at least in the early stages of the investigation, for the discontinuity we observed between secondary school and college courses nor did we anticipate the complexity of the relationships between course features and students' study activities. To try to make sense of this complexity, we identified three general classes of factors that appeared to prompt or inhibit students' engagement in autonomous learning activities.

First, courses can impose different *demands* on students' autonomous learning activities. Demands are standards that must be met, tasks that must be carried out, or criterion performance capabilities that must be demonstrated in order to complete a course successfully. For example, the requirement to compose a term paper places demands on students' time management activities that are absent in courses in which the sole requirement is to take notes on lectures and prepare for exams. Ideally, demands prompt students to engage in demand-responsive autonomous learning activities. Demands may also prompt students to modify or discard habitual strategies or to develop new strategies.

In our investigation of social science courses, analyses of course documents revealed significant increases in information load (e.g., the number of pages of assigned reading per day) and decreases in demand for verbatim information (the extent to which tests required the reproduction of information) between secondary school and college levels (Strage, Tyler, Rohwer, & Thomas, 1987). More important for our goals, we were able to link these demand differences to differences, between these levels, in the quality of students' study activities (Christopoulos et al., 1987). Increases in information load were accompanied by increased engagement in selective notetaking; decreases in demand for verbatim reproduction of information were accompanied by decreases in students' engagement in what we referred to as "duplicative processing" (e.g., repeating information to oneself over and over) in both routine studying and test preparation activities.

A second category of course features we referred to as *supports*. Supports are teacher- or test-provided aids that serve to prompt or sustain students' engagement in particular demand-responsive study activities. These aids can take the form of information, training, rewards, opportunity for practice, or psychological support. For example, whereas increasing students' workload is presumed to increase the demand placed on students' autonomous learning activities, training students to set proximate goals for completing this workload on a routine basis may serve to support students' engagement in demand-appropriate, effort management activities (Bandura & Schunk, 1981).

The effect of supports appears to be linked to that of demands. In our investigation of high school social studies courses, we found that the likelihood that students engage in higher level cognitive-processing activities while studying (noting relationships between ideas, extending concepts and principles to contexts outside the course) was higher in courses that included a larger number of integrative items or problem-solving exercises on unit tests and lower in courses in which the majority of test items tapped knowledge of facts and details. Yet, requiring integrative processing on test items was no guarantee that students would engage in appropriate integrative processing activities while studying. The tendency for integrative tests to prompt integrative study practices seemed to depend on the presence of instructor-provided supports such as study advice, practice questions, and integrative frameworks provided as handouts (Christopoulos et al., 1987; Thomas & Rohwer, in press). Similarly, results from other surveys indicate that the institution of explicit demands for integrative processing seems to affect students' autonomous learning activities in demand-responsive ways when combined with goal clarity and explicit encouragement of independent learning (Ramsden, Martin, & Bowden, 1989).

A third class of course characteristics, *compensations,* are course features that either reduce or eliminate demands. Some compensations provide students with the product of autonomous learning activities (e.g., handing out the test items prior to the test). Minimizing the demands of tests by providing students with an alternative path to achievement (e.g., makeup tests) or by obscuring individual performance (e.g., giving grades to groups vs. individuals) are other possible compensations. Some compensatory practices are quite similar to supports in that they tend to facilitate students' performance on criterion tasks (e.g., handing out copies of test questions vs. giving students nonidentical, model test questions). However, whereas supports prompt students to cope with demands on their own, compensations reduce the effect of demands, thus reducing the need for students to engage in autonomous learning activities.

In our investigation of social studies courses, we attempted to describe the links between the demand of unit testing and the kinds of cognitive-processing activities students engage in when preparing for these tests. To do so, we devised a classification system whereby we looked at the kind of capability that a test item seemed to call for (i.e., recognition vs. reproduction; comprehension vs. integration) as well as the relative similarity in treatment of an objective between the test and course documents. Because we had collected teacher handouts as well as texts for these courses, we also examined these handouts in search of additional coverage of particular objectives.

What we found, to our surprise, was that, in secondary-level courses, more often than not, (a) content presented on the test was invariably covered in the handouts as well as in the text, and (b) the treatment of a particular objective (item of information, definition, concept, principle) on the test was usually very similar to or identical to that in the handouts. Rather than adding to students' information load in any meaningful way, handouts served to reduce the demand on students' study activities. In most secondary-level courses we observed, in order for students to receive a passing grade on a unit test, it appeared to be unproductive for them to do more than memorize the information on teacher handouts. And to assist in this activity, all the teachers we surveyed at the secondary level also held in-class review sessions on the day or days just prior to the test. Most teachers reviewed their handouts; some were observed to review questions, or questions and answers, that subsequently appeared in verbatim form on the test (Strage, Tyler, Thomas, & Rohwer, 1987).

Thus, conditions that can limit students' engagement in autonomous learning activities include the presence of low demands, low supports, and compensatory practices. In addition, combinations of these conditions create further, sometimes highly subtle, limits on the development of autonomous learning proficiency. For example, when both demands and compensations are high, the course may appear to be quite rigorous. However, the effective result may be that demands are lowered covertly and that students are discouraged from engaging in productive study activities on their own. When demands are high and both compensations and supports are low, on the other hand, the presumed value of high demand for prompting students to engage in demand-responsive study activities may not hold for students who depend on supports to initiate or sustain effective study practices.

Impediments Associated with Demand Conditions

Demands set the tasks or the work of a course. Table 1.1 presents an abbreviated description of some of the limiting conditions that may be associated with the documents, coursework, testing practices, test items, and grading practices that define a course of instruction. Some of these demand features occupy a central position in recent conceptions of academic studying (Brown et al., 1983; Entwistle, 1987; Thomas & Rohwer, 1986).

Considerable research has focused on the relationship between features of texts and students' study practices. Specific features such as the unfamiliarity or abstractness of idea units, the presence of imbedded ambiguity, and the length of sentences have all been shown to affect reading activities (Singer & Donlan, 1989). However, in our analyses, readability differences between texts were relatively insignificant across the age range of adolescence. In contrast, it was more common for course documents to differ on the basis of whether important material could be identified easily, or whether it had to be distinguished from irrelevant material. Although this contrast can be observed between courses that assign different texts, it is more common between courses that assign primary versus secondary sources. Primary sources often require students to read scores of pages in order to identify and understand major points. Secondary sources often distill this same material into a few succinct paragraphs. Although the requisite research has not been conducted, we would expect courses using primary sources to place greater demands on students' selective processing activities than other courses (Thomas & Rohwer, in press). Likewise, texts that abbreviate, consolidate, and signal (e.g., highlighting) important points should prompt minimal levels of autonomous selective processing on the part of students.

The influence of information load or coursework load on students' study activities has been described by some investigators as debilitating for younger students (Brown, 1978) as well as high school (Entwistle, Kozecki, & Tait, 1989) and college-level students (Entwistle & Ramsden, 1983). In Entwistle and Ramsden's research, students who reported that their courses are characterized by a high versus a moderate amount of workload also reported engaging in study activities characterized by "superficial processing" versus "deep processing."

In contrast, a survey conducted with first-year, community college students enrolled in a remedial study skills program lends at least indirect evidence for the idea that a low degree of workload is associated with the failure, on the part of students, to develop the kinds of cognitive and effort management strategies that are at a premium in college settings (Losak, Schwartz, & Morris, 1982). In this survey, 77% of the remedial students regretted having taken high school courses that required little or no reading. Conditions of moderate workload might be expected to prompt students to engage in learning-enhancing autonomous learning activities, whereas very low or very high levels of workload might be expected to prompt either nonengagement or superficial engagement in learning activities.

TABLE 1.1
Course Characteristics Hypothesized to Impede the Use and
Development of Autonomous Learning Activities: Demand Conditions

Feature	Impeding Condition	Hypothesized Effect
Documents	• Ratio of important to unimportant course content	
	* High irrelevant content load	• Focus on low-level knowledge products
	* Low irrelevant content load	• Low demand on selective processing activities
Course Work	• Information load (e.g., pages of reading, volume of lectures)	
	* High load	• Superficial processing, stress, dilatory effort management activities
	* Low load	• Low demand on selection, integrative processing, effort management activities
	• Number of assignments per unit of instructional time	
	* High load	• Superficial processing, stress, dilatory effort management activities
	* Low load	• Low demand on time management activities
Testing Practices	• Tests cover few vs. many content categories	• Low demand on memory augmentation activities
	• Tests cover all topics vs. a selection of content topics	• Low demand on selective processing activities
Test Item Demands	• Test items require students to recognize vs. produce responses	• Low demand on interpretation and memory augmentation activities
	• Test items require low-level vs. high-level transformations	• Low demand on integrative processing activities
	• Test items tap low-level vs. high-level knowledge products	• Focus on facts/details vs. concepts and principles
	• Test item content is tied to the text vs. novel content	• Low demand on extensive processing
Grading Practices	• Importance of tests	
	* High importance	• Superficial processing, stress, dilatory effort mgt.
	* Low importance	• Low demand on all test preparation activities

16

Tests and testing practices are perhaps the most important source of course demands. Curriculum-imbedded tests, usually teacher-developed indices, are often the most important index of student achievement in schools. Their centrality in determining course grades seems to increase with grade level. Test scores become especially important in high school where acceptance into honors programs and then colleges and universities is contingent on grade point averages that are computed mainly from performance on these teacher-developed tests.

Moreover, tests play a major role in students' decisions about what and how to learn from a given course. Many students exert effort in a course in direct correspondence to what they know or believe about the instructors' criteria for dispensing grades. First, students are inclined to learn only that which they expect will be on the test (Laurillard, 1979; Miller & Parlett, 1974). Second, past performance determines in large measure students own sense of self-worth (Covington & Beery, 1976). This in turn sets limits on students' aspirations, achievement motivation, and disposition to engage in generative study activities in subsequent learning situations (Covington, 1984; Thomas, Iventosch, & Rohwer, 1987; Thomas & Warkentin, 1991).

Test items can vary in the kinds of cognitive transformations of course content that must be made in order to construct an answer. Surveys of teacher-developed tests administered at the secondary level reveal that the majority of items on these tests are written in a way that requires relatively low-level reproductive responses on the part of students. Fleming and Chambers (1983), in their survey of classroom tests, classified teacher-developed test items on the basis of a popular taxonomy of instructional objectives. They found that across all grades (elementary through high school), 80% of the items on teachers' tests were constructed to tap the lowest of the taxonomic categories, knowledge (of items, facts, or principles). At the high school level, the percentage of knowledge items on teachers' tests dropped to 69%. However, the percentage of application items was just 2% of all items at this level. Fleming and Chambers observed significant variation between disciplines, with most of the application items found in mathematics and the least in social studies courses. In social studies courses, 99% of the test items tapped knowledge-level capabilities.

Similarly, in our survey of American history courses, we collected the teacher-developed tests administered in a sample of junior high school, high school, and college courses. Items were classified on the basis of whether they called on students to reproduce or recognize items of information, interpret information, or integrate information (relate two or more ideas). A comparison of the items administered at the three levels of schooling revealed that the percentage of items that called on students to integrate information in constructing their answers did not increase by grade level from junior high (18%) to high school (14%), but the difference between the secondary and college levels was particularly remarkable. At the college level, fully 99% of the items on instructor-developed tests required the integration of ideas; only 1% of the items we collected required reproduction or comprehension of items of information. We hypothesized that this discontinuity in the level of processing required by test items might account for some of the differences we observed between these levels in students' engagement in the kinds of generative, selective processing activities displayed in Fig. 1.1 (Christopoulos et al., 1987), as well as for the difficulties college students experience in their ability to cope with the demands of college courses (Thomas & Rohwer, in press).

Tests also vary in item format. In the investigation conducted by Fleming and Chambers (1983), essay tests were found to account for less than 1% of items on the 342 tests reviewed. The most common type of item on these tests was the matching item. Teachers' test construction practices with respect to item format are presumed to affect students' expectations about item format, and these expectations, in turn, are presumed to influence the kinds of cognitive-processing activities students engage in when they study for tests in these courses. In a study by d'Ydewalle et al. (1983), students who prepared for a recall test allocated more study time, used more study time, and performed better than students who prepared for a recognition test, regardless of the test they received. In other studies, students who expect an essay versus a multiple-choice test were observed to take notes on ideas of higher structural importance (Rickards & Friedman, 1978) and to pay more attention to the relationship among ideas to be remembered (Connor, 1977). Yet, there are counterexamples to these findings. Researchers have failed to observe variations in students' study activities in response to information about the format of an upcoming test (e.g., Feldt, 1990; Hakstian, 1971). However, the available evidence suggests that, when the information about test format is specific or when students have the opportunity to assess the effectiveness of their studying given different information about the test (support conditions), the demand for extended production versus recognition responses has been found to prompt high-level cognitive-processing activities (Anderson & Armbruster, 1984; Pressley & Ghatala, 1990).

Finally, in a recent survey of students' study practices in high school biology courses, we found limited support for the influence of two additional demand factors on particular study activities (Bol & Thomas, 1991). In this study the disposition on the part of students to engage in memory augmentation activities in preparing for a unit test in their courses depended on two demand factors: the weight of the test ($r = .53$) and the number of content categories that the test covered ($r = .46$).

Impediments Associated with Support Conditions

Courses can fail to provide students with the models, rewards, training, and other supportive aids necessary to prompt and sustain effective autonomous learning. For some students and at some grade levels, these supports appear crucial. In their absence, variations in demand conditions may have little effect. For example, in the absence of feedback designed to demonstrate to students the connection among item types, particular study strategies, and achievement, variations in test format or item type may fail to prompt students to change their study practices (Pressley & Ghatala, 1990). Table 1.2 presents a selection of support provisions whose absence may impede students' engagement in demand-responsive study activities in the short run and their development of proficient autonomous learning strategies in the long run.

TABLE 1.2
Course Characteristics Hypothesized to Impede the Use and
Development of Autonomous Learning Activities: Support Features

Feature	Impeding Condition	Hypothesized Effect
Documents	• Lack of coherent structure	• Reduced engagement in integrative processing
	• Lack of imbedded models and organizers	• Reduced engagement in integrative, extensive processing
Course Work	• Minimal Practice Opportunities	• Reduced engagement in cognitive processing, all levels
	• Low accountability	• Reduced engagement in cognitive processing all levels, minimal effort management
	• Absence of routine performance events (e.g., quizzes)	• Reduced selective and integrative processing, memory augmentation
	• Absence of guidance/ training in processing strategies	• Low-level processing and memory augmentation activities

Teaching Practices	• Feedback
	  * Lack of feeback re: mastery
	  * Lack of feedback re: study activities
		• Minimal development re: strategy selection and proficiency
		• Minimal development re: strategy proficiency

Testing Practices	• Predictability/Clarity/ Correspondence between coursework and tests
	  * High predictability/tests and coursework are identical
	  * Low predictability/low clarity/capricious test construction practices
		
		• Minimal cognitive processing activities low effort expenditure
		• Superficial cognitive processing, stress, dilatory effort management activities

Grading Practices	• Goal structure * Competitive performance goals	 • Superficial cognitive processing, stress, dilatory effort management activities

The role of support features in fostering productive study practices is well known. Support features that have been shown to facilitate students' study practices include ("considerate") text structures (Armbruster & Anderson, 1981; Pressley, 1983), imbedded text aids (Mayer, 1984), cooperative and individualistic versus competitive classroom goal structures (Ames, 1984; Ames & Archer, 1987; Covington, 1984; Nicholls, 1983), and the provision of direct, explicit instruction in study strategies (Weinstein & Mayer, 1986). Less well appreciated perhaps are instances where the absence of supports leads to debilitating behavior on the part of students.

Consider the effect, in a course, of instructors' relative explicitness concerning the goals of learning and the nature of criterion performance expectations. On the one hand, supportive information in the form of advance knowledge about criterion test characteristics (Anderson & Armbruster, 1984) or specific statements of learning goals (La Porte & Nath, 1976; Muth, Glynn, Britton, & Graves, 1988) has been found to improve students' study practices and boost their subsequent achievement. In a study by Duckworth, Fielding, and Shaughnessey (1986), students were asked to rate the degree to which they knew what they were expected to be learning in the course. This measure, which Duckworth et al. called "clarity," correlated .40 with student ratings of effort and .61 with their ratings of efficacy in the course. Likewise, students ratings of "communication" (the extent to which they thought that teachers give advance notice about tests) correlated positively with effort and efficacy, .44 and .65, respectively.

However, instructors may withhold such information on the assumption that inexplicitness supports learning. Whether intended to "keep students on their toes," to encourage students to put equal effort into studying all course material, or to avoid "teaching to the test," some instructors may purposefully keep students in the dark about their tests or develop test items designed to surprise students. In his review of classroom tests developed by 9th- through 12th-grade teachers, Haertel (1986) found that, often, test development practices are capricious and tests are not well articulated with the curriculum: "Problems were included to see if students had done the required reading or had paid attention in class but not whether they were assimilating an organized body of knowledge" (p. 16). Evidence that courses with a low degree of correspondence between tests and coursework can impede the effectiveness of students' autonomous learning activities in these courses is provided in the study by Duckworth et al.. Students were asked to rate the degree to which tests in their courses cover what they expect them to cover. This measure referred to as "correspondence" correlated .46 with students' ratings of how thoroughly they studied for the course (referred to as "effort") and .57 with student ratings of their efficacy in the course.

Feedback is another instructional provision that may affect students' engagement in productive autonomous learning activities in a course. The effectiveness of feedback on learning and on subsequent test performance is generally acknowledged (Crooks, 1988; Kulhavy, 1977; Rudman et al., 1980) and has been suggested as a key ingredient in college-level courses that promote more effective study practices (Light, 1990). The effect of feedback on high school students' study practices and coursework effort is not as well known. There is some indication in the study by Duckworth et al. (1986) that the provision of feedback prompted students' engagement in productive study activities. Students were asked to rate the degree to which they agreed with the statement, "the results from the test let me see easily what I need to review to get a good grade," an index that correlated .29 with teachers' indications that they usually discuss test items with students following test events. Students' perceptions that their teacher provided feedback was found to correlate positively with students' ratings of effort expended in the course ($r = .30$) and with their ratings of efficacy in the course ($r = .53$). In our investigation of high school biology courses, the extensiveness of feedback given to students following test events was found to correlate positively with students' reported engagement in cue-seeking study activities ($r = .70$), with engagement in higher level effort management activities ($r = .50$), and with the construction of learning aids during test preparation ($r = .56$).

Although the importance of feedback is generally acknowledged by teachers (Thomas, Strage, Bol, & Warkentin, 1990), their routine feedback practices have been criticized for emphasizing social comparison rather than some measure of mastery (Crooks, 1988; McPartland, 1987) and for failing to praise student effort as opposed to normative performance (Natriello, 1987). More important perhaps, typical feedback practices do not often extend down to the level of student performance on individual concepts or principles. In the survey we conducted with high school biology teachers, we found that although the majority of these teachers collected and graded homework assignments only 37% returned homework with written comments. Similar results were obtained for quizzes; 80% of teachers graded quizzes, but only 25% provided written comments. Although giving grades on quizzes and homework may be informative with respect to a student's standing in the course, it does not help students to know how to alter their study practices in future study sessions.

Impediments Associated with Compensatory Conditions

Whereas the absence of supports may fail to encourage or sustain students' engagement in productive autonomous learning activities, the provision of compensations is presumed to discourage such activities. In a course in which performance on tests nominally determines students' standing, instructors can discourage students' engagement in autonomous learning activities by (a) providing students, in advance of test events, with one or more of the products of studying, (b) reducing the degree of intellectual challenge associated with the test, or

(c) providing alternative paths to achievement or otherwise reducing the importance of the test for obtaining a satisfactory grade in the course. Table 1.3 lists some of the compensatory practices that are hypothesized to impede the development of autonomous learning proficiency in academic contexts.

One of the most common compensatory practices, at least at the secondary level, is the provision, by the instructor, of handouts intended to help students prepare for unit tests. In a survey of 38 high school biology instructors (Thomas et al., 1990), 71% of these instructors reported that they distribute handouts to their students to help them prepare for tests in their courses. Overall, 53% reported that they hand out a list of terms, 63% provided study questions, 26% provided summaries of important information, and 26% reported reviewing actual test questions prior to the test. When asked if they "give students advice concerning what to study," 82% of the teachers surveyed answered in the affirmative. In addition, 50% of teachers reported that they reviewed test-related handouts in class on the day prior to the test.

Advance information about the content to be covered on the test can, of course, have a positive influence on students' study activity. Such information

TABLE 1.3
Course Characteristics Hypothesized to Impede
the Use and Development of Autonomous Learning Activities:
Compensatory Practices

Feature	Impeding Condition	Hypothesized Effect
Documents	• Provision of lists of important information in texts	• Low demand on selective processing activities
	• Presence of integrative summaries in texts	• Low demand on integrative processing activities
Teaching Practices	• Provision of lists of important information to aid test preparation	• Low demand on selective processing activities
	• Presence of integrative summaries to aid test preparation	• Low demand on integrative processing activities
	• Provision of (verbatim) test items	• Low demand on all levels of processing activities
Testing Practices	• Provision of "open-book" tests	• Low demand on memory augmentation activities
	• Setting the difficulty level of tests below that of practice material	• Low demand on test preparation review activities
Grading Practices	• Provision of "safety nets" to minimize failure (e.g., extra credit, makeup tests)	• Low demand on all classes of autonomous learning activities
	• Lack of accountability (e.g., grading for group work)	• Low demand on all classes of autonomous learning activities

tends to orient students to the goals of the course and can contribute to their feelings of confidence that time spent studying should have a positive payoff (Duckworth et al., 1986). Furthermore, handouts can serve an important modeling function. For example, the provision of adjunct questions and statements of objectives can help students select important information when studying, whereas providing skeletal outlines can help students generate connections between ideas (Mayer, 1984).

However, the kind of information found frequently on instructors' handouts constitutes something other than a guide for subsequent study efforts. Instead of providing orienting information (e.g., a list of content areas to be responsible for), or a model for processing (e.g., a chart for students to fill in), teachers often provide students with what would otherwise be the very products of their own studying. These products include a list of the specific items of information that will be on the test and interpretive and integrative summaries of the main ideas of the course. Such provisions significantly reduce the demand on the part of students to engage in selective and generative processing on their own. Furthermore, teachers often supplement these handouts with drill and practice sessions held on the day before the test, thus reducing the need for students to engage in memory augmentation activities on their own.

Although these provisions might be justified by instructors in that they probably improve student performance on the upcoming test, they may have some long-range unintended consequences. First, they may reduce the quality and quantity of the autonomous study activities that students engage in throughout the remainder of the course. Second, to the extent that the need to engage in autonomous selective processing, comprehension-enhancing, and integrative activities is lessened under compensatory conditions, the degree to which students come to be able to apply the to-be-learned material to content other than course content may also be lessened. Third, these provisions may make it less likely that students will acquire and develop personally-effective study strategies on their own, thus leading to their lack of preparedness for courses in which compensatory material is not provided.

A second type of compensatory practice sometimes associated with high school instructors' test review practices is the practice of developing or choosing test items that match, in verbatim fashion, information that has been reviewed or ones that have been practiced by students prior to the test. In our observations, this identity between test items and prior content occurs when test items are drawn from teachers' handouts or when the questions or answers that make up tests are specifically rehearsed beforehand. Either way, the demand posed by classroom tests would seem to be reduced substantially when the test questions constitute reproductions of items that students have experienced prior to the test. In Haertel's (1986) examination of tests developed by high school teachers, he concluded that "These tests sometimes fall short of measuring attainment of teachers' instructional objectives, often calling for little more than repetition of material presented in the textbook or in class or solution of problems almost exactly like those encountered during instruction" (pp. 4–5) . . . "Students were not asked to apply their knowledge or understanding and even items that appeared to call for analysis or supported augmentation proved in fact to require no more than reproduction of what had been said in class" (p. 16). Again, such practices, although they may boost student achievement on tests, should, we hypothesize, lower the probability that students will engage in high-level processing during test preparation activities, increase the probability that students will engage in duplicative processing activities, and make it less likely that students will be able to apply what they have learned in new contexts.

In our investigation of biology courses, we constructed and administered a criterion test of our own design to all participating students. All the items on the criterion test were based on course material covered by all instructors, no matter what text was used in a particular course. None of the items on our criterion test had been seen or practiced by students prior to the administration of the test. In comparing the performance of students across different courses, we measured the correlation between the number of test items on teacher-developed tests that were identical to items provided on handouts, on the one hand, and students' achievement on our experimenter-developed criterion test on the other hand. This correlation was found to be substantial and negative ($r = -.54$). Furthermore, the course feature defined as the percentage of test items drawn from handouts was also found to relate negatively to students' self-reported engagement in cue-seeking activities while preparing for a test ($r = -.63$). These results suggest that students enrolled in courses in which a relatively large percentage of test items are routinely drawn from teachers' handouts may be less likely to take initiative in study activities and end up less proficient in course content than students enrolled in courses in which instructors construct nonverbatim test items.

Instructors can also reduce the demand associated with classroom tests by providing alternative means for obtaining a passing grade. Sanford (1987) referred to these practices as "safety nets." In our investigation of high school biology courses, half the sample of 12 teachers allowed students to make up a failing grade by means of extracredit work, and one additional teacher allowed students who failed a test to take a makeup exam. Practices such as these seem to reduce the risk of student failure. But, they also may act to reduce the demand on students to expend effort and to be strategic in their study activities. In the previously mentioned investigation of high school biology courses, a strong negative correlation was obtained between the provision of extracredit and Autonomous Management scores ($r = -.77$); that is, in courses in which extracredit was offered as an alternative means of obtaining a passing grade, students tended to engage less frequently in self-directed learning activities such as preparing study materials and testing themselves when studying for a unit test than did students enrolled in courses without such "safety nets."

Other compensatory practices common at the high school level are described well by Sanford (1987). These practices include assignments of group work, peer assistance, balancing difficult or unfamiliar content on tests with overlearned familiar content, allowing students to revise products, providing less exacting grading standards for low-achieving students, grading on completion of tasks rather than performance, and using flexible grading systems that can be altered when the class does poorly on a particular test. An additional compensatory practice, observed in about half of the high school biology courses we surveyed, involves setting the relative difficulty of the tests below the average difficulty of practice items given out for homework or on quizzes.

The prevalence of compensatory practices may help to explain many anomalous findings from surveys and laboratory studies in which the spontaneous study activities of students have been found to be desultory or nonexistent. For example, surveys of high school students reveal that students fail to use certain strategies such as notetaking, found to be effective in laboratory settings (Annis & Annis, 1982; Christopoulos et al., 1987), and some laboratory studies report that students fail to detect inconsistencies while studying texts (Pressley & Ghatala, 1990) and underestimate their readiness for tests (Snyder & Pressley, 1989).

Although the requisite research has not yet been conducted to test it, one inference from these studies is that these same students who appear to be deficient are relatively successful in the courses they take; that is, they have relied successfully over the years of secondary schooling on serviceable, low-level cognitive processing (e.g., reading and rereading) and effort management (e.g., studying while watching television) strategies. Further, encoding, selection, integration, extension, and effort-planning difficulties that might have emerged in different curricular domains were anticipated and avoided by well-meaning instructors whose concern for avoiding student failure led to their use of compensatory practices. Because of such practices, students have no cause to abandon their serviceable strategies and little reason to improve their study activities. According to this analysis, progress in promoting autonomous learning proficiency on the part of secondary-level students will not be accomplished without difficulty. Many of the limitations that have been discussed have some apparent benefits for both students and teachers.

COURSE-SPECIFIC FACILITATORS OF ENGAGEMENT IN AUTONOMOUS LEARNING

Course characteristics expected to facilitate engagement in productive autonomous learning activities include combinations of the demands, supports, and compensations identified in the preceding section. Such facilitators include the use of more challenging tests, the provision of students with more opportunities to obtain feedback concerning the effectiveness of their study activities, and the reduction of compensatory practices. However, these reforms must be implemented with careful attention to interdependencies among demands and supports, the role of individual differences, the importance of performance expectations in different domains, and the need to minimize student failure. More specifically, the challenge for instructors and instructional designers is to construct courses that have the following characteristics.

Explicit Articulation of Demand Conditions and Support Practices. Making courses more challenging for the development of autonomous learning proficiency, and doing so successfully, will require (a) setting course demands at a level that constitutes a moderate degree of difficulty for students without exceeding the limits of students' abilities, (b) withdrawing compensations but doing so gradually and explicitly, and (c) establishing multiple support practices matched to course demands.

Provision of Authentic Self-Directed Learning Responsibilities and Tasks. Most secondary-level and many postsecondary courses do not specifically require students to engage extensively and meaningfully in autonomous learning activities. Reforming courses so that self-directed learning is an explicitly central part of the course may require the assignment of more independent projects and greater responsibility for managing learning over tasks and time. But, it is also expected to require instructors to relinquish some of the responsibility they now hold for administering the instructional process (Bereiter & Scardamalia, 1987; Brown, 1987). If students are to become better at learning on their own, they must not be left simply to read texts or to do exercises on their own. Students must be allowed to discover what is important in a domain, to define as well as solve problems, to construct rather than learn about relationships between concepts, to set not merely meet goals, to construct schedules not just follow them, and to learn to live with ambiguity.

Opportunities to Assess the Effectiveness of Existing Strategies and to Learn New Ones. Successful training studies stress the importance of combining training in cognitive-processing and effort management activities with the institution of supportive environments for learning, environments that allow learners to develop expertise on their own. Component features of these guided development environments include feedback, such that students come to be able to assess the effectiveness of learned strategies (Pressley & Ghatala, 1990; Zimmerman, 1990), instruction attuned to helping students to make connections between effort and efficacy (Carr & Borkowski, 1987), providing students with the opportunity to discuss their thinking with others (Brown & Palincsar, 1989; Paris & Newman, 1990), and apprenticeship arrangements whereby peers, tutors and students, or teachers and students are given the opportunity to observe others, take on aspects of skilled performance at their own rate, and get nonevaluative feedback on their performance. Over time in such environments, students move from dependence to independence and from external guidance to internalization of skills and knowledge (Brown & Palincsar, 1989).

The outcomes of learning depend on the kinds of learning in which students engage. In turn, the kinds of learning students engage in depend on features of the contexts in which their activity takes place. In contexts that provide and require autonomy, and that embody practices of importance to them, students will engage in forms of learning that result in productive outcomes. In contexts where control resides in instructors or supervisors, and where autonomy is neither required nor encouraged, students will engage in learning that results in diluted outcomes. Regrettably, the latter kind of context appears to be the norm in schools, and, perhaps, in many workplaces as well. The challenge, then, is to transform these contexts into ones that demand and support the kinds of learning that would justify the enormous amounts of time and effort invested there.

REFERENCES

Ames, C. (1984). Competitive, cooperative, and individualistic goal structures: A cognitive motivational analysis. In R. E. Ames & C. Ames (Eds.), *Motivation in education* (Vol. 1, pp. 177–208). New York: Academic Press.

Ames, C., & Archer, J. (1987, April). *Achievement goals in the classroom: Student learning strategies and motivation processes.* Paper presented at the annual meeting of the American Educational Research Association, Washington, DC.

Anderson, T. H., & Armbruster, B. B. (1984). Studying. In P. D. Pearson (Ed.), *Handbook of reading research* (pp. 657–680). New York: Longman.

Annis, L., & Annis, D. (1982). A normative study of students' preferred study techniques. *Reading World, 21,* 201–207.

Armbruster, B. B., & Anderson, T. H. (1981). Research synthesis on study skills. *Educational Leadership, 39,* 154–156.

Bandura, A., & Schunk, D. H. (1981). Cultivating competence, self-efficacy, and intrinsic interest through proximal self-motivation. *Journal of Personality and Social Psychology, 41,* 586–598.

Barnett, J. E., Di Vesta, F. J., & Rogozinski, J. T. (1981). What is learned in note taking. *Journal of Educational Psychology, 73,* 181–192.

Bates, J. A. (1979). Extrinsic reward and intrinsic motivation: A review with implications for the classroom. *Review of Educational Research, 49,* 557–576.

Bereiter, C. (1990). Aspects of an educational learning theory. *Review of Educational Research, 60,* 603–624.

Bereiter, C., & Scardamalia, M. (1987). Intentional learning as a goal of instruction. In L. B. Resnick (Ed.), *Knowing, learning, and instruction: Essays in honor of Robert Glaser* (pp. 361–392). Hillsdale, NJ: Lawrence Erlbaum Associates.

Biggs, J. B. (1978). Individual and group differences in study processes. *British Journal of Educational Psychology, 48,* 266–279.

Biggs, J. B., & Collis, K. F. (1982). *Evaluating the quality of school learning.* New York: Academic Press.

Bol, L., & Thomas, J. W. (1991, April). *The relationship between teachers' classroom practices and students' study activities in high-school biology courses.* Paper presented at the annual meeting of the American Educational Research Association, Chicago.

Bransford, J. D., Nitsch, K. E., & Franks, J. J. (1977). Schooling and the facilitation of knowing. In R. C. Anderson, R. J. Spiro, & W. E. Montague (Eds.), *Schooling and the acquisition of knowledge* (pp. 31–64). Hillsdale, NJ: Lawrence Erlbaum Associates.

Bransford, J. D., Stein, B. S., Shelton, T. S., & Owings, R. A. (1981). Cognition and adaptation: The importance of learning to learn. In J. H. Harvey (Ed.), *Cognition, behavior, and the environment* (pp. 93–110). Hillsdale, NJ: Lawrence Erlbaum Associates.

Brooks, L. W., & Dansereau, D. F. (1983). Effects of structural schema training and text organization on expository prose processing. *Journal of Educational Psychology, 75,* 811–820.

Brown, A. L. (1978). Knowing when, where, and how to remember: A problem of metacognition. In R. Glaser (Ed.), *Advances in instructional psychology* (Vol. I, pp. 77–165). Hillsdale, NJ: Lawrence Erlbaum Associates.

Brown, A. L. (1987). Metacognition, executive control, self-regulation, and other more mysterious mechanisms. In F. E. Weinert & R. H. Kluwe (Eds.), *Metacognition, motivation, and understanding* (pp. 65–116). Hillsdale, NJ: Lawrence Erlbaum Associates.

Brown, A. L., Armbruster, B. B., & Baker, B. B. (1986). The role of metacognition in reading and studying. In J. Orasanu (Ed.), *Reading comprehension: From research to practice* (pp. 49–75). Hillsdale, NJ: Lawrence Erlbaum Associates.

Brown, A. L., Bransford, J. D., Ferrara, R. A., & Campione, J. C. (1983). Learning, remembering, and understanding. In J. H. Flavell & E. H. Markman (Eds.), *Handbook of child psychology: Cognitive development* (Vol. 3, pp. 77–176). New York: Wiley.

Brown, A. L., & Campione, J. C. (1978). Memory strategies in learning: Training children to study strategically. In H. L. Pick, Jr., W. W. Leibowitz, J. E. Singer, A. Steinschneizler, & W. H. Stevenson (Eds.), *Psychology: From research to practice* (pp. 47–73). New York: Plenum Press.

Brown, A. L., Campione, J. C., & Barclay, C. R. (1979). Training self-checking routines for estimating test readiness: Generalizations from list learning to prose recall. *Child Development, 50,* 501–512.

Brown, A. L., Campione, J. C., & Day, J. D. (1981). Learning to learn: On training students to learn from text. *Educational Researcher, 10,* 14–21.

Brown, A. L., & Palincsar, A. S. (1989). Guided cooperative learning and individual knowledge acquisition. In L. B. Resnick (Ed.), *Knowing, learning, and instruction: Essays in honor of Robert Glaser* (pp. 393–451). Hillsdale, NJ: Lawrence Erlbaum Associates.

Brown, A. L., Smiley, S. S., & Lawton, S. W. C. (1978). The effects of experience on the selection of suitable retrieval cues for studying texts. *Child Development, 49,* 829–835.

Carr, M. M., & Borkowski, J. G. (1987, April). *Underachievement: The importance of attributional retraining of comprehension strategies.* Paper presented at the annual meeting of the American Educational Research Association, Washington, DC.

Christopoulos, J., Rohwer, W. D., Jr., & Thomas, J. W. (1987). Grade-level differences in students' study activities as a function of course characteristics. *Contemporary Educational Psychology, 12,* 303–323.

Connor, J. M. (1977). Effects of organization and expectancy on recall and recognition. *Memory and Cognition, 5,* 315–318.

Corno, L. (1986). The metacognitive control components of self-regulated learning. *Contemporary Educational Psychology, 11,* 333–346.

Corno, L. (1987). Teaching and self-regulated learning. In D. Berliner & B. Rosenshine (Eds.), *Talks to teachers* (pp. 249–266). New York: Random House.

Covington, M. V. (1984). The motive for self-worth. In R. Ames & C. Ames (Eds.), *Motivation in education, Vol. I: Student motivation* (pp. 78–113). New York: Academic Press.

Covington, M. V. (1986, April). *Reading, thinking, and the fear of failure.* Invited address given at the annual meeting of the American Educational Research Association, San Francisco.

Covington, M. V., & Beery, R. G. (1976). *Self-worth and school learning.* New York: Holt Rinehart & Winston.

Cronbach, L. J., & Snow, R. E. (1977). *Aptitudes and instructional methods.* New York: Irvington.

Crooks, T. J. (1988). The impact of classroom evaluation practices on students. *Review of Educational Research, 58,* 438–481.

Culler, R. E., & Holahan, C. J. (1980). Test anxiety and academic performance: The effects of study-related behaviors. *Journal of Educational Psychology, 72,* 16–20.

Dansereau, D. F. (1985). Learning strategy research. In J. W. Segal, S. F. Chipman, & R. Glaser (Eds.), *Thinking and learning skills* (pp. 209–240). Hillsdale, NJ: Lawrence Erlbaum Associates.

Day, J. D. (1986). Teaching summarization skills: Influence of student ability level and strategy difficulty. *Cognition and Instruction, 3,* 193–210.

Duckworth, K., Fielding, G., & Shaughnessey, J. (1986). *The relationship of high school teachers' class testing practices to students' feelings of efficacy and efforts to study.* Eugene, OR: Center for Educational Policy and Management, Oregon University.

d'Ydewalle, G., Swerts, A., & DeCorte, E. (1983). Study time and test performance as a function of test expectations. *Contemporary Educational Psychology, 8,* 55–67.

Einstein, G. O., Morris, J., & Smith, S. (1985). Note-taking, individual differences, and memory for lecture information. *Journal of Educational Psychology, 77,* 522–532.

Entwistle, N. J. (1987). *A model of the teaching learning process.* In J. T. E. Richardson, M. W. Eysenck, & D. Warren Piper (Eds.), *Student learning: Research in education and cognitive psychology* (pp. 13–28). London: S.R.H.E./Open University Press.

Entwistle, N. J. (1988). Motivational factors in students' approaches to learning. In R. R. Schmeck (Ed.), *Learning strategies and learning styles* (pp. 21–52). New York: Plenum Press.

Entwistle, N. J., Kozecki, B., & Tait, H. (1989). Perceptions of schools and teachers II: Relationships with motivation and approaches to learning. *British Journal of Educational Psychology, 59,* 340–350.

Entwistle, N. J., & Ramsden, P. (1983). *Understanding student learning.* London: Croom Helm.

Feldt, R. C. (1990). Test expectancy and performance on factual and higher-level questions. *Contemporary Educational Psychology, 15,* 212–233.

Flavell, J. H., & Wellman, H. M. (1977). Metamemory. In R. Kail, Jr., & J. Hagen (Eds.), *Perspectives on the development of memory and cognition* (pp. 3–33). Hillsdale, NJ: Lawrence Erlbaum Associates.

Fleming, M., & Chambers, B. (1983). *Teacher-made tests: Windows on the classroom.* San Francisco: Jossey-Bass.

Franks, J., Vye, N. J., Auble, P. M., Mezynski, K. J., Perfetto, G. A., Bransford, J. D., Stein, B. S., & Littlefield, J. (1982) Learning from explicit versus implicit texts. *Journal of Experimental Psychology, General, iii,* 414–422.

Fransson, A. (1977). On qualitative differences in learning: IV—Effects of intrinsic motivation and extrinsic test anxiety on process and outcome. *British Journal of Educational Psychology, 47,* 244–257.

Glaser, R. (in press). On the nature of expertise. In C. Schooler & W. Schaie (Eds.), *Cognitive functioning and social structure over the life course.* Norwood, NJ: Ablex.

Goldman, R., & Warren, R. (1973). Discriminant analysis of study strategies connected with college grade success in different major fields. *Journal of Educational Measurement, 10,* 39–47.

Haertel, E. (1986, April). *Choosing and using classroom tests: Teachers perspectives on assessment.* Paper presented at the annual meeting of the American Educational Research Association, San Francisco.

Hakstian, A. R. (1971). The effects of type of examination anticipated on test preparation and performance, *Journal of Educational Research, 64,* 319–324.

Kulhavy, R. W. (1977). Feedback in written instruction, *Review of Educational Research, 47,* 211–232.

La Porte, R. E., & Nath, R. (1976). Role of performance goals in prose learning. *Journal of Educational Psychology, 68,* 260–264.

Laurillard, D. (1979). The processes of student learning. *Higher Education, 8,* 395–410.

Lave, J. (1988). *Cognition in practice*. Cambridge: Cambridge University Press.

Light, R. J. (1990). *The Harvard Assessment Seminars: Explorations with student and faculty about teaching, learning, and student life: First report*. Cambridge, MA: Harvard Graduate School of Education.

Losak, J., Schwartz, M. I., & Morris, C. (1982). College students in remedial courses: Report on their high school preparation. *College Board Review, 125,* 21–22, 29–30.

Markham, E. M. (1979). Realizing that you don't understand: Elementary school children's awareness of inconsistencies. *Child Development, 50,* 643–655.

Marton, F., & Saljo, R. (1984). Approaches to learning. In F. Marton, D. Hounsell, & N. Entwistle (Eds.), *The experience of learning*. Edinburgh: Scottish Academic Press.

Mayer, R. E. (1984). Aids to text comprehension. *Educational Psychologist, 19,* 30–42.

Mayer, R. E. (1987). Instructional variables that influence cognitive processes during reading. In B. Britton & S. Glynn (Eds.), *Executive control processes in reading* (pp. 201–216). Hillsdale, NJ: Lawrence Erlbaum Associates.

McPartland, J. M. (1987, April). *Changing testing and grading practices to improve student motivation and teacher–student relationships: Designs for research to evaluate new ideas for departmental exams and progress grades*. Paper presented at the annual meeting of the American Educational Research Association, Washington, DC.

Meyer, B. J. F. (1984). Text dimensions and cognitive processing. In H. Mandl, N. L. Stein, & T. Trabasso (Eds.), *Learning and comprehension of text* (pp. 3–51). Hillsdale, NJ: Lawrence Erlbaum Associates.

Meyer, B. J. F., Brandt, D. N., & Bluth, G. J. (1980). Use of the top level structure in text: Key for reading comprehension of ninth-grade students. *Reading Research Quarterly, 16,* 72–103.

Miller, C. M. L., & Parlett, M. (1974). *Up to the mark: A study of the examination game*. London: Society for Research into Higher Education.

Muth, K. D., Glynn, S. M., Britton, B. K., & Graves, M. F. (1988). Thinking out loud while studying text: Rehearsing key ideas. *Journal of Educational Psychology, 80,* 315–318.

Natriello, G. (1987). The impact of evaluation processes on students. *Educational Psychologist, 22,* 15–175.

Nicholls, J. G. (1983). Conceptions of ability and achievement motivation: A theory and its implications for education. In S. G. Paris, G. M. Olson, & H. W. Stevenson (Eds.), *Learning and motivation in the classroom* (pp. 211–237). Hillsdale, NJ: Lawrence Erlbaum Associates.

Paris, S. G., Lipson, M. Y., & Wixson, K. K. (1983). Becoming a strategic reader. *Contemporary Educational Psychology, 8,* 293–316.

Paris, S. G., & Newman, R. S. (1990). Developmental aspects of self-regulated learning. *Educational Psychologist, 25,* 87–102.

Pask, G. (1976). Styles and strategies of learning. *British Journal of Educational Psychology, 46,* 128–148.

Pressley, M. (1983). Making meaningful materials easier to learn: Lessons from cognitive strategy research. In M. Pressley & J. R. Levin (Eds.), *Cognitive strategy research: Educational applications* (pp. 239–266). New York: Springer–Verlag.

Pressley, M., Borkowski, J. G., & O'Sullivan, J. (1985). Children's metamemory and the teaching of memory strategies. In D. L. Forrest-Pressley, G. E. MacKinnon, & T. G. Waller (Eds.), *Metacognition, cognition, and human performance: Theoretical perspectives* (Vol. 1, pp. 111–154). New York: Academic Press.

Pressley, M., & Ghatala, E. S. (1990). Self-regulated learning: Monitoring learning from text. *Educational Psychologist, 25,* 19–33.

Ramsden, P., Martin, E., & Bowden, J. (1989). School environment and sixth form pupils' approaches to learning. *British Journal of Educational Psychology, 59,* 129–142.

Rickards, J. P., & Friedman, F. (1978). The encoding versus the external storage hypothesis. *Journal of Educational Psychology, 3,* 136–143.

Rigney, J. W., Munro, A., & Crook, D. E. (1979). Teaching task-oriented selective reading: A learning strategy. In H. F. O'Neil, Jr. & C. D. Spielberger (Eds.), *Cognitive and affective learning strategies* (pp. 177–205). New York: Academic Press.

Rohwer, W. D., Jr. (1980). An elaborative conception of learner differences. In R. E. Snow, P. A. Federico, & W. E. Montague (Eds.), *Aptitude, learning and instruction: Cognitive process analyses of aptitude, learning and problem solving* (Vol. 1, pp. 23–46). Hillsdale, NJ: Lawrence Erlbaum Associates.

Rohwer, W. D., Jr. (1984). An invitation to a developmental psychology of studying. In F. J. Morrison, C. A. Lord, & D. P. Keating (Eds.), *Advances in applied developmental psychology* (Vol. 1, pp. 1–57). New York: Academic Press.

Rohwer, W. D., Jr., & Thomas, J. W. (1987). The role of mnemonic strategies in study effectiveness. In M. A. McDaniel & M. Pressley (Eds.), *Imaginal and mnemonic processes* (pp. 428–450). New York: Springer-Verlag.

Rudman, H. C., Kelly, J. L., Wanous, D. S., Mehrens, W. A., Clark, C. M., & Porter, A. C. (1980). *Integrating assessment with instruction*. East Lansing, MI: The Institute for Research on Teaching.

Sanford, J. P. (1987). Management of science tasks and effects on students' learning opportunities, *Journal of Research in Science Teaching, 24,* 249–265.

Schmeck, R. R., & Grove, E. (1979). Academic achievement and individual difference in learning processes. *Applied Psychological Measurement, 3,* 43–49.

Schoenfeld, A. H. (1985). Metacognitive and epistemological issues in mathematical understanding. In E. A. Silver (Ed.), *Teaching and learning in mathematical problem solving: Multiple research perspectives* (pp. 361–379). Hillsdale, NJ: Lawrence Erlbaum Associates.

Singer, H., & Donlan, D. (1989). *Reading and learning from text.* Hillsdale, NJ: Lawrence Erlbaum Associates.

Smith, H. K. (1967). The responses of good and poor readers when asked to read for different purposes. *Reading Research Quarterly, 3,* 53–84.

Snyder, B. L., & Pressley, M. (1989). *How do adult students use textbook restudy opportunities: They start at the beginning and reread.* Manuscript submitted for publication.

Strage, A., Tyler, A. B., Thomas, J. W., & Rohwer, W. D., Jr. (1987). An analytic framework for assessing distinctive course features within and across grade levels. *Contemporary Educational Psychology, 12,* 280–302.

Svensson, L. (1977). Symposium: Learning processes and strategies—III; On qualitative differences in learning: III—Study skills and learning. *British Journal of Educational Psychology, 47,* 233–243.

Thomas, J. W., Iventosch, L., & Rohwer, W. D., Jr. (1987). Relationships among student characteristics, study activities, and achievement as a function of course characteristics. *Contemporary Educational Psychology, 12,* 344–364.

Thomas, J. W., & Rohwer, W. D., Jr. (1986). Academic studying: The role of learning strategies. *Educational Psychologist, 21,* 19–41.

Thomas, J. W., & Rohwer, W. D., Jr. (1987). Grade-level and course-specific differences in academic studying: Summary. *Contemporary Educational Psychology, 12,* 381–385.

Thomas, J. W., & Rohwer, W. D., Jr. (in press). Studying across the life span. In S. R. Yussen & M. C. Smith (Eds.), *Reading across the life span.* New York: Springer-Verlag.

Thomas, J. W., Strage, A., Bol, L., & Warkentin, R. W. (1990, April). *Features of high school science courses expected to prompt students' study activities.* Paper presented at the annual meeting of the American Educational Research Association, Boston.

Thomas, J. W., & Warkentin, J. W. (1991, April). *The relationship between students' feelings of self-efficacy and their study activities and subsequent achievement in high-school biology courses.* Paper presented at the annual meeting of the American Educational Research Association, Chicago.

Weinstein, C. E., & Mayer, R. E. (1986). The teaching of learning strategies. In M. E. Wittrock (Ed.), *Handbook of research on teaching* (3rd ed., pp. 315–327). New York: MacMillan.

Weinstein, C. E., Zimmerman, S. A., & Palmer, D. R. (1988). Assessing learning strategies: The design and development of the LASSI. In C. E. Weinstein, E. T. Goetz, & P. A. Alexander (Eds.), *Learning and study strategies: Issues in assessment, instruction, and evaluation* (pp. 25–40). New York: Academic Press.

Zimmerman, B. J. (1990). Self-regulated learning and academic achievement: An overview. *Educational Psychologist, 25,* 3–17.

2 Toward Integrated Curricula: Possibilities From Anchored Instruction

The Cognition and Technology Group at Vanderbilt

During the past decade, educators have increasingly emphasized the importance of developing educational environments that enhance thinking and independent learning (e.g., Bransford, Goldman, & Vye, 1991; Chipman, Segal, & Glaser, 1985; Nickerson, 1988; Resnick, 1987; Resnick & Klopfer, 1989; Scardamalia & Bereiter, 1991; Segal, Chipman, & Glaser, 1985; Sternberg, 1986). One reason for educators' concern comes from existing data that suggest that students' abilities to think and reason are much less developed than is desirable. For example, after an extensive review of literature relevant to thinking, Nickerson (1988) concluded: "it is possible to finish 12 or 13 years of public education in the United States without developing much competence as a thinker" (p. 5).

It is important to note that the concern is not simply that some of our nation's students must learn to think more effectively. Educators such as Resnick (1987) argue that thinking must be a priority for all students, not only a select few. One of the reasons is dramatic changes in workplace requirements; it is no longer sufficient for an individual to learn one set of skills and expect to be able to exercise them for a lifetime. Today's employees must be problem solvers who help maintain quality and find ways to make the workplace more efficient, and they must be lifelong learners who are capable of adapting to change. Increasingly fast-paced changes in society also mean that thinking and learning abilities are important for effective citizenship and a promising life.

A number of curricula are being developed that are designed to promote thinking (e.g., Beck, in press; Resnick & Klopfer, 1989). A noteworthy feature of nearly all of them is that they involve the principle that "less is more." Rather

33

than spend the majority of their time attempting to memorize a wide variety of facts about a discipline, students are encouraged to explore specific areas of a discipline in depth. The good news of this approach is that opportunities to explore topics in depth can be more motivating to students and help them learn to think more deeply about issues (e.g., Bransford, Vye, Kinzer, & Risko, 1990; Collins, Hawkins, & Carver, 1991; CTGV, 1990). The bad news is that students cover less content at a time when the world's knowledge is accumulating at an increasingly fast pace. A major challenge for educators is to provide opportunities for sustained thinking about important areas while at the same time helping students acquire a range of skills and knowledge that will prepare them for lifelong learning. It is not a challenge that is easily met.

Our goal in this chapter is to discuss one component of a strategy for the design of curricula and instruction that can help us begin to meet the challenge of teaching thinking while also covering a sufficient range of skills and content. The component that we consider involves attempts to integrate instruction across different subject matters rather than to teach each one as a discrete entity. The importance of connecting instruction in one area to other curriculum areas and to events outside the classroom, and especially of helping students make connections among mathematics, science, and technology, has been emphasized by the National Council of Teachers of Mathematics (1989) and the American Association for the Advancement of Science (1989). Other educators have suggested models for integrating additional subject areas (e.g., Fogarty, 1991). Our goal in this chapter is to discuss some of the issues that arise when one attempts to create integrated curricula for schools.

Before beginning our discussion, it is important to identify an issue that we do not attempt to cover; namely, the identification of key "foundational concepts" that should be introduced in Grades K through 12 in order to facilitate knowledge integration and to prepare students for lifelong learning. A discussion of possible candidates for foundational concepts (e.g., systems theory, structure–function relationships, change) is clearly important but is beyond the scope of this chapter. Our goal is to consider some of the cognitive and educational benefits that one should attempt to ensure as the process of identifying foundational concepts takes place.

We begin our discussion by considering why it is valuable to help students integrate their knowledge across subject areas. We then note important barriers to such integration, the most notable being that this approach to instruction requires that teachers command an even larger knowledge base than is presently required. We end by discussing an approach to instruction, one that we call *anchored instruction* (CTGV, 1990), that has the potential to overcome these barriers, and we provide examples of the approach.

SOME REASONS FOR ENCOURAGING KNOWLEDGE INTEGRATION

Instructional Time

There are several arguments that provide a rationale for the design of curricula that can help students integrate their knowledge across subject areas. One involves the issue of making better use of the time available during school. During the past several years, members of our center have had the opportunity to meet with groups of mathematicians, scientists, geographers, historians, reading specialists, artists, musicians, and so forth. Invariably, each group would like more time for instruction, which means that less time is available to teach something else.

We remember a cartoon published several years ago (we think by Gary Trudeau) that illustrates the "time for instruction" dilemma. It begins by mentioning test scores that indicate that American students are terrible at geography. We then see a teacher who is extremely upset by this fact and vows to spend the rest of the year correcting this problem with his students. The cartoon ends with someone saying to the teacher: "But you're the mathematics teacher." Unless the teacher can integrate the teaching of mathematics with the teaching of geography, something is going to be lost.

A perusal of typical curriculum materials suggests that there is considerable room to provide students with opportunities to learn multiple areas of knowledge simultaneously. As an illustration, consider elementary and middle school instruction that involves mathematical word problems. Bransford, Sherwood, and Hasselbring (1988) noted that many word problems tend to involve arbitrary rather than real situations. An example might be a distance–rate–time problem involving some unknown person "Sam" who is going from point A to B in some type of vehicle. It is possible to create analogous distance–rate–time problems using real historic figures such as Mark Twain on a raft or steamboat; Charles Lindbergh or Amelia Erhardt and their respective airplanes, and so forth. Under these conditions, students could learn something about history and geography (including authentic numerical values) at the same time that they are learning about mathematics. Furthermore, they could learn to compare changes in speeds of travel as technology has advanced.

The opportunities to learn about multiple areas simultaneously are also made possible by combining areas such as engineering and science with mathematics, literature with mathematics and science, literature with history and geography, and so forth. We argue that these opportunities become richer when instruction is organized around more general themes or projects that serve as "anchors" (CTGV, 1990) for instruction. We say more about anchored instruction in our discussion of the Jasper series later on.

Inert Knowledge

A second more fundamental reason for integrating inquiry across subject areas relates to a problem discussed many years ago by Alfred Whitehead (1929) and re-emphasized in the past decade: *the inert knowledge problem*. Whitehead noted that students are often asked to learn individual concepts and procedures that they can remember when explicitly asked to do so—when given a multiple choice test, for example. Nevertheless, when asked to solve problems where these concepts and procedures would be useful, the students often fail to do so. Their knowledge remains inert.

A study by Gick and Holyoak (1980) provides an excellent illustration of the inert knowledge problem. They presented college students with the following passage about a general and a fortress:

> A general wishes to capture a fortress located in the center of a country. There are many roads radiating outward from the fortress. All have been mined so that while small groups of men can pass over the roads safely, a large force will detonate the mines. A full-scale direct attack is therefore impossible. The general's solution is to divide his army into small groups, send each group to the head of a different road, and have the groups converge simultaneously on the fortress. (p. 309)

Students memorized the information in the passage and were then asked to use it to solve the tumor problem that is illustrated next.

> You are a doctor faced with a patient who has a malignant tumor in his stomach. It is impossible to operate on the patient, but unless the tumor is destroyed the patient will die. There is a kind of ray that may be used to destroy the tumor. If the rays reach the tumor all at once and will sufficiently high intensity, the tumor will be destroyed. At lower intensities the rays are harmless to healthy tissue, but they will not affect the tumor either. What type of procedure might be used to destroy the tumor with the rays, and at the same time avoid destroying the healthy tissue? (p. 307–308)

Few college students were able to solve this problem if they were not provided with hints. In contrast, when students were asked to use the information in the fortress problem to solve the ray problem, over 90% were able to solve the problem. These students perceived the analogy between dividing the troops into small units and using a number of small-dose rays that each converge on the same point—the cancerous tissue. Each ray is therefore too weak to harm tissue except at the convergence point.

Note that the group in the Gick and Holyoak study that scored 90% on the ray problem was *explicitly informed* that information about the fortress was relevant. In most problem-solving situations we do not have the luxury of someone telling us which aspect of our knowledge is relevant. If we cannot access relevant knowledge spontaneously, it does us little good.

From the perspective of spontaneous access, the most interesting part of the Gick and Holyoak study involved a group of college students who also memorized the fortress story and were then presented with the ray problem. However, students in this group were not explicitly told to use the information about the fortress to solve the problem involving rays. For this group of students, the solution rate for the ray problem was only 20%. These results illustrate the value of using the "spontaneous access" methodology (see also Asch, 1969; Perfetto, Bransford, & Franks, 1983; Stein, Way, Benningsfield, & Hedgecough, 1986; Weisberg, DiCamillo, & Phillips, 1978). People may be able to retrieve and use knowledge when explicitly asked to do so and yet fail to spontaneously access it or use it. Under these conditions, the knowledge does them little good.[1]

Making Knowledge Less Inert Through Integrated Knowledge Structures. A number of laboratory and classroom-based experiments, plus new formulations of the nature of knowledge, have helped educators better understand how to avoid inert knowledge (e.g., Bransford et al., 1991; Bransford, Sherwood, Vye, & Rieser, 1986; Gick & Holyoak, 1980, 1983; Simon, 1980). Basically, students need a deeper understanding of why, how, and when various concepts and procedures are useful, and they need the kinds of experiences that will allow them to develop organized knowledge structures that are richly interconnected (e.g., Chi, Bassok, Lewis, & Glaser, 1989; Resnick & Klopfer, 1989). When one attempts to create such experiences for students, it becomes natural to use information from one domain to clarify another and vice versa.

Bransford (1979) provided an illustration of the arbitrariness of information that often leads to inert knowledge. He discusses a story taken from a fourth-grade reader that contained statements like the following: "The Indians of the Northwest Coast lived in slant-roofed houses built of cedar plank. . . . Some Californian Indian tribes lived in simple earth-covered or brush shelters. . . . The Plains Indians lived mainly teepees. . . ."

The story provided no information about why certain Indians chose certain houses; hence no attempt was made to relate the passage to geography and explain how the area where Indians lived related to the kinds of houses they built. Adults reading this story might be able to make these connections on their own, but children are likely to have difficulty doing so. Without this extra information, the relationships between particular Indian tribes and their houses seem arbitrary, and we should expect story comprehension and memory to suffer. In addition, without knowledge of the relationships between Indian lifestyles, habitat, and

---

[1]A common offshoot of the kind of instruction that produces inert knowledge is a dislike for the subject matter. Several of us have asked college freshmen in our class to describe their feelings about mathematics and to interview their friends about the same topic. Almost to a person, there was a strong dislike for mathematics—even by people who were getting As in courses such as calculus. A complaint voiced by nearly every student was the seeming irrelevancy of the subject matter for anything except a course grade. For example, they had no idea why one would ever need calculus.

geographic area, even students who memorized the arbitrary information would not be expected to be able to use this information to predict the structure of a new house given knowledge of how and where a new tribe lived.

There are many additional areas in which knowledge seems destined to remain inert because it is taught in isolation and hence seems arbitrary. Consider the following interview with a fifth-grade student:

Interviewer (I): Do you know anything about Geometry?
Student (S): Sure. We study it in school.
I: What do you do in Geometry?
S: Measure angles. We use a protractor.
I: Why do people measure angles?
S: To find out if they are obtuse or acute and stuff.
I: Why is it useful to know that?
S: To pass the fifth grade.

Other parts of the interview revealed that this student had learned many facts and procedures that are relevant to geometry. She knew the difference between acute and obtuse angles, could use a protractor, and had even memorized the definitions of a point and a line. However, we could find no evidence that she had the slightest idea about actual uses of geometry. We also believe that this is typical of most students (and even of adults).

Interviews that we have conducted suggest that geometry becomes more meaningful when students can see its usefulness for solving problems. One class of problems involves those faced by engineers who are trying to measure and map the environment; another involves navigators who are trying to locate a particular source by means of triangulation and must then navigate in order to find that source. Two of the adventures in our Jasper series focus on geometry; both are based on the assumption that an introduction to these areas of application can help students transform their impression of geometry from one involving the (sterile) measurement of triangles, circles, squares, and so forth (see the preceding interview with the fifth grader) into something that is more inspiring, namely, the powerful idea of using the "secrets" (invariant properties) of basic shapes (e.g., triangles, circles, squares) to measure, locate, and communicate about important aspects of the world.

Problems of inert knowledge also abound in science classes. A number of researchers have shown that students often begin instruction in physics with misconceptions about natural phenomenon that affect how they think about them (e.g., they intuitively adopt an Aristotelian rather than Newtonian perspective on the world). Ideally, science courses that introduce students to technically correct information should change the way they view their world. Unfortunately, this often does not happen. Students learn to deal with the technical definitions and formulas during their science courses, but they tend to leave these courses with the same misconceptions that they held when they started (e.g., see Clement,

1987; Minstrell, 1989). For example, Caramazza, McCloskey, and Green (1981) found that students who had taken a year of college-level physics courses and who were able to solve textbook problems ignored Newtonian principles of motion and gravity when asked to solve "real-world" versions of these same problems. When asked to sketch the path of the weight of a swinging pendulum whose string had been cut, students drew straight lines—ignoring the factor of gravity and reverting to a more naive intuition. In short, the technical knowledge acquired in their science classes remained inert. It had little effect on how the students thought about their world.

As in other disciplines, concepts in science become clearer when students can explore their implications in a variety of settings. We have been able to help students understand the usefulness of a concept such as density by creating video scenarios that involve objects that are supposedly pure gold (e.g., the golden idol in "Raiders of the Lost Ark" or a "golden statuette" used in one of our video stories; CTGV, in press a). How could one tell whether the objects are actually made of gold or made of something else? In order to solve such problems, students have to determine the mass of the objects and then the volume (Archimedes faced a similar challenge and solved it with his insight about displacement as a way to measure volume). Most high school students with whom we have worked had very little idea about how to approach these problems even though they had studied density and displacement in their science classes (another example of the inert knowledge problem). After being helped to understand the video scenarios, students report a much clearer idea of the importance of discoveries such as density and displacement. Prospective science teachers also needed help in this regard (CTGV, in press a).

The Importance of Exploring Shared Concepts and Methods of Inquiry

In addition to attempts to deal with the problem of limits on instructional time and the problem of inert knowledge, a third reason for integrating instruction is that it allows students to see how common concepts and methods of inquiry may be relevant to a number of areas. For example, important areas of study such as systems theory are relevant to a variety of disciplines, and the idea of quantifying information and of developing mathematical models in an effort to explain important phenomena is ubiquitous in science, business, engineering, and a host of other fields (e.g., Collins, 1991). In addition, the idea of using technology-based tools to create models of phenomena is becoming so commonplace in science and business environments that it provides a natural link between areas.

Technology is also a powerful tool for effective communication of ideas, which is important for all areas of inquiry. The availability of desktop multimedia programs makes it possible for students to publish text, animations, still pictures, moving video clips, and so forth. In short, principles of effective writing and communication (e.g., Hull, 1989) can be integrated in a variety of different content domains.

The Importance of Multiple Perspectives

A final reason for attempting to integrate curricula involves a special case of the inert knowledge problem that is particularly important—the idea of approaching problems from multiple perspectives. Elsewhere, we argue that the typical compartmentalization of courses tends to inhibit people's tendencies to apply knowledge from one area to other areas. The following quotation by Bransford, Sherwood, Hasselbring, Kinzer, and Williams (1990) refers to college students, but similar issues exist for students in K through 12:

> Currently, most students who take courses in the humanities, social science and physical science learn about each area as a separate entity. They rarely have the opportunity to apply ideas from one area to a problem that is also being addressed from the perspective of the other areas. Students therefore lack a common ground for comparing the effects of adopting different perspectives. Because of the specialized nature of their training, most college professors share a similar fate. (p. 134)

Adams (1979) provided an excellent illustration of the importance of adopting multiple perspectives. He wrote that, many years ago, a group of engineers was attempting to solve the "bruised tomato" problem. Mechanical pickers were needed to make tomatoes cheap enough to market but they were bruising the tomatoes. Something needed to be done.

Adams noted that a group of engineers began to work on the problem, which they defined as "designing a mechanical tomato picker that is less likely to bruise tomatoes." They considered a number of options such as putting padding on the picking arms of the mechanical devices and slowing them down somewhat. Although the engineers made some progress in their thinking, they spent a considerable amount of time without generating a truly breakthrough idea.

At some point some biologists entered the picture. They argued that the engineers had adopted the wrong implicit goal and suggested another one that would be more successful. Rather than attempt to "design a mechanical tomato picker that is less likely to bruise tomatoes," they attempted to "design a tomato that is less likely to be bruised." This eventually led to the development of a tomato that had thicker skin and hence was less likely to be bruised when picked and shipped.

One can also approach the tomato problem from the perspective of an ethicist. Making tomatoes with thicker skins enhances the ability to pick and ship them but also makes them considerably less tasty. (Compare the skins of store-bought tomatoes to those people grow in their own gardens.) At some point, the disadvantages of proposed solutions to problems begin to outweigh the advantages that they may have.

The Adams example involved different groups of people approaching a problem. Ideally, individuals learn to approach problems from multiple perspectives even though a great deal of everyday problem solving involves group activities. Without having a sense of the importance of multiple perspectives, individuals are less likely to choose to work in groups or to know the kinds of expertise that can help them solve the problems that they confront.

Elsewhere we discuss several studies that indicate that the tendency to approach problems from multiple perspectives can be enhanced by relating different ideas to a common "case" or set of examples (Bransford, Vye, Kinzer, & Risko, 1990; Michael, Klee, Bransford, & Warren, in press). For example, in a pilot study we used the bruised tomato problem as a transfer task for problem solving. We wanted to compare the effects of two different types of acquisition conditions on transfer to this problem.

One kind of acquisition condition used in the study was designed to mirror the kind of compartmentalized approach to teaching that we noted earlier. Students in this condition were provided with information that was potentially relevant to the tomato problem, but each type of information was presented in a different context. Thus, an engineer's idea of creating a better mechanical device to pick fruit was discussed in the context of apples; a geneticist's idea of creating a source of food that was less likely to be damaged while being gathered was discussed in the context of eggs; a transportation expert's idea of limiting damage to food by stacking it in specific ways while being shipped was discussed in the context of peaches; a horticulturalist's idea of creating fast-growing seeds that could be shipped directly to consumers who would grow them in window gardens was discussed in the context of carrots, and so on.

Students in the second group in the pilot study read the same set of passages prior to the transfer text. However, prior to reading, they were asked to think about the implications of each of the inventor's ideas for solving the problem of providing watermelons to consumers that were less likely to be damaged on the outside. The purpose of this condition was to mirror situations where a common problem or case is viewed from multiple points of view.

The results of the experiment showed large differences in the degree to which the two groups of students spontaneously generated a variety of possible solutions to the tomato problem. Those who had participated in the "multiple perspectives on the same problem" group, the second group, generated approximately twice as many unique perspectives on the tomato problem as did those in the first group. The results are not surprising on an intuitive level. Nevertheless, they have important implications for attempts to create curricula that develop flexible problem solvers who approach problems from multiple points of view.

BARRIERS TO INTEGRATED CURRICULA

Despite the potential advantages of knowledge integration, there are clear barriers to attempts to create integrated curricula. A major barrier is that it places an exceptionally heavy burden on teachers. It is very difficult to develop the content knowledge and pedagogical skills necessary to be an outstanding science teacher, mathematics teacher, writing teacher, history teacher, and so forth. To be able to teach all these areas well is extremely difficult. A related problem is that there is very little time during school hours for teachers to learn about new instructional ideas and to discuss these ideas with one another.

The goal of integrating curricula becomes especially difficult to achieve if one wants students to learn with understanding rather than simply to become familiar with surface features of an area. For example, it seems clear that scientific inquiry provides an excellent domain for helping students understand the value of mathematics as a tool for inquiry. Nevertheless, the mathematics educators whom we know also want students to learn to explore mathematics as a formal system as well as use it as a tool for exploring other issues (e.g., Schoenfeld, 1988, 1989). Many science teachers know how to use mathematics as a tool but do not deeply understand it as a formal system.

Related to the preceding point is the fact that good mathematics teachers help students develop deep conceptual understandings of mathematical concepts and procedures. The ability of a science teacher to use mathematics to solve a problem does not guarantee that he or she knows how to help students understand the mathematical knowledge at a conceptual level. As a simple example, imagine a sixth-grade science teacher who is using a cylinder of some unknown metal to teach about the concept of density and, in the process of calculating its volume, needs to teach the students to use the value pi. It is one thing to teach students that pi is approximately 3.1416; it is quite a different matter to help students understand that pi represents the ratio of circumference to diameter and constitutes an invariant property of all circles. Good mathematics teachers know how to develop conceptual (rather than mere procedural) understanding for a wide variety of concepts (e.g., NCTM, 1989). To develop the knowledge and skills needed to teach conceptually is no trivial matter.

The preceding argument can be made in reverse if one considers the possibility of having mathematics teachers teach science. It is easy to assume that people with strong backgrounds in mathematics can teach science effectively because much of it involves solutions to mathematical formulas and equations. However, there are extremely important differences between approaches that teach students to deal with formulas (e.g., $F = MA$) and those that help students understand at a conceptual level. We noted earlier that a number of researchers have shown that students often begin science instruction with misconceptions about natural phenomenon (e.g., they assume an Aristotelian rather than a Newtonian world), and that these misconceptions persist if students are taught to deal only with facts and formulas (e.g., see Clement, 1987; Minstrell, 1989). There are important gaps between "learning to do the calculations" and understanding the concepts that are being taught.

The fact that most school schedules allow only a limited amount of planning time for teachers makes it extremely difficult for them to increase their abilities to integrate math, science, and other subject matters—especially given the fast-paced changes in these areas. One solution to this problem might be to create classroom-based events that allow teachers to learn along with their students. In our discussion of teleconferencing that appears later, we discuss some possibilities for achieving this goal.

ANCHORED INSTRUCTION AS AN APPROACH TO INTEGRATIVE COLLABORATIVE INQUIRY

During the past several years, we have been exploring the potential of anchored instruction (CTGV, 1990) to overcome some of the barriers to knowledge integration discussed previously. One of the advantages of the anchored instruction approach is its potential to facilitate collaboration among specialists in a variety of domains. When this approach is augmented by telecommunications and teleconferencing, it provides a way for teachers to learn along with their students.

Common Grounds for Collaboration.   The anchored instruction approach that we have been developing involves the use of specially designed, inquiry-based video environments. They serve as "anchors" or "cases" that provide a common ground for exploration and collaboration. These environments are very different from the typical educational video that usually shows a lecture on videotape. Our environments depict real-life adventures that can be explored at many levels. They are designed to allow teachers as well as students to connect knowledge of mathematics, science, history, and literature by exploring the environments from different points of view.

The Need for Multidisciplinary Teams

The video environments and the materials and activities to accompany them are being developed by our Learning Technology Center at Vanderbilt. Our center is multidisciplinary and includes specialists in cognitive science (including cognitive development), education, mathematics, the sciences, and computer and video design. In effect, our center is designed to provide the kinds of collaborative efforts that seem necessary in order to keep instruction from falling into the same disciplinary boxes that have existed in the past.

One of the advantages of our multidisciplinary group is that many people who work on a project are not necessarily experts in the area. Thus, nonscientists and scientists work together, nonmathematicians and mathematicians work together. The experts in each area play a crucial role, of course, but they also have a disadvantage. They are often so close to their subject matter that they have lost their intuitions about what is clear and unclear to novices. Our team approach helps us find the kinds of examples and experiences that make areas of inquiry make sense.

Our center also works very closely with teachers and their students. One of our projects involves fifth- and sixth-grade classrooms in nine different states (Pellegrino et al., 1991). This is providing us with a great deal of valuable information that comes from formal evaluations of students' problem solving, from teacher's insights about ways to do things better, and from a deeper understanding of the constraints on teachers and students that affect what they do (e.g., CTGV, in press c). The need to "cover the existing curriculum" and to worry about scores on standardized tests are two examples of constraints. The lack of time available during school hours for planning new lessons is another important constraint.

Theoretical Rationale

As noted earlier, the videodisc environments that we have created are designed to allow students and teachers to experience the kinds of problems and opportunities that experts in various areas encounter. Theorists such as Dewey (1933), Schwab (1960), and Hanson (1970) emphasized that experts in an area have been immersed in phenomena and are familiar with how they have been thinking about them. When introduced to new theories, concepts, and principles that are relevant to their areas of interest, the experts can experience the changes in their own thinking that these ideas afford. For novices, however, the introduction of concepts and theories often seems like the mere introduction of new facts of mechanical procedures to be memorized. Because the novices have not been immersed in the phenomena being investigated, they are unable to experience the effects of the new information on their own noticing and understanding. Under these circumstances, their knowledge tends to remain inert.

The general idea of anchored instruction has a long history. Dewey (1933) discussed the advantages of theme-based and project-based learning. In the 1940s, Gragg (1940) argued for the advantages of case-based approaches to instruction—approaches that are currently used quite frequently in areas such as medicine, business, and law (Williams, 1991). Each of our videodisc environments can be viewed as providing a context for a case-based project that provides a common ground for collaborative exploration. A major goal of uses of these cases is to allow students to experience changes in their own noticing and understanding as they discover and are introduced to new ideas about these cases. A related goal is to ensure that each case is explored from multiple points of view.

AN ENVIRONMENT FOR ANCHORED INSTRUCTION

For purposes of this chapter, we try to illustrate the concept of anchored instruction by focusing on one of our center's videodisc projects, our "Jasper Woodbury Problem Solving Series."[2] The primary focus of the Jasper series is on mathematical thinking. However, we also designed the series so that there is considerable potential to integrate mathematical and scientific inquiry. In addition, it is designed to help students create links to history, literature, and other areas.

The Jasper series consists of a set of specially designed video-based adventures that provide a motivating and realistic context for problem solving and reasoning. Each video in the Jasper series has a main story that is 14 to 18 minutes in length. At the "end" of each video narrative, one of the characters (Jasper in the first episode; Emily in the second, etc.) is faced with a realistic problem that has to be solved. Students are challenged to solve the problem. They have to generate the relevant subproblems comprising the overall problem and decide on the relevant data and mathematical procedures. All the data needed to solve the problems are provided in the video, and the problem to be solved is very complex (see Table 2.1 for a description of the full set of design principles underlying the Jasper series). Each Jasper adventure also shows a conclusion to the adventure that students can watch after they have solved the problem themselves.

The Jasper adventures are organized into pairs; both members of each pair involve similar types of problems (i.e., trip planning for the first pair, using statistical data to develop a business plan in the second pair; making decisions from data gathered from meaningful uses of geometry in the third). There are also many links in each video that allow students and teachers to extend their explorations across the curricula. We discuss these in more detail later on.

A Description of "Rescue at Boone's Meadow"

The first episode of the pair of trip-planning videos, "Journey to Cedar Creek," has been described elsewhere (e.g., CTGV, in press b). We describe the second episode, "Rescue at Boone's Meadow." This episode opens with a view of Larry Peterson flying his ultralight airplane. We soon learn that Larry also teaches others to fly and we see him with one of his pupils, Emily Johnson. Through a series of lessons, Larry introduces Emily (and the viewers) to a variety of information about his ultralight such as fuel capacity, speed, payload limits, how

[2]We thank Joe B. Wyatt, Chancellor of Vanderbilt University, for his leadership and support in helping us develop the Jasper series, finding school-based sites in nine states, and making possible the kinds of collaborative ventures (e.g., making science-based hypercard stacks) that provide deeper understandings of events in the Jasper series. Support for Development of the Jasper Series has also been provided by a grant from the National Science Foundation.

45

TABLE 2.1
Seven Design Principles Underlying the Jasper Adventure Series

Design Principle	Hypothesized Benefits
1. Video-Based Format	A. More motivating. B. Easier to search. C. Supports complex comprehension. D. Especially helpful for poor readers yet it can also support reading.
2. Narrative with realistic problems (rather than a lecture on video)	A. Easier to remember. B. More engaging. C. Primes students to notice the relevance of mathematics and reasoning for everyday events.
3. Generative format (i.e., the stories end & students must generate the problems to be solved).	A. Motivating to determine the ending. B. Teaches students to find and define problems to be solved. C. Provides enhanced opportunities for reasoning.
4. Embedded data design (i.e., all the data needed to solve the problems are in the video).	A. Permits reasoned decision making. B. Motivating to find. C. Puts students on an "even keel" with respect to relevant knowledge. D. Clarifies how relevance of data depends on specific goals.
5. Problem Complexity (i.e., each adventure involves a problem of at least 14 steps).	A. Overcomes the tendency to try for a few minutes & then give up. B. Introduces levels of complexity characteristic of real problems. C. Helps students deal with complexity. D. Develops confidence in abilities.
6. Pairs of Related Adventures	A. Provides extra practice on core schema. B. Helps clarify what can be and what cannot. C. Ilustrates analogical thinking.
7. Links Across the Curriculum	A. Helps extend mathematical thinking to other areas (e.g. history, science). B. Encourages the integration of knowledge. C. Supports information finding and publishing.

the shape of the wing produces lift, and so forth. Emily learns her lessons well and soon flies solo. To celebrate, she and Larry join Jasper Woodbury at a local restaurant.

At the restaurant, we learn that Jasper is planning to take his annual fishing trip. He is going to drive to Hilda's (where she has her house and runs a gas station) and then hike approximately 15 miles into the woods to Boone's Meadow. The conversation reveals other information such as the fact that Larry flew his ultralight to see Hilda the previous week and set it down in the field beside her house. At the end of the restaurant scene both Larry and Emily weigh themselves. Data from this as well as other scenes become relevant later on.

As the adventure proceeds we see Jasper on his fishing trip. As he is eating his catch he hears a shot and goes out to investigate. He finds a wounded eagle and uses his CB radio to call for help.

Hilda answers Jasper's call and relays the message to Emily. Emily consults with Doc Ramirez, the veterinarian, who supplies additional information about eagles, distances, and so on. His map reveals that there are no roads between Cumberland City (where Larry and Emily are located) and Boone's Meadow (the location of Jasper and the Eagle). The doctor has another patient to attend to but emphasizes to Emily that time is of the essence in rescuing the eagle.

The adventure ends with a view of Emily posing the problem that confronts her: "What is the fastest way to rescue the eagle and how long will that take?" This is the challenge that is presented to the students. It is at this point that students move from the passive television-like viewing to an active generation mode. They must solve Emily's problem; to do so they have to generate the subgoals and constraints that she must consider to find the fastest way to rescue the Eagle. All the data needed to solve the problem were presented in the video. Students go back and search for the information they need.

The problem looks deceptively simple, but in reality there are numerous possible solutions and each involves many subproblems. For example, once students decide on a **route,** they must also identify a specific **agent** (person) and a **vehicle** (car, ultralight, or hiking). Then, students must determine the feasibility of the route by evaluating the plan against multiple constraints: landing area, payload, and the range of the vehicle. If the ultralight is in the plan, range is determined by a complex calculation involving fuel capacity, fuel consumption, and distance. In addition, the ultralight's range can be extended by carrying an extra gallon of gas. But carrying the extra gas and the cargo box will affect payload.

Overall, there are a number of possible (and impossible) solutions and some are faster than others. In order to adequately explore and discuss the possibilities, students generally need three or four class periods. Even college students find the Jasper problems challenging. Data showing the effects of working with Jasper on students' abilities to generate and solve complex problems are discussed elsewhere (e.g., Goldman, Vye, Williams, Rewey, & Pellegrino, 1991; Pellegrino, Heath, Warren & CTGV, 1991; Van Haneghan et al., 1992).

Analogs and Extensions

In addition to the major problem for each Jasper adventure, we are also designing additional print and video materials that present analog problems as well as extensions. We provide these as prototypes and models, with the expectation that the most effective learning comes when teachers and students learn to generate similar types of problems on their own.

Analogs.   Analogs are problems that are very similar to the original Jasper adventure. The purpose of the analogs is to invite students to think about the implications of slight changes in the adventure. For example, students may be asked to imagine that Emily had access to a different ultralight with different features (fuel capacity and consumption, payload limits, etc). Given this set of constraints, is there a different flight plan that would be more ideal?

Students can also be asked to consider whether Emily's solution with the original ultralight would have worked if there were a 6-mile per hour headwind while she flew from Cumberland City to Boone's Meadow (it would not). Problems become increasingly tricky if Emily encounters a wind from the side rather than a direct headwind. Now students can see the need for trigonometry and the concept of vectors. We do not expect fifth- and sixth-grade students to master such information. Nevertheless, by understanding how this knowledge fits into the greater scheme of things, students stand a much better chance of wanting to learn about these areas later in their academic careers.

Extensions.   In addition to Jasper, analog problems are extensions that allow students to see how the planning involved in Emily's rescue is similar to the planning involved in other events. One extension problem for "Rescue at Boone's Meadow" involves a consideration of the planning that Charles Lindbergh had to do in order to prepare for his flight from New York to Paris. Another involves the planning required for the first trip to the moon. By exploring these issues, students learn history, geography, and other subject matters at the same time that they receive increased opportunities to think mathematically. We believe that the mathematical analyses of the planning involved in these historical events provide students with a richer understanding than they receive by merely reading about what happened and when the event occurred.

Other types of extensions provide the opportunity for integrating a number of different areas in mathematics and science. In "Rescue at Boone's Meadow," an exploration of principles of flight is an obvious area for further inquiry. So is an examination of radio waves and how they can be transmitted without wires (Jasper uses his CB radio to tell Hilda about the wounded eagle who then contacts Emily by phone). An examination of endangered species is also made relevant by the eagle in the story. We especially want to develop extension materials that allow students to perform their own experiments in order to draw conclusions (e.g., Schwab, 1962). An example involves the construction of various kinds of devices for measuring wind speed. Another involves investigations of the kinds of materials (e.g., lead) that block various types of radio waves.

Other Jasper adventures provide opportunities that allow students to learn about, and perform experiments on, concepts of flotation, density, leverage, recycling, statistical probability, and so forth. In several of the adventures (especially "The Big Splash" and "A Capital Idea"), students have the opportunity to create written handouts to accompany presentations to be made to important audiences in order to convince them of the possibility of achieving certain goals. The possibilities for meaningful extensions of each Jasper adventure continue to expand as one begins to work with people from a variety of different areas and disciplines. By creating HyperCard stacks that all relate to a common Jasper anchor, experts who might never have the time to meet together can share their ideas. Students are able to share their ideas in similar ways.

Our ultimate hope for the Jasper series is to have it set the stage for student-generated activities centered around issues that are relevant to the students' community. For example, two of our adventures involve the use of statistical data to construct a business plan that enables our Jasper characters to achieve some important goals. We would like our adventures to motivate students to find a worthy goal of their own, construct a plan for achieving the goal, convince someone that the plan is feasible, and then actually carry it out. Similarly, we are hopeful that the emphasis on ecology and recycling that is emphasized in one of our Jasper adventures will motivate students to do something about these issues in their own community. Reports from our collaborative school sites suggest that activities such as these are being generated by students and are actually being carried out (CTGV, in press c).

Multimedia Publishing Software

The Jasper series includes specially designed multimedia publishing software that allows students and teachers to publish their research about various topics (e.g., about principles of flight or about endangered species) in a multimedia format (e.g., CTGV, in press b). One of the adventures of this software is that it provides a very simple-to-learn mechanism for accessing video segments from other discs that are relevant to the authors' topic (there are a growing number of videodiscs published by the Smithsonian, Nova, National Geographic, NASA, and so forth). The software also makes it very easy to scan in pictures from stills, to record sounds, and to create hypertext that includes links to a variety of relevant concepts. Students and teachers can also export the stacks they create and send them via telecommunications to others around the nation and the world. For teachers, a collection of HyperCard stacks can provide a rich source of materials that they can use to help students learn about various events. As in other areas of communication, it is important to help students learn to create unique products rather than simply rely on "knowledge telling" (Scardamalia & Bereiter, 1991). This is an area where collaboration with expert writing teachers can be excellent for teachers who specialize in other content domains.

Tools for Modeling

We are also beginning to develop tools for modeling that students can use in their explorations of various Jasper adventures. Some of the models work like a spreadsheet and let students see the effects of possible changes in the problems to be solved (e.g., a change in a headwind, in the speed of the aircraft, etc.). Other models let students experiment with aspects of sampling and statistics that are relevant to some of the Jasper adventures. In all cases, our goal is to help students see how the construction of models can simplify the task of making predictions and of understanding complex events.

Anchored Collaboration Through Teleconferencing

The rapidly increasing availability of teleconferencing links to schools makes it possible to extend the concept of "anchored collaboration" even further. Imagine that students work on a videodisc-based adventure (Jasper or otherwise) for several weeks and, at the end of this time, know that they will have the opportunity to participate in an interactive teleconference with other schools across the country (currently, such teleconferences are less expensive when students see a downlinked video but respond by phone). The teleconference focuses on the adventure on which the students have been working. Students prepare by learning to ask relevant questions about the Jasper adventure, by attempting to solve particular analog and extension "challenges," and perhaps by creating their own hypermedia stack that explores an issue relevant to the Jasper adventure. Students can compare their abilities to deal with analog problems to those of other classes, attempt to create presentations that are good enough to appear on the broadcast, and set up joint research projects with classes from different areas of the country (e.g., to estimate the number of eagles in their states and compare state laws about endangered species). Overall, these anchored events have the potential to increase students' motivation to learn because they represent exciting events (analogous to the "musical recital" or the "big game" for which students and teachers prepare). Furthermore, they provide forums for helping students and teachers continually expand their horizons and set new standards for themselves.

Teleconferencing and other forms of communication networks also address a dilemma alluded to earlier. It is unrealistic to expect individual teachers to be able to provide the kinds of instruction that leads to a deep understanding of the multitude of concepts and principles that emerge in the context of exploring a video anchor. With teleconferencing, expert scientists can be brought into the classroom during "preparation" periods for the main "challenge" teleconferencing and hence can enhance the learning of teachers as well as students. Text descriptions of the experts' ideas can be made available through electronic means. So can multimedia stacks that include animations and other forms of presentation that help clarify the information to be learned.

The theoretical perspective that underlies our work suggests that a key to the success of the kinds of telecommunication-based broadcasts that we have in mind is the fact that everyone involved has had a chance to explore a particular adventure prior to the broadcast. As noted previously, new ideas are more fully appreciated when people first have the opportunity to explore an environment on their own and are then able to experience the changes in their own noticing and understanding that accompany the introduction of new ideas and perspectives. Under these conditions, they are much more receptive and much more likely to learn (e.g., Bransford, Vye, et al., 1990; Bransford, Franks, Vye, & Sherwood, 1989).

SUMMARY AND CONCLUSIONS

We have attempted to make and provide support for the following arguments:

1. There are a number of reasons for attempting to integrate instruction across traditional disciplinary boundaries. These include the fact that (a) instructional time is limited and could be used much more efficiently; (b) integration across content domains can help students acquire knowledge that is less likely to remain inert; (c) integration can help students appreciate the power of common concepts and methods of inquiry that transcend domains; (d) integration can facilitate the degree to which students learn to adopt multiple perspectives when attempting to solve problems.

2. Despite these advantages, there are barriers to integrating instruction across disciplinary boundaries. The most notable one is that it places an extremely heavy burden on teachers. This problem is exacerbated by the extremely limited amount of planning time that is available to most teachers—especially planning time that involves the opportunity to interact with other colleagues.

3. There are ways to get around these barriers. One approach involves the use of videodisc-based anchors to create environments that can be explored and discussed collaboratively. Our Jasper Woodbury Problem Solving Series (consisting of a set of main adventures plus analog and extension problems and computer tools) provides an example of this approach to instruction.

4. Classroom-based programs such as Jasper become even more powerful when used in conjunction with telecommunications and teleconferencing technologies that allow students and teachers to create a broad community of learners. Under these conditions, it becomes possible to engage in a process of collaborative inquiry that provides opportunities to see differences in what is noticed and understood as people from different areas explore the same general situations from their particular points of view.

5. The approach to instruction that we described is definitely not limited to Jasper. Through the development of new project-based anchors and the use of telecommunications and teleconferencing, it should become possible to have a positive impact on cross-curricular inquiry on a wide scale.

ACKNOWLEDGMENTS

An initial draft of this chapter was presented at the Wingspread Conference on Integrated Science and Mathematics Teaching and Learning sponsored by the NSF (April 26, 1991), Racine, WI. Preparation of this chapter was supported, in part, by grants from the James S. McDonnell Foundation (No. 87-39) and the National Science Foundation (No. NSF-MDR 9050191). The ideas expressed herein do not necessarily reflect their views. Members of the Cognition and Technology Group who contributed to this chapter are Linda Barron, John D. Bransford, Olin Campbell, Bill Corbin, Dave Edyburn, Ben Ferron, Laura Goin, Elizabeth Goldman, Susan R. Goldman, Ted Hasselbring, Allison Heath, Charles Kinzer, James W. Pellegrino (in his pre-dean years), Kirsten Rewey, Vicki Risko, Diana Sharp, Bob Sherwood, Marcy Singer, Nancy J. Vye, Susan Warren, and Susan Williams.

REFERENCES

Adams, J. L. (1979). *Conceptual blockbusting: A guide to better ideas.* New York: Norton.

American Association for the Advancement of Science (1989). *Science for all Americans. A project 2061 report on literacy goals in science, mathematics, and technology.* Washington, DC: Author.

Asch, S. E. (1969). A reformulation of the problem of associations. *American Psychologist, 24,* 92–102.

Beck, I. L. (1991). *Reading and learning from social studies texts.* Paper presented at the Maryland Conference on Literacy in the 90's: Perspectives on Theory, Research, and Practice, Baltimore.

Brand, S. (1989). Science by mail. *The Online Journal of Distance, Education and Communication, 3*(1), Item #5.

Bransford, J. D. (1979). *Human cognition: Learning, understanding, and remembering.* Belmont, CA: Wadsworth.

Bransford, J. D., Franks, J. J., & Vye, N. J., & Sherwood, R. D. (1989). New approaches to instruction: Because wisdom can't be told. In S. Vosniadou & A. Ortony (Eds.), *Similarity and analogical reasoning* (pp. 470–497). New York: Cambridge University Press.

Bransford, J. D., Goldman, S. R., & Vye, N. J. (1991). Making a difference in peoples' abilities to think: Reflections on a decade of work and some hopes for the future. In L. Okagaki & R. J. Sternberg (Eds.), *Directors of development: Influences on children* (pp. 147–180). Hillsdale, NJ: Lawrence Erlbaum Associates.

Bransford, J., Kinzer, C., Risko, V., Rowe, D., & Vye, N. (1989). Designing invitations to thinking: Some initial thoughts. *Cognitive and social perspectives for literacy research and instruction.* 38th Yearbook—National Reading Conference, Chicago.

Bransford, J., Sherwood, R., & Hasselbring, T. (1988). Effects of the video revolution on cognitive development: Some initial thoughts. In G. Foreman & P. Pufall (Eds.), *Constructivism in the computer age* (pp. 173–201). Hillsdale, NJ: Lawrence Erlbaum Associates.

Bransford, J. D., Sherwood, R. S., Hasselbring, T. S., Kinzer, C. K., & Williams, S. M. (1990). Anchored instruction: Why we need it and how technology can help. In D. Nix & R. Spiro (Eds.), *Cognition, education, and multi-media: Explorations ideas in high technology* (pp. 115–141). Hillsdale, NJ: Lawrence Erlbaum Associates.

Bransford, J. D., Sherwood, R., Vye, N., & Rieser, J. (1986). Teaching thinking and problem solving: Research foundations. *American Psychologist,* 1078–1089.

Bransford, J. D., Vye, N., Kinzer, C., & Risko, V. (1990). Teaching thinking and content knowledge: Toward an integrated approach. In B. Jones & L. Idol (Eds.), *Teaching thinking* (pp. 381–413). Hillsdale, NJ: Lawrence Erlbaum Associates.

Briggs, H. (1624). *Arithmetica logarithmica*. Londini: Excudebat Gulielmus Iones.

Brown, J. S., Collins, A., & Duguid, P. (1989). Situated cognition and the culture of learning. *Educational Researcher, 17*, 32–41.

Caramazza, A., McCloskey, M., & Green, B. (1981). Naive beliefs in "sophisticated" subjects: Misconceptions about trajectories of objects. *Cognition, 9*, 117–23.

Chi, M. T., Bassok, M., Lewis, P. J., & Glaser, R. (1989). Self-explanations: How students study and use examples in learning to solve problems. *Cognitive Science, 13*, 145–182.

Chipman, S. F., Segal, J. W., & Glaser, R. (Eds.). (1985). *Thinking and learning skills: Research and open questions* (Vol. 2). Hillsdale, NJ: Lawrence Erlbaum Associates.

Clement, J. (1987). Overcoming students' misconceptions in physics: The role of anchoring intuitions and analogical validity. In J. Novak (Ed.), *Proceedings of the Second International Seminar on Misconceptions on Educational Strategies in Science and Mathematics* (Vol. III, pp. 84–96). Ithaca, New York: Columbia University.

Cognition and Technology Group at Vanderbilt (in press a). Anchored instruction and science education. In R. Duschl & R. Hamilton (Eds.), *Philosophy of science, cognitive psychology and educational theory and practice*. New York: SUNY Press.

Cognition and Technology Group at Vanderbilt. (in press b). Technology and the design of generative learning environments. *Educational Technology*.

Cognition and Technology Group at Vanderbilt (in press c). The Jasper series: A generative approach to improving mathematical thinking. *This year in school science*. Washington, DC: American Association for the Advancement of Science.

Cognition and Technology Group at Vanderbilt. (1990). Anchored instruction and its relationship to situated cognition. *Educational Researcher, 19*(3), 2–10.

Collins, A. (1991). The role of computer technology in restructuring schools. *Phi Delta Kappan*, 28–36.

Collins, A., Hawkins, J., & Carver, S. M. (1991). A cognitive apprenticeship for disadvantaged students. In B. Means, C. Chelemer, & M. S. Knapp (Eds.), *Teaching advanced skills to at-risk students* (pp. 216–243). San Francisco: Jossey-Bass.

Curlitz, R. D. (1989). A global network for children second installment. *The Online Journal of Distance Education and Communication, 3* (1), Item #1.

Dewey, S. (1933). *How we think: Restatement of the relation of reflective thinking to the educative process*. Boston: Heath.

Feuerstein, R., Rand, Y., Hoffman, M. B., & Miller, R. (1980). *Instrumental enrichment*. Baltimore: University Park Press.

Fogarty, R. (1991). Ten ways to integrate curriculum. *Educational Leadership*, 61–65.

Gick, M. L., & Holyoak, K. J. (1980). Analogical problem solving. *Cognitive Psychology, 12*, 306–365.

Gick, M. L., & Holyoak, K. J. (1983). Analogical problem solving. *Cognitive Psychology, 15*, 1–38.

Goldman, S. R., Vye, N. J., Williams, S. M., Rewey, K., & Pellegrino, J. W. (1991). *Problem space analyses of the Jasper problems and students' attempts to solve them*. Paper presented at the American Educational Research Association, Chicago.

Gragg, C. I. (1940, October 19). Because wisdom can't be told. *Harvard Alumni Bulletin*, 78–84.

Hanson, N. R. (1970). A picture theory of theory meaning. In R. G. Colodny (Ed.), *The nature and function of scientific theories* (pp. 233–274). Pittsburgh: University of Pittsburgh Press.

Hull, G. A. (1989). Research on writing: Building a cognitive and social understanding of composing. In L. B. Resnick & L. E. Klopfer (Eds.), *Toward the thinking curriculum: Current cognitive research* (pp. 104–128). Alexandria, VA: ASCD.

Kurshan, B. (1990). Educational telecommunications connections for the classroom—Part 1. *The Computing Teacher, 17*(6), 30–35.

Lampert, M. (1990). When the problem is not the question and the solution is not the answer. Mathematical knowing and teaching. *American Educational Research Journal, 27,* 29–63.

Michael, A. L., Klee, T., Bransford, J. D., & Warren, S. (in press). The transition from theory to therapy: Test of two instructional methods. *Applied Cognitive Psychology.* New York: Wiley.

Minstrell, J. A. (1989). Teaching science for understanding. In L. B. Resnick & L. E. Klopfer (Eds.), *Toward the thinking curriculum: Current cognitive research* (pp. 129–149). Alexandria, VA: ASCD.

National Council of Teachers of Mathematics. (1989). *Curriculum and evaluation standards for school mathematics.* Reston, VA: Author.

Nickerson, R. S. (1988). On improving thinking through instruction. *Review of Research in Education, 15,* 3–57.

Pellegrino, J. W., Heath, A., & Warren, S., with the Cognition and Technology Group at Vanderbilt (1991). *Collaboration at a distance: A Jasper implementation experiment in nine states.* Paper presented at the annual meeting of the American Educational Research Association, Chicago.

Pellegrino, J. W., Hickey, D., Heath, A., Rewey, K., Vye, N. J., & Cognition and Technology Group at Vanderbilt (1991). *Assessing the outcomes of an innovative instructional program: The 1990–1991 implementation of the "Adventures of Jasper Woodbury"* (Tech. Rep. No. 91-1). Nashville, TN: Vanderbilt University, Learning Technology Center.

Perfetto, G. A., Bransford, J. D., & Franks, J. J. (1983). Constraints on access in a problem solving context. *Memory and Cognition, 11,* 24–31.

Resnick, L. (1987). *Education and learning to think.* Washington, DC: National Academy Press.

Resnick, L. B., & Klopfer, L. E. (Eds.). (1989). *Toward the thinking curriculum: Current cognitive research.* Alexandria, VA: ASCD.

Scardamalia, M., & Bereiter, C. (1991). Higher levels of agency for children in knowledge building: A challenge for the design of new knowledge media. *Journal of the Learning Sciences, 1*(1), 37–68.

Schoenfeld, A. H. (1988). Problem solving in context(s). In R. Charles & E. A. Silver (Eds.), *The teaching and assessing of mathematical problem solving* (pp. 82–92). Hillsdale, NJ: Lawrence Erlbaum Associates and National Council of Teachers of Mathematics.

Schoenfeld, A. H. (1989). Teaching mathematical thinking and problem solving. In L. B. Resnick & L. E. Klopfer (Eds.), *Toward the thinking curriculum: Current cognitive research* (pp. 83–103). Alexandria, VA: ASCD.

Schwab, J. J. (1960). What do scientists do? *Behavioral Science, 5,* 1–27.

Schwab, J. J. (1962). The teaching of science as enquiry. In J. Schwab & P. Brandwein, *The Teaching of Science* (pp. 3–103). Cambridge, MA: Harvard University Press.

Segal, J. W., Chipman, S. F., & Glaser, R. (Eds.) (1985). *Thinking and learning skills: Relating instruction to research* (Vol. 1). Hillsdale, NJ: Lawrence Erlbaum Associates.

Sherwood, R. D., Kinzer, C. K., Bransford, J. D., & Franks, J. J. (1987). Some benefits of creating macro-contexts for science instruction: Initial findings. *Journal of Research in Science Teaching, 24*(5), 417–435.

Simon, H. A. (1980). Problem solving and education. In D. T. Tuma and R. Reif (Eds.), *Problem solving and education: Issues in teaching and research* (pp. 81–96). Hillsdale, NJ: Lawrence Erlbaum Associates.

Stein, B. S., Way, K. R., Benningsfield, S. E., & Hedgecough, C. D. (1986). Transfer in problem solving tasks. *Memory & Cognition, 14,* 432–441.

Sternberg, R. J. (1986). *Intelligence applied.* San Diego: Harcourt Brace Jovanovich.

Van Haneghan, J. P., Barron, L., Young, M. F., Williams, S. M., Vye, N. J., & Bransford, J. D. (1992). The Jasper series: An experiment with new ways to enhance mathematical thinking.

In D. F. Halpern (Ed.), *Enhancing thinking skills in the sciences and mathematics* (pp. 15–38). Hillsdale, NJ: Lawrence Erlbaum Associates.

Vygotsky, L. S. (1978). *Mind in society.* Cambridge, MA: Harvard University Press.

Weisberg, R., DiCamillo, M., & Phillips, D. (1978). Transferring old associations to new situations: A nonautomatic process. *Journal of Verbal Learning and Verbal Behavior, 17,* 219–228.

Whitehead, A. N. (1929). *The aims of education.* New York: MacMillan.

Williams, S. M. (1991). *Putting case-based instruction into context: Examples from legal, business, and medical education* (Tech. Rep.). Learning Technology Center, Vanderbilt University, Nashville, TN.

3

The Role of Self-Referent Cognitions in Goal Setting, Motivation, and Performance

Daniel Cervone
University of Illinois at Chicago

It's hard to take pride in a bridge you're never gonna cross, in a door you're never gonna open. You're mass-producing things and you never see the end result of it. (Muses) I worked for a trucker one time. And I got this tiny satisfaction when I loaded a truck. At least I could see the truck depart loaded.
—Mike Lefevre, steel worker, interviewed in Terkel (1972, pp. 1–2)

On the face of it, loading trucks does not seem more rewarding than working in a steel mill. And, in general, it probably is not. The comments of Mike Lefevre suggest that any activity may contain particular features that can improve people's thoughts and feelings about their work—and perhaps the quality of their work, as well. Two features of Mr. Lefevre's trucking job stand out: Employees had clear information, or feedback, on the progress of their work (they could see the truck being loaded and pulling away), and this feedback indicated progress toward a specific, well-defined goal (fully loading a truck). A wealth of psychological research highlights these same factors. Clear goals and feedback foster more motivating and satisfying work environments (Locke & Latham, 1990a).

The first section of this chapter briefly reviews empirical research on the effects of goals and feedback on motivation and achievement. The second section takes up the main goal of this chapter, which is to examine cognitive processes that regulate goal-directed action. Performance goals and feedback affect behavior through the mediating influence of cognitive self-regulatory processes, self-referent thinking processes through which people appraise and evaluate their progress toward valued goals. A general model of self-referent cognitive processes in goal-directed behavior is presented. The next two sections of the chapter review empirical research by my colleagues and myself, and others, that directly bears upon this model. The first of these sections examines the effects of goals and self-referent thinking on activities for which success requires sustained effort and task persistence; such activities have received the greatest attention in the goals literature. The following section examines a relatively neglected class of activities, namely, complex tasks on which success requires more than a simple application of effort. Recent findings reveal that the same motivational factors can have different effects on simple versus highly complex tasks. The chapter's final section investigates an issue that is fundamental to any cognitive model of motivation: the issue of causality. Do cognitive processes truly function as proximal determinants of behavior? I review a series of studies that addresses this issue by integrating research on cognition and motivation with work on heuristics and biases in human judgment (Tversky & Kahneman, 1974). By investigating the behavioral effects of biased self-judgments, this work provides a particularly stringent test of the hypothesis that self-referent thinking causally contributes to motivation.

Before beginning, let us consider how the work discussed in this chapter relates to the broad theme of this volume, cognitive science and its application to instruction. The present analysis of goal motivation, like other contributions to this text, is concerned fundamentally with human cognition. People's evaluations of their attainments, judgments of their capabilities for performance, and plans for future courses of action are cognitive processes that enable individuals to direct their own behavior, motivating themselves in the pursuit of desired goals. Although it is accurate to label these processes "cognitive," they do differ from the aspects of thinking that have been the typical object of study in cognitive science. In a recent essay, Bruner (1990) argues that, in developing computational models of mental processes, cognitive psychology has neglected "old-fashioned mental states identifiable by . . . their subjective marking" (p. 8). He further suggests that "cognitive science . . . is still chary of a concept of agency. For 'agency' implies the conduct of action under the sway of intentional states . . . (which) is now regarded as something to be eschewed by right-minded cognitive scientists (Bruner, 1990, p. 9)." This characterization certainly is not universally applicable; some recent information-processing analyses provide great insight into personality functioning and the self-regulation of behavior (e.g., Cantor & Kihlstrom, 1987). Nonetheless, the present analysis of subjectively experienced cognitive states and self-directed motivation gives this chapter a focus that clearly differs from that of mainstream cognitive science, and from other contributions to this volume.

Much of the chapter reviews theory and laboratory research on cognition and motivation. Despite this theoretical bent, the work strongly relates to a number of applied and instructional interests. Educational psychologists employ goal-setting procedures to enhance motivation and academic achievement (Ames,

1986; Schunk, 1984). Clinical psychologists apply self-management techniques to teach clients to monitor and regulate their own behavior as they work toward therapeutic goals (Rehm & Rokke, 1988). Industrial–organizational psychologists extensively have applied goal setting procedures to enhance work motivation and productivity. In this domain, scores of studies, conducted in a wide spectrum of settings, demonstrate that goal setting research indeed has yielded "a motivational technique that works" (Locke & Latham, 1984). The importance of these applications attests to the value of elucidating the mechanisms through which performance goals enhance motivation and achievement.

GOALS, MOTIVATION, & PERFORMANCE

Goal-setting research focuses on such volitional purposive behavior through which individuals are striving to reach a certain end state. Psychologists working from a variety of theoretical perspectives have analyzed people's goals and personal standards for performance, and goal-directed action (Pervin, 1989). Kurt Lewin and his colleagues studied "level of aspiration," the difficulty level individuals set as their aim on an activity (Lewin, Dembo, Festinger, & Sears, 1944). Situational factors such as prior goal attainment or nonattainment were found to strongly affect aspiration levels for future performance (Festinger, 1942). Control theories have employed cybernetic, negative feedback models in conceptualizing the regulation of action (Campion & Lord, 1982; Carver & Scheier, 1981, 1990; Miller, Galanter, & Pribram, 1960). Here, human behavior is seen as simply a way for a control system to minimize deviations between environmental inputs and internal reference values, or standards. Theories of achievement motivation (e.g., Heckhausen, 1967) accord prominent status to people's standards for behavior and reactions to feedback indicating whether their performance was a success or a failure in relation to those standards. Social cognitive theories of personality and social behavior, discussed in greater detail later, long have focused on standards, goals, and goal-directed action (e.g., Bandura & Kupers, 1964) and have argued that the capacity of self-direction is a central feature of human personality (Bandura, 1986; Cantor & Kihlstrom, 1987; Cervone & Williams, in press; Dweck & Leggett, 1988; Mischel, 1973).

   The study of self-regulated, or "self-managed," behavior also has been of interest to clinical psychologists (e.g., Thoresen & Mahoney, 1974; Watson & Tharp, 1977). Rather than merely imposing environmental contingencies to alter undesirable behavior, one could attempt to foster long-term behavior change by training clients to monitor and modify their own actions. Once clients learn to "carry the contingencies with them," behavior change may be maintained beyond the duration of the formal therapeutic program. Theoretical models of self-managed behavior change focus on people's monitoring of their performance, evaluation of performance outcomes, and self-rewarding of desirable actions

(Kanfer, 1980). Such work has fostered numerous successful therapeutic applications (Kanfer, 1980; Kanfer & Schefft, 1987), although some limitations to this work have been noted (Kirschenbaum, 1987).

Perhaps the most extensive body of empirical research on goal setting, motivation, and performance is that associated with goal theory (Locke & Latham, 1990a). Locke (1968) proposed that performance goals, aims one is trying to achieve on an activity, serve as immediate regulators of action. Scores of subsequent studies, conducted in laboratory and field settings, find that individuals working toward specific challenging goals outperform those aiming for easy goals or not working toward any specific goal (Locke & Latham, 1990a; Mento, Steel, & Karren, 1987; Tubbs, 1986). Such goal-setting effects are one of the most robust phenomena in the literature on human motivation. Oddly, this extensive body of research on human motivation has not been a part of the mainstream literature in personality and social psychology until quite recently. This, in large part, is simply because most goal theory work was conducted in industrial settings and published in applied journals. In recent years goal theory analyses have begun to enter the psychological mainstream (e.g., Lee, Locke, & Latham, 1989; Locke & Latham, 1990b).

A key insight of goal theory is the recognition that performance goals differ along a variety of dimensions, and that these goal dimensions are systematically related to performance. One important dimension is goal difficulty: People's aims can vary in the level or quality of performance that they require. One may commit oneself to running either 2 miles or 4 miles in an evening. Employees may work toward production targets that vary in the quality or quantity of performance demanded. Numerous laboratory and field studies document a strong linear relation between goal difficulty and task performance. As long as individuals accept and remain committed to their goals, more difficult goals foster higher levels of achievement (Mento et al., 1987; Tubbs, 1986; Wood, Mento, & Locke, 1987).

Goals also can differ in specificity. Consider a student faced with a seemingly endless textbook. She or he could decide to "get as much reading done as I can" in a given evening, or, alternatively, could set a specific goal of trying to read X number of pages or chapters. Numerous studies have compared specific goals to conditions involving nonspecific aims such as instructions to "do your best." More than 90% of these studies demonstrate the clear superiority of specific goal setting (Locke, Shaw, Saari, & Latham, 1981).

Finally, goals can differ in proximity. Although "graduating 4 years from now with a 3.5 GPA" and "getting a 3.5 GPA this semester" may be equally difficult and specific ideals, their considerable difference in proximity may have important motivational implications. Motivation is most reliably enhanced by proximal goals that give immediate direction to one's action and, when achieved, provide salient markers of progress. This point is illustrated in a study in which schoolchildren exhibiting deficits in arithmetic skills were instructed to aim toward either proximal or distal goals in a self-study mathematics program (Bandura & Schunk, 1981). Children received either a proximal goal of trying to complete 6 pages of instructional material each day, or a distal goal of completing 42 pages of material by the conclusion of the 7-day program. (The children, being deficient in arithmetic, were unable to divide the distal goals into proximal guides.) Proximal goals enhanced children's perceptions of their efficacy at mathematics, interest in math, and arithmetic performance. Although overly stringent proximal goals and plans occasionally can prove burdensome (Kirschenbaum, 1985, 1987), in many contexts the setting of short-term proximal subgoals significantly enhances motivation and performance (Stock & Cervone, 1990).

In order for these goal influences to have a strong motivational impact, individuals must receive feedback on their ongoing performance. Lasting motivational effects result not merely from having a challenging aim in mind, but from also being able to monitor one's progress toward that aim. Even if one is committed to an exercise goal of running 4 miles in a half hour, turning that commitment into effective action requires clear distance markers and a stopwatch. Experimental results illustrate the necessity of combining goals with feedback. Strang, Lawrence, and Fowler (1978) varied whether subjects were assigned a challenging or easy goal, and whether or not they received knowledge about the quality of their performance, as they worked on a series of arithmetic problems. Subjects receiving both a challenging goal and task feedback were the fastest to complete the problems. In an interesting field study, Becker (1978) assigned easy or challenging conservation goals to households participating in an energy conservation program. Some households received energy use feedback, via a chart that was taped to the patio window of the home. Households receiving both a challenging goal and feedback used the least energy and were the only homes to use less energy than a no-goal, no-feedback control group. Analogous findings derive from studies of subjects' ability to generate sentences that followed specified linguistic constraints (Kazdin, 1974), tolerate pain in a cold-pressor paradigm (Stevenson, Kanfer, & Higgins, 1984), and exert sustained physical effort on an aerobic task (Bandura & Cervone, 1983). Feedback facilitates the effects not only of assigned goals but also of self-set goals (Erez, 1977) and most strongly affects performance when past attainments are markedly short of one's standard (Matsui, Okada, & Inoshita, 1983).

Note that feedback can be of two types (Payne & Hauty, 1955): (a) knowledge about the type or direction of past errors, which allows one to correct performance, and (b) information about the overall quality of one's performance, or "knowledge of results." The latter feedback can be on an absolute scale, in comparison to one's own past performance, or in reference to a social norm. By varying feedback on performance quality, the aforecited goal-setting research demonstrates that knowledge of one's progress toward a goal greatly enhances motivation and performance—even when that knowledge provides no information about how best to perform the task.

One important qualification to these goal-setting effects involves the complexity of the task on which individuals are working. Until quite recently, most of the research documenting goal effects has involved relatively simple activities (e.g., anagrams, simple addition, typing) for which subjects already possessed the rudimentary knowledge and skills necessary to succeed (Mento et al., 1987; Wood et al., 1987). Although useful, such tasks may not tap processes critical to performance on cognitively complex activities, such as the development of task strategies (Christensen-Szalanski, 1980; Locke, Frederick, Lee, & Bobko, 1984). A recent meta-analysis indicates that assigned goals have weaker effects on performance of cognitively complex tasks (Wood et al., 1987), on which successful performance requires the development and testing of strategic knowledge. The effects of assigned goals on complex performance may, however, be enhanced by training or information that aids strategy development (Earley, Connolly, & Ekegren, 1989). Thus, although challenging goals can enhance complex performance, these effects are not as robust and reliable as those obtained with relatively simple activities.

The extensive body of findings on the effects of goal setting naturally raises the question of how goals enhance achievement. Why is it that individuals with concrete, challenging, proximal goals ("read three chapters tonight," "reduce food intake to 1400 calories a day," "increase sales by 10% this month") so frequently outperform those with only ambiguous, vague, or long-range aims ("do better in this class," "drop some of this darn weight," "try to increase sales")? There are two senses in which one can answer this question. The first addresses behavioral mechanisms through which goals enhance achievement (i.e., the classes of behavior that are reliably affected by challenging goals and, in turn, enhance performance outcomes).

As extensively reviewed by Locke and Latham (1990a, Chapter 4), goals affect performance in at least three different ways, the first two of which involve motivational mechanisms. First, commitment to challenging goals enhances effort. Much work indicates that people exert greater physical effort (e.g., Bandura & Cervone, 1983; Earley, Wojnaroski, & Prest, 1987) and work at higher rates of performance (e.g., Sales, 1970) under challenging goal conditions. A second related mechanism is task persistence. Performance success often requires "sticking to" an activity, even when it appears difficult or potentially unmanageable. Challenging proximal goals have been shown to enhance task persistence on a diverse range of activities including prose learning (LaPorte & Nath, 1976), bargaining (Huber & Neale, 1987), and complex problem solving (Stock & Cervone, 1990). Third, goals serve a directional function. Specific goals direct effort and attention to important aspects of an activity (Rothkopf & Billington, 1975, 1979) and guide information processing such that individuals more thoroughly process goal-relevant information (Cohen & Ebbesen, 1979; Hoffman, Mischel, & Mazze, 1981).

Even a detailed explication of behavioral mechanisms does not yield a full understanding of the effects of goals and feedback. Left unanswered is the question of the psychological processes through which goals affect these behaviors. A basic theoretical goal here is to identify a relatively simple set of processes that can be shown to account for each of the findings we have reviewed: the impact of challenging specific goals; the benefits of proximal goal setting; and the moderating influence of task complexity. In much of the remainder of this chapter, I attempt to accomplish this objective by adopting a social cognitive theory perspective on goal setting, motivation, and performance (Bandura, 1986; Bandura & Cervone, 1983, 1986).

SELF-REFERENT COGNITIONS IN GOAL MOTIVATION

From a social cognitive theory perspective, the motivational power of goal setting derives not from the goals themselves, but from the influence of a set of self-referent thinking processes, or self-regulatory processes. When people work toward a specific goal or standard, they periodically will gauge the relation between this standard and their actual attainments. The comparison forms the basis of people's reactions to their performance. Three classes of self-reactions are central to the regulation of goal-directed action: self-evaluative reactions to one's performance, judgments of self-efficacy, and personal goal setting.

Self-Evaluative Reactions.   People often react evaluatively to their performances. Attainments generate satisfaction with oneself, whereas substandard outcomes foster self-criticism and discontent with one's performance and with the prospect of continued inadequate attainments. Such reactions are important in their own right. Negative evaluations that stem from excessively high standards may predispose one to depression (Ahrens, 1987; Rehm, 1977). Lowered self-esteem may result from negatively evaluating one's performance on highly valued activities. Additionally, self-evaluative reactions serve an important motivational function. People have the capacity to guide and motivate their own behavior by making self-satisfaction contingent upon achieving desired outcomes. When performances are seen as falling short of standards, self-dissatisfaction spurs individuals to take corrective action. Those who are highly dissatisfied with substandard performances exert great effort to change, whereas individuals who react to the same performances in a complacent manner show little subsequent improvement (Bandura & Cervone, 1983, 1986). Through self-evaluative processes, people can motivate themselves to work toward challenging standards of achievement even in the relative absence of external constraints or rewards for behavior. The achievements of artists, writers, and athletes in solitary training testify to this capacity for self-direction.

Performance outcomes and self-evaluations are reciprocally linked; they "reciprocally determine" (Bandura, 1978) one another. Superior attainments generally will foster more positive self-evaluations. However, factors other than sheer positivity and negativity of outcome influence people's reactions to their attainments. People who view a performance standard as internally generated experience different reactions to failure than those whose standards are externally imposed (Higgins, 1987). Level of attainment and self-evaluations are more strongly linked among individuals who highly value an activity (Simon, 1979). Satisfaction is related not only to the magnitude of outcomes, but to the rate at which outcomes change over time (Hsee & Abelson, 1991; Hsee, Abelson, & Salovey, 1991).

Perceived Self-Efficacy.   Sustained performance toward a goal requires a robust sense that one actually can attain the desired outcome. Self-efficacy judgments, people's self-assessments of the level or type of performance they can achieve in a given setting (Bandura, 1977), are a second key motivational process. Much work demonstrates that perceptions of efficacy are critical to human achievement. Research manipulating and assessing perceived self-efficacy demonstrates that people who have greater confidence in their performance capabilities display greater effort and persistence in facing challenges and difficulties (Brown & Inouye, 1978; Cervone, 1989; Cervone & Peake, 1986; Peake & Cervone, 1989; Schunk, 1984; Stock & Cervone, 1990), experience less anxiety arousal prior to and during stressful performance (Bandura, Cioffi, Taylor, & Brouillard, 1988; Bandura, Taylor, Williams, Mefford, & Barchas, 1985), and more readily enter into challenging environments (Betz & Hackett, 1986).

As with self-evaluative reactions, self-efficacy judgments and performance are reciprocally linked. Assessments of one's efficacy affect future performance, and that performance experience, in turn, can alter one's efficacy judgments. Such first-hand performance experience generally exerts the strongest influence on self-efficacy perceptions (Bandura, 1977). However, this effect of performance outcomes is not automatic. Self-efficacy perceptions are a product of cognitive processing in which individuals may access and integrate information in an idiosyncratic manner. Thus, similar attainments can have different effects on efficacy perceptions for different people (Bandura, Reese, & Adams, 1982). Those who focus on difficult or unmanageable aspects of an activity (Cervone, 1989), attribute successes to external unstable factors (Weiner, 1985), or are in a negative mood state that biases information processing (Kavanagh & Bower, 1985) may judge themselves relatively inefficacious in the absence of corresponding negative outcomes. Conversely, many people maintain overly positive and optimistic perceptions of self-efficacy; these illusions actually may promote mental health (Taylor & Brown, 1988).

Personal Goal Setting.   Self-efficacy judgments can influence behavior both directly and through their effect on a third self-regulatory mechanism: personal standards, or self-set goals for performance (Bandura, 1989). In the course of performing an activity, individuals may redefine or reinterpret their aims, raising or lowering their personal performance goals (Campion & Lord, 1982). Commitment to this adjusted standard can strongly influence subsequent efforts. Various social and personal factors influence the standards that people adopt for themselves, and their degree of commitment to those aims. When goals are externally assigned, more authoritative figures foster greater goal commitment (Locke & Latham, 1990a). Those who view models displaying high performance standards tend to adopt stringent standards for themselves (Bandura, Grusec, & Menlove, 1967; Bandura & Kupers, 1964; Lepper, Sagotsky, & Mailer, 1975). Individuals with a stronger sense of self-efficacy set higher personal goals (Bandura & Cervone, 1986; Wood, Bandura, & Bailey, 1990) and remain more committed to achieving their aims (Locke et al., 1984). In the absence of assigned performance goals, people may create highly motivating circumstances for themselves by setting challenging standards for future performance (Bandura & Cervone, 1983).

Personal factors other than these three self-referent processes clearly also play a significant role in goal motivation. The self-processes are seen as immediate regulators of behavior that mediate the impact of other factors. For example, people's causal attributions for unexpected outcomes can strongly affect cognitive and affective reactions following success or failure (Russell & McAuley, 1986; Weiner, 1985). Attributing failure to personal, controllable, changeable factors may serve to increase self-dissatisfaction with performance, maintain strong perceptions of self-efficacy despite the setback, and heighten personal goals for future performance. The motivational effects of anticipated external rewards similarly may be at least partly mediated by self-regulatory influences such as personal goal commitment (Locke & Latham, 1990a). When highly valued rewards are contingent on goal attainment, people may remain more committed to challenging standards and become more dissatisfied when their efforts fall short of requirements.

Differential Engagement of Self-Regulatory Influences

These self-regulatory influences are not static motivational forces but dynamic psychological processes that are differentially activated, or engaged, by different performance environments. Different settings, in other words, are posited to affect the degree to which self-referent thinking processes contribute to performance. In particular, both a well-defined performance goal and feedback of current progress may be necessary to fully activate self-influences. When either of these factors is lacking, relations between performance and self-regulatory processes are relatively weak. For example, the relations between performance and self-evaluative reactions should be weaker when individuals are not working toward a specific performance goal. As noted before, people often engage in activities without clearly defining a specific standard of achievement they are trying to reach; indeed, a key component of self-managed behavior change is translating vague aims, such as "lose some weight," into specific goals such as "eat no more than 500 calories at dinner" (Watson & Tharp, 1977). Without a specific performance goal individuals may lack a clear unambiguous standard against which to evaluate their progress. Particular outcomes therefore may not elicit strong self-reactions, and subsequent motivation, in turn, may be only weakly affected by self-evaluations. The absence of clear feedback about one's progress similarly should moderate relations between self-evaluations and action. Performances cannot take on evaluative significance without information that enables individuals to gauge the quality of their attainments.

Relations between performance and perceived self-efficacy also may be moderated by goal setting. When people receive feedback on their progress toward a well-defined goal, they use this information to assess their capability of reaching the goal and rely on these self-efficacy judgments in regulating subsequent efforts. In contrast, without a goal or standard against which to compare attainments, performance feedback may not reliably indicate self-efficacy or inefficacy. In addition, the absence of task goals may produce low levels of motivation and effort (Locke & Latham, 1990a). Self-efficacy judgments then may not strongly regulate subsequent effort, because people lack an incentive for attaining superior levels of performance. Further, past performance may not strongly affect self-efficacy for future performance when effort is low, because inferior outcomes achieved with little effort may not indicate a lack of capabilities (Nicholls, 1984).

The critical factor determining the strength of relations between performance and self-reactive influences is not necessarily the presence or absence of an assigned goal but the presence of clear and accepted standards for performance. Such standards may be either socially determined or internally generated. In many settings, an authority figure (e.g., a teacher, supervisor, experimenter) will assign a goal that serves as the standard that is adopted in evaluating one's performance. However, with extended experience on tasks of personal importance, individuals generally will develop clear internal standards and employ these personal standards in the comparison judgments underlying self-evaluations. Those who have neither a socially based standard nor a clear internal standard for self-evaluation should experience less pronounced self-reactions and consequently should be less motivated to seek improvements in their performance.

GOALS, SELF-REFERENT PROCESSES, AND MOTIVATION

This social cognitive theory analysis of goal motivation makes a number of distinct types of predictions about relations among environmental influences, self-referent thinking, and motivated behavior. Situational factors such as assigned performance goals and task feedback should strongly influence evaluations and appraisals of one's own performance. These self-reactions, in turn, should affect subsequent performance, mediating the impact of goals and feedback. Finally, the strength of relations between performance and self-referent processes should vary as a function of the presence or absence of clear environmental goals and feedback.

A key to empirically analyzing these complex relations among the environment, cognition, and action has been the use of independent indices of the self-referent processes. People's evaluations of their performance, appraisals of their capabilities, and plans and goals for the future are consciously experienced and readily accessible cognitions that can be directly tapped through self-report. A number of procedural issues must be considered in taking such assessments; in particular, the timing of these self-report measures is important. Research that assesses self-referent thinking after individuals have been exposed to relevant social information (e.g., performance feedback) but before the behavior of interest provides the strongest test of hypotheses about the mediating role of self-referent cognitions. In contrast, taking these measures after the behavior has occurred raises the possibility that subjects' retrospections about what they *had been* thinking will be inaccurate, having been biased by theories about or rationalizations for their actions (Ericcson & Simon, 1980; Nisbett & Wilson, 1977). The strongest tests of our theoretical predictions have derived from studies employing independent self-report measures of the self-regulatory processes, and examining the sequential, reciprocal relations between self-referent thought and action. This research strategy has been used to elucidate the role of self-referent processes in goal setting and effortful performance (Bandura & Cervone, 1983, 1986).

Challenging Goals and Performance Feedback

Our initial study investigated the role of self-referent processes in mediating the impact of challenging goals and performance feedback on physical effort expenditure (Bandura & Cervone, 1983). In this research, subjects performed a rather grueling aerobic task: an arm-powered exercise bicycle, or ergometer. In addition to yielding an objective measure of effort expended, this task had the advantage of being relatively novel; thus, subjects did not begin with a strong preconception of their exact performance capabilities. A further advantage was that, when performing the task over a number of trials, subjects could not intuit their exact change in performance from one trial to the next. This allowed us to provide convincing experimentally controlled performance feedback.

In this study, subjects performed the ergometer task for three 5-minute periods. Four experimental conditions factorially manipulated the presence or absence of challenging assigned goals, and the presence or absence of performance feedback. Goals were assigned after the first performance period. Subjects were asked to improve their initial performance by 40% in each of the two subsequent trials. Performance feedback was given after the second period. Subjects were informed that they had increased their output by 24% from the first session to the second. Thus, in the experimental condition combining goals and feedback, subjects knew they had improved their performance, yet still faced a marked negative discrepancy between their attainments and the goal. The self-referent processes were assessed via a questionnaire completed during a "break period" between the second and third sessions. Subjects indicated (a) their perceived self-efficacy for the task, their confidence that they could maintain or increase their performance by designated percentage increments from the second session to the third, and (b) their evaluative reactions to their performance, their satisfaction or dissatisfaction with their performance thus far, and with the prospect of maintaining a similar level of performance in the third session. The central dependent measure was the extent to which subjects increased their output from the second session to the third.

In this experimental design, there were a number of interrelated predictions. The first concerned the impact of goal and feedback conditions on effortful performance. As shown in Fig. 3.1, (left panel), the combination of challenging goals and clear feedback substantially increased performance, with subjects increasing their performance by an average of more than 50%—a particularly notable increase, as this was the third session of a highly fatiguing task. The other three conditions were, in terms of mean output, equivalent and substantially below the Goal + Feedback group. Neither goals in the absence of per-

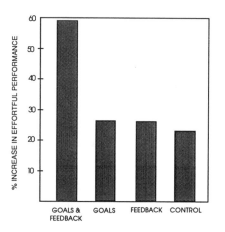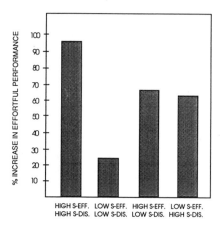

FIG. 3.1.   Mean percentage increase in effortful performance (Bandura & Cervone, 1983). The left panel displays mean change in performance in experimental conditions combining goals with feedback, providing goals alone, feedback alone, or neither of these factors. The right panel displays performance within the condition combining goals and feedback, as a function of differential combinations of self-dissatisfaction with performance and perceived self-efficacy for goal attainment. Reprinted by permission of the American Psychological Association.

formance feedback, nor knowledge of one's performance in the absence of challenging goals, increased motivation in this session.

The second aspect of the results concerns the role of self-efficacy and self-evaluative processes in mediating these motivational effects. Although, in general, the combination of challenging goals and feedback markedly increased performance, there were substantial individual differences in performance *within* this experimental condition. When faced with a discrepancy between their goals and attainments, some subjects were highly dissatisfied with their performance, whereas others reacted with relative complacency. Some remained confident of their capabilities on the task, whereas others suffered from a low sense of efficacy. These differential reactions strongly predicted variations in performance within this condition (Fig. 3.1, right panel). Subjects who retained a high sense of efficacy and were highly dissatisfied with substandard attainments nearly doubled their output. Those who were satisfied with their performance and lacked a strong sense of efficacy showed only marginal increments in output. People's reactions to their performance influenced not only overall output but changes in performance within the third session as well. Subjects who were dissatisfied with their inadequate attainments and confident that they could improve speeded up during the final 5-minute session. Those who felt less efficacious and were less self-critical of their substandard performance slowed down throughout this session. Both self-efficacy and self-evaluative reactions predicted significant unique percentages of the variance in performance. (Levels of satisfaction with performance and perceived self-efficacy were not significantly intercorrelated.) Thus, subjects influenced their own levels of motivation through their evaluations of themselves and appraisals of their capabilities.

As predicted, these relations between performance and both self-evaluation and perceived self-efficacy held only with the condition combining assigned goals with feedback. In the other conditions, these relations were variable, and substantially weaker. For example, in the absence of both goals and feedback, neither of the self-processes significantly predicted overall performance or changes in performance within the third session. These results provide evidence that the self-processes are not static motivational forces. Rather, self-referent processes contribute to motivation in contexts in which people can gauge the relation between their performance and a clearly defined standard.

The goals people set for themselves also predicted changes in effortful performance. In a postexperimental questionnaire, some subjects who received performance feedback but no assigned goal indicated that they spontaneously set for themselves a goal of improving their performance from the second session to the third. These subjects showed marked increases in performance, upping their output by an average of 40%. One must, of course, interpret these results cautiously, as postexperimental reports of personal goal setting may be influenced by past accomplishments and therefore may not accurately reflect the preperformance goals people had held. In our subsequent work (e.g., Bandura & Cervone, 1986), self-set goals were assessed prior to performance.

In a following study (Bandura & Cervone, 1986), we examined the role of perceived self-efficacy, self-evaluative reactions, and personal goal setting under conditions that systematically varied the discrepancy between goals and current attainments. Falling far short of a valued goal can generate a qualitatively different set of cognitive and affective reactions than if one comes close to meeting a challenging standard. We assigned all subjects the goal of trying to increase their performance by 50% above baseline on the ergometer task. All subjects received feedback on their performance after the second session. This information was systematically varied to create varying discrepancies between goals and attainments. Three experimental conditions exposed subjects to either a very large, a moderate, or a very small negative discrepancy. In a fourth group, the feedback was suprastandard (i.e., it indicated that subjects had slightly exceeded the 50% goal in the second session).

The impact of the self-processes on performance varied markedly as a function of the discrepancy between assigned goals and attainments (Table 3.1). The Large and Moderate substandard conditions replicated the findings of the previous study, with higher perceptions of self-efficacy and greater self-dissatisfaction spurring individuals to greater effort. Regression analyses indicated that both of the self-processes independently predicted changes in performance in the face of markedly substandard efforts. When subjects' second-session performance fell just slightly short of their goal, however, the determinants of motivation were strikingly different. Under this circumstance, some subjects remained committed to their 50% increment goal. Others responded to their near miss by setting higher goals for themselves. Still others apparently became discouraged by exert-

TABLE 3.1
Predictors of Changes in Effort

	Discrepancy Between Goal and Prior Attainment							
	Large Sub-standard		Moderate Substandard		Small Substan-dard		Small Supra-standard	
Predictor	r	R²inc	r	R²inc	r	R²inc	r	R²inc
Self-Dissatisfaction	.53	.29**	.44	.19*	−.12	.02	.29	.08
Self-Efficacy	.69	.24**	.57	.19*	.20	.03	.52	.20*
Self-Set Goals	.64	.05	.69	.17*	.84	.66***	.59	.16*

*p < .05; **p < .01; ***p < .001.
Note. Relations between self-referent processes and changes in subsequent performance in experimental conditions varying the magnitude of discrepancy between goals and prior attainments. (Increments to R² are based on hierarchical regressions in which the predictors were entered in the order listed). Adapted from Bandura & Cervone (1986).

ing great effort yet falling short of their assigned goal. They abandoned the challenging standard, setting lower personal goals for the third session. These variations in self-set goals were highly predictive of changes in performance; indeed, personal goal setting accounted for nearly two-thirds of the variance in performance change. Interestingly, under this circumstance, subjects' self-set goals were unrelated to their perceptions of self-efficacy or evaluative reactions to their performance. There was no simple linear relation between attainments and either of these two self-processes.

The determinants of motivation under "near miss" conditions are deserving of further study. People may categorize such situations in distinctly different ways: as a clear sign that they can surpass their goal in the future; as a missed opportunity that may not come again due to the difficulty of mounting a similar effort in the future; and so on. People's reactions may depend, in part, on whether they easily can envision alternative actions that would have brought success (Kahneman & Tversky, 1982). Whatever the factors that underlie these reactions, our results suggest that the goals people set for themselves are major determinants of subsequent performance in such "near miss" contexts.

Both self-efficacy perceptions and personal goal setting contributed to performance when subjects received feedback indicating they had surpassed the assigned standard (Bandura & Cervone, 1986). Achieving one's goal on this arduous task does not necessarily imply that one can do so again in the future. As with many everyday activities that require sustained effort, repeating one's prior success is not a routine matter. Despite feedback indicating that they had succeeded in reaching their goal, subjects displayed wide variations in subsequent self-efficacy perceptions and personal goals. Note that this finding contrasts with traditional level-of-aspiration results (e.g., Festinger, 1942). On simple tasks requiring little effort, people generally raise their aspiration level after achieving a given standard. However, this result appears to have limited generality. On activities requiring considerable effort, goal attainment can generate diverse patterns of self-reactions and goals for the future.

Research by Podsakoff and Farh (1989) provides additional evidence of the differential engagement of perceived self-efficacy in goal-directed performance. Subjects received either positive or negative feedback, in the form of evaluative statements and normative data, as they performed an object-listing task. Measures of perceived self-efficacy strongly predicted increments in performance when subjects received negative feedback but were unrelated to performance in the positive feedback condition. On this cognitive task—on which performance is not highly taxing, so successful efforts are easily replicable—success feedback is likely to quell any doubts people may have about their personal efficacy. People are more likely to dwell on their performance capabilities and base future actions on these self-judgments when faced with failure than when informed that they are succeeding.

Proximal Goal Setting

In contrast to the extensive and consistent literature documenting the effects of challenging goals versus no specific goals, the literature on proximal goal setting is somewhat sparse and equivocal. Some studies indicate that performance is enhanced by setting proximal subgoals that can be reached as one works toward more distal aims (Bandura & Schunk, 1981; Bandura & Simon, 1977). However, other work has not found proximal goal setting to be superior (Dubbert & Wilson, 1984; Locke & Bryan, 1967, Expt. 2). If proximal plans are overly specific and restrictive, they may not allow individuals enough flexibility in choosing among activities (Kirschenbaum, Humphrey, & Malett, 1981; Kirschenbaum, Malett, Humphrey, & Tomarken, 1982; also see Kanfer & Grimm, 1978). The assignment of restrictive proximal goals can diminish intrinsic motivation on tasks that individuals already find to be highly interesting (Manderlink & Harackiewicz, 1984).

Progress in understanding proximal goal effects has been hampered by a key methodological problem: Because most people feel it is advantageous to set proximal goals (Kirschenbaum, Tomarken, & Ordman, 1982), many subjects who are assigned distal goals spontaneously set proximal subgoals for themselves. This precludes true experimental comparisons between proximal and distal goal setting. For example, in a 4-week weight-loss program (Bandura & Simon, 1977), subjects assigned proximal and distal goals lost similar amounts of weight. However, internal analyses revealed that half of the distal goal subjects spontaneously set proximal weight-loss goals for themselves. This subgroup of individuals who held both a specific distal goal and proximal subgoals exhibited the greatest weight loss. Although these results support the efficacy of proximal goal setting, they must be interpreted cautiously because the results favoring proximal subgoals did not involve a true experimental comparison. Subjects who spontaneously set proximal goals for themselves may have differed from other subjects in important respects; for example, those setting proximal goals may have been more committed to losing weight or more knowledgeable about weight-loss strategies. Dubbert and Wilson (1984) similarly found that proximal goal setting did not enhance weight loss more than more long-term distal goals. Again, however, some subjects failed to adhere to their assigned goal-setting strategy.

Our recent work has attempted to circumvent this problem, while simultaneously examining self-referent processes through which subgoals may exert their effects (Stock & Cervone, 1990). The social cognitive theory analysis of goal motivation suggests a number of distinct processes through which proximal goal setting can enhance motivation and performance. First, setting proximal goals can increase initial perceptions of self-efficacy by making a task appear more manageable. When conceptualized in terms of a number of discrete steps, a task may appear within the range of one's capabilities. Second, attaining a proximal subgoal provides an indicator of progress that is likely to further boost perceptions of self-efficacy. Finally, subgoal attainment also may affect self-evaluative reactions to performance. Reaching a proximal subgoal may enhance an individual's level of self-satisfaction with his or her current attainments and increase dissatisfaction with the prospect of not eventually reaching the final goal.

In this research, subjects were assigned to one of three types of goal-setting conditions as they performed a complex problem-solving task commonly known as the Missionaries and Cannibals problem (Simon & Reed, 1976; or "Hobbits and Orcs" problem; Thomas, 1974). The problem involves working through a sequence of steps, moving missionaries and cannibals while following various constraints; one's overall final goal is to transfer all the missionaries from one location to another. An important aspect of this task was that subjects did not know how many steps were required. They thus could not meaningfully fractionate the task into smaller units to set proximal goals. Proximal goals were experimentally varied by informing subjects of designated intermediate steps in the problem that they should work toward on their way to its final solution. In the various experimental conditions, subjects (a) worked toward a subgoal that they achieved after a number of problem steps, (b) received no subgoal instructions, or (c) worked toward a subgoal that was not reached because it was outside the problem space. This latter condition allowed for the separate assessment of the effects of initially setting, and subsequently attaining, a proximal subgoal.

Proximal goal setting had a number of distinct effects on self-referent thinking. First, proximal subgoals enhanced initial, preperformance self-efficacy perceptions (Fig. 3.2, left panel). When subjects conceptualized the activity as one that involved their first working toward an intermediate problem stage, they became more confident in their ability to solve the entire problem. Mentally "dividing up" a task in this manner can make it appear more manageable. As an illustration, students appear far less daunted by a course syllabus that describes "4 or 5 readings each week" than one that raises the specter of a semester with "more than 60 papers!"

Second, achieving the proximal subgoal provided a marker of progress that greatly boosted efficacy perceptions (Fig. 3.2, right panel). When the second self-efficacy assessment was taken, all subjects had reached the same step in the problem and had attained that step in equivalent amounts of time. Despite these objectively equivalent experiences, reaching this step had differential effects on self-perceptions. For those who first had established this problem step as a proximal goal, reaching it carried added significance as an indicant of personal efficacy.

In addition to self-efficacy perceptions, proximal goal setting enhanced subjects' evaluations of their performance. Subjects who had achieved the proximal goal were significantly more satisfied with their performance than those in the other conditions—again, despite all subjects having achieved the same objective level of progress.

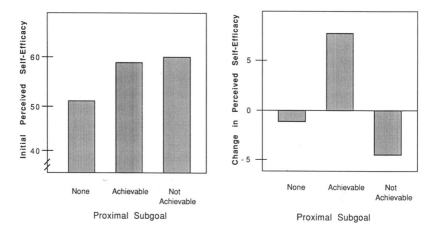

FIG. 3.2. The left panel displays initial mean strength of self-efficacy among subjects who either had no subgoal or received one of two proximal subgoals toward which to direct their efforts. The right panel displays changes in perceived self-efficacy after all subjects reached the same intermediate stage of the Missionaries and Cannibals problem, the stage that served as the subgoal in the Achievable Subgoal condition. From Stock, J., & Cervone, D. (1990). Proximal goal-setting and self-regulatory processes. *Cognitive Therapy and Research, 14,* 483–489. Reprinted by permission of Plenum Press.

Finally, proximal goal setting enhanced subjects' persistence on the Missionaries and Cannibals problem. Subjects who had set and achieved a proximal goal expended more time and effort on the task. Importantly, regression analyses demonstrated that the changes in self-efficacy that resulted from proximal goal attainment mediated these behavioral effects. In other words, if one statistically controlled for self-efficacy, there was no relation between proximal goal attainment and behavior. This finding has an important applied implication. When proximal goal setting is employed in programs of behavior change, one should monitor individual differences in perceptions of self-efficacy for subgoal attainment. Even a goal-setting strategy that has general utility will not help a particular individual who lacks a sense of efficacy for attaining the subgoals or fails to experience a boost in self-efficacy perceptions following subgoal attainment.

GOAL SETTING AND COMPLEX TASK PERFORMANCE

Thus far, our analysis of self-referent processes has provided a detailed understanding of the motivational effects of goal setting. Why do challenging proximal goals and performance feedback enhance motivation? It is because they foster a set of self-referent cognitive processes through which people guide and motivate their own efforts.

Ideally, an analysis of self-referent processes would provide insight not only into goal setting's robust effects, but also into those circumstances under which goals and feedback do not reliably influence performance. As reviewed earlier, the most notable moderator of goal effects is task complexity: Challenging goals have relatively weaker effects on highly complex tasks (Wood et al., 1987).

Our recent work (e.g., Cervone, Jiwani, & Wood, 1991) has investigated the role of self-referent processes in goal-directed performance on a particular highly complex activity. In this program of research, subjects perform a dynamic decision-making task, a computer-based simulation of managerial decision making (Wood & Bailey, 1985). They manage a small business organization, the "Special Orders Department," of a hypothetical furniture factory. In each of a series of trials, subjects assign employees to each of eight jobs ("assembling parts," "upholstering," etc.). They then make three additional decisions about motivational factors that affect employee performance: Subjects assign performance goals to the employees, chosen from among various types of supervisory feedback, and administer rewards. Subjects receive numerical feedback on the performance of each employee after each set of decisions. By using this feedback to vary and test decision options systematically, subjects can discover relations between decision options and organizational performance and thereby increase the organization's efficiency.

This type of activity was chosen for a number of reasons. Such dynamic decision making requires considerable self-directed effort. Subjects must attend to multiple cues, monitor the effects of decision options, and develop and test task strategies. Unlike activities typically employed in research on goal setting, motivation, and performance, success on this task results not from the sheer application of effort but from the systematic development and application of knowledge about the task. Self-reactions to performance are particularly important here because, although systematically testing strategic options is necessary for success, novel task strategies occasionally do fail. One's reactions to such setbacks can influence subsequent decision efforts and the eventual quality of performance. In their model of strategy development and performance, Wood and Locke (1990) included two appraisal processes in strategy selection: whether the strategy will work, and whether "I" (the decision maker) am capable of implementing the strategy. A series of studies by Wood and Bandura (1989; Bandura & Wood, 1989; Wood, Bandura, & Bailey, 1990) demonstrated that self-efficacy perceptions influence the quality of analytic thinking and problem solving on complex tasks. Individuals with a strong sense of self-efficacy develop more effective strategies than those who feel less efficacious. They learn more from feedback, respond more adaptively to the decision environment, and, over time, are better able to translate their learning into improved performance.

The decision-making paradigm has afforded a unique opportunity to systematically analyze the sequential reciprocal relations between performance and self-reactions. In our work, the experimental performance period is divided into trial blocks. Self-regulatory processes are assessed between blocks. These self-assessments appear on the computer screen. Subjects indicate their perceived self-efficacy (their confidence in attaining specified levels of performance in future trials), self-evaluative reactions (their degree of satisfaction of dissatisfaction with their current attainments), and personal goals (the level of performance they personally are aiming for in upcoming trials). Taking these assessments between blocks enables one to analyze the effects of past performance on self-reactions, and the influence of self-reactive processes on subsequent performance.

In our initial study in this area (Cervone et al., 1991), subjects performed the decision task under experimental conditions that involved either no specific goal (subjects were instructed to "do your best"), or one of two assigned goals, a moderately challenging or an extremely difficult standard. These standards were numerical goals representing overall levels of organizational performance; subjects received feedback on the organizations' performance levels after each trial. Thus, both of the assigned goal conditions contained the two comparative factors, clear goals and performance feedback, that should most fully activate self-referent processes.

In accord with our theoretical model, self-regulatory processes and performance were strongly linked in the experimental conditions that provided a specific goal (Table 3.2). When subjects worked toward a specific standard of achievement, higher levels of initial performance predicted greater self-satisfaction, higher perceived self-efficacy, and more challenging personal goal levels. In contrast, when subjects were not working toward a specific goal, prior performance outcomes were unrelated to these self-reactions. Goal setting thus appears to influence the manner in which people interpret performance outcomes. By providing an unambiguous reference point against which to compare attain-

TABLE 3.2
Correlations Between Decision Performance and Self-Reactive Processes

	Goal Condition	
	No Goal	Specific Goal
Block 1 Performance with Subsequent Assessments		
Self-Efficacy	−.014	.353*
Self-Evaluation	.108	.363*
Self-Set Goal	.226	.631**
Assessments after Block 1 with Subsequent Performance		
Self-Efficacy	−.231	.424*
Self-Evaluation	.088	.400*
Self-Set Goal	.285	.657**

*$p < .05$; **$p < .01$.
Note. From Cervone, Jiwani, & Wood (1991).

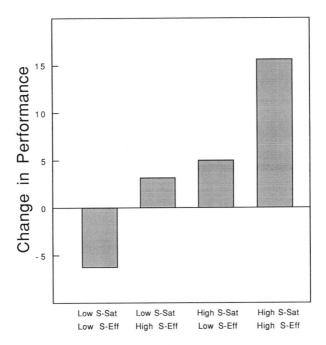

FIG. 3.3. Median levels of change in decision performance among subjects working toward a specific performance goal, as a function of differential combinations of self-satisfaction with prior performance and perceived self-efficacy (Cervone, Jiwani, & Wood, 1991). Reprinted by permission of the American Psychological Association.

ments, specific goals may prompt individuals to categorize outcomes as being clearly acceptable or inadequate (as "successes" or "failures"). As a result, feedback elicits self-evaluative reactions and serves as an indicant of efficacy or inefficacy. In contrast, when working toward a vague goal (e.g., "trying to do as well as I can on this task"), the same objective performance information can have different meaning. Because of the ambiguity of one's standard, it can be unclear whether a given attainment is adequate or not.

Specific goal assignment also moderated the effect of self-referent processes on future decision performance. In the absence of a challenging performance goal, self-reactions were not predictive of performance. In contrast, all three of the self-processes significantly predicted performance within the challenging goal conditions (Table 3.2). Multiple regression analyses provided evidence of the unique causal contribution of the self-processes, and the moderating effects of goal assignment. Even when controlling for initial performance, the interaction of goal condition and both self-evaluative processes and self-efficacy perceptions significantly predicted future performance. It is evident in Fig. 3.3 that combination of subjects' evaluative reactions and self-efficacy judgments strongly predicted changes in performance. Those who were highly efficacious and satisfied with their performance greatly improved. Subjects who were dissatisfied with their performance and had a low sense of efficacy showed deteriorating decision performance.

In some respects, these findings parallel those obtained with cognitively simple activities (Bandura & Cervone, 1983, 1986). Self-regulatory processes are more strongly linked to performance when subjects work toward a specific goal. A stronger sense of self-efficacy predicts superior levels of subsequent performance. The findings do, however, differ from earlier results in two important and potentially interrelated respects. First, goal assignment only weakly affected mean levels of performance, a result consistent with recent reviews (Wood et al., 1987). Subjects who received a specific goal attained slightly higher performance levels during the first block of trials; the groups did not differ in the second block. A second difference concerns the impact of self-evaluation on performance. Here, the results are *the very opposite of* those found previously. On measures of motivation and effort expenditure, dissatisfaction with one's efforts predicted *superior* outcomes (Bandura & Cervone, 1983, 1986). On the decision task, subjects who were more dissatisfied with their progress toward a performance goal achieved *inferior* levels of performance. Bandura and Jourdan (1991) recently reported a similar detrimental effect of dissatisfaction on decision performance.

As these findings attest, effortful physical performance and complex decision making are qualitatively different phenomena, with fundamentally different relations between motivational processes and performance outcomes. When there is a simple and direct relation between effort and performance, self-dissatisfaction that enhances effort will positively affect attainments. However, on complex tasks the effect of effort on performance is mediated by mechanisms that include the testing and appraisal of alternatives, and the development of novel creative strategies. Here, the negative affect due to self-evaluations can undermine performance by deleteriously affecting required short-term memory functions (Humphreys & Revelle, 1984), biasing recall of previously encoded information (Isen, 1987; Isen, Shalker, Clark, & Karp, 1978), or diverting attention from task-relevant thoughts (Sarason, 1975; Sarason, Sarason, & Pierce, 1990). Negative self-evaluations that lead to private ruminations about oneself may divert essential attentional resources away from task execution, thereby undermining performance.

To gain further insight into these relations between self-evaluation and performance, we analyzed not only performance outcomes but the quality of subjects' decision strategies. In this complex setting, changing multiple decision parameters for each employee is a deficient strategy for testing hypotheses about the impact of motivational factors, because it confounds the contribution of factors to outcomes. The most efficient way to develop one's knowledge about the task is to change only one factor at a time, while holding other decision parameters constant. Our task strategy analyses revealed that subjects who became dissatisfied with their performance changed a great many decision parameters; they did, in a sense, exert a great deal of effort in an attempt to improve. However, many of their changes were confounded and thereby led to poorer performance. Thus, the generally useful heuristic of substantially changing one's strategy when faced with unsatisfactory outcomes failed in this extremely complex setting. Even if subjects had devoted all their attentional resources to the task, those who varied a substantial percentage of the decision parameters may have been literally incapable of adequately assessing the effects of these decisions. The information associated with an exceedingly large number of changes simply may have exceeded the normal capacity of working memory. Thus, people who became dissatisfied with their performance created for themselves a decision environment in which they are incapable of succeeding due to "information overload."

This pattern of results provides some insight into the question of why goal effects are weaker on complex tasks. On both simple and complex activities, a commitment to challenging goals will foster dissatisfaction with substandard performance. On simple activities, this dissatisfaction enhances effort and thereby contributes to the power of goal setting (Bandura & Cervone, 1983). On complex tasks, the same self-reactions can interfere with cognitive processes critical to success, thereby attenuating the performance effects of challenging goals. Negative discrepancies between attainments and standards have the same effect on self-evaluations on simple and complex tasks, but self-evaluative processes have an opposite effect on subsequent performance.

Complementary findings have been obtained in a recent study that factorially manipulated the presence or absence of assigned goals and organizational performance feedback on the decision task (Cervone & Wood, 1991). In No Feedback conditions, subjects did not receive information on the overall performance of the organization after each trial (although they did receive information about the performance of each of the individual Furniture Factory employees). In the Assigned Goal conditions, subjects received a highly challenging goal for performance. In accord with our theoretical model, self-efficacy perceptions and personal goal setting strongly predicted future performance in the condition combining challenging goals and performance feedback, but not in the other conditions. Regression analyses revealed that the absence of clear goals, performance feedback, or both significantly moderated the effects of these two self-regulatory processes. Performance feedback powerfully affected the strength of relations between performance and self-referent thinking. When subjects received feedback on their goal-directed efforts, both self-efficacy judgments ($r = .45$) and personal goal setting ($r = .84$) strongly predicted attainments. When they received a goal but no feedback, neither efficacy judgments ($r = .22$) nor personal goals ($-.01$) predicted subsequent decision performance. As in the prior study (Cervone et al., 1991), self-satisfaction with past attainments predicted superior decision performance; those who were *dis*satisfied with their efforts performed more poorly. Somewhat unexpectedly, self-evaluations were strongly linked to performance in both of the goal conditions (i.e., whether or not subjects received overall organizational feedback). In retrospect, in this particular paradigm, information about the performance of the individual simulated employees enables one to make general inferences about how performance compares to the goal. Thus, even "no feedback" subjects were able to evaluate their goal-directed efforts.

Types of Goals and Goal Orientations

One's aims on an activity may differ not only in level (challenging versus easy performance goals) but in type. People have different types of aims when engaged in an activity. For example, one may read an essay for entertainment ("it looked interesting"), to learn (perhaps in preparation for an upcoming discussion or exam), or because one's comprehension of the material will be immediately tested (as in a standardized exam with reading comprehension questions). Different types of aims and goals may be associated with qualitatively different affective reactions and self-referent cognitions. Competitive goal structures lead individuals to make ability attributions, whereas goals involving personal improvement foster cognitions about effort and effort-related strategies (Ames, 1986). Subjective experience during performance differs strikingly when individuals are ego involved, with the goal of demonstrating ability relative to others, as opposed to task involved, with the goal of improving personal mastery (Nicholls, 1984). In a conception closely related to the present analysis, Dweck and her colleagues (Dweck & Leggett, 1988; Elliott & Dweck, 1988) found that different patterns of cognition and behavior emerge from varying goal orientations and perceptions of one's ability. When aiming to obtain positive evaluations of one's capability, high and low perceptions of capability lead, respectively, to mastery or helpless patterns of response. When aiming to increase personal competence, a mastery-oriented pattern may emerge from either high or low perceptions of present ability.

Our recent work (Cervone & Kopp, 1990) examined the role of self-regulatory processes in decision performance under two types of performance settings. In a Performance Goal condition, subjects attempted to reach a specific challenging standard throughout two blocks of trials on the decision task. In a Learning Goal condition, subjects aimed to learn as much as they could about the task during the initial block of trials. This learning was in preparation for the subsequent trials, during which their performance would be assessed. As hypothesized, the self-regulatory processes more strongly affected decision performance in Performance Goal conditions than under Learning Goal instructions (Table 3.3). When aiming to learn about the task, there was no specific standard of achievement against which to evaluate attainments; thus, evaluative reactions had little facilitative or detrimental effect on subsequent performance. Similarly, learning goals should make one less prone to interpret occasional inferior outcomes as indicants

TABLE 3.3
Correlations Between Self-Reactive Processes and Performance

	Goal Condition	
	Learning	Performance
Assessments after Block 1 with Block 2 Performance		
Self-Efficacy	.146	.314+
Self-Evaluation/Past Performance	.263	.606***
Self-Set Goal	−.104	.196
Assessments after Block 2 with Block 3 Performance		
Self-Efficacy	.583**	.796***
Self-Evaluation/Past Performance	.433*	.797***
Self-Set Goal	.486**	.546**

$+p < .075$; $*p < .05$; $**p < .01$; $***p < .001$.

Note. All subjects worked toward a specific performance goal during the third trial block. Data from Cervone & Kopp (1990).

of personal inefficacy (Dweck & Leggett, 1988). Indeed, when merely attempting to learn about a task, people may less frequently dwell on perceptions of their performance capabilities or rely on such self-perceptions in regulating their actions. Under learning goal conditions, efficacy judgments and performance were not significantly related (Table 3.3). Note that the type of goal subjects aimed toward varied both between and within subjects. Subjects in the Learning Goal conditions did have a specific performance goal in the second block of trials. In accord with our theoretical predictions, the self-regulatory processes strongly predicted decision performance in this second trial block, but not in the first.

Goal Mechanisms in Everyday Social Behavior

Throughout this discussion of goals, motivation, and performance, we have reviewed studies in which some agent (e.g., a job supervisor, an experimenter) assigns goals to individuals. This fact should not be taken to mean that goal-directed behavior always involves the external imposition of burdensome tasks that individuals find aversive. To the contrary, many everyday activities naturally involve concrete challenges. It is precisely these activities that individuals find to be stimulating and enjoyable. Csikszentmihalyi (e.g., Csikszentmihalyi & LeFevre, 1989) examined people's experiences as they engage in everyday activities that vary in the challenges they present, and in the skills that people perceive they have to meet those challenges. When both challenges and perceived skills are high, individuals report feeling more active, alert, happy, and satisfied with what they are doing (Csikszentmihalyi, 1990; Csikszentmihalyi & LeFevre, 1989). Challenging goals can relieve one of boredom and serve as a stimulus to creativity and self-development.

CAUSAL ANALYSIS OF THOUGHT AND ACTION

An issue of central importance to any cognitive model of motivation is the question of causality. Are the cognitive components of the model truly *determinants of* behavior? In the context of the present analysis of goal motivation: Do appraisals of oneself and one's capabilities for performance truly function as *causal* factors?

To the layperson, speaking of mental processes as causes of action is not controversial. We commonly explain people's behavior in terms of their expectations, plans, or feelings about various courses of action. Many psychologists, however, have viewed such explanations as fundamentally flawed (e.g., Skinner, 1953). The Behaviorist would argue that such cognitions are not causes of action but are themselves "behaviors" that may accompany an overt action of interest, and that themselves need to be explained in terms of environmental factors that act upon the person.

The causal status of cognitive states is a question that can be addressed empirically. We consider work exploring the causal impact of self-efficacy judgments. A number of research strategies have been employed to assess the impact of efficacy judgments on behavior. Because some have argued that self-efficacy judgments are mere reflections of past behavior, with no causal impact of their own (Borkovec, 1978), one strategy is to examine relations between perceived efficacy and action while statistically controlling for the effects of past performance. As noted earlier, research on complex decision making demonstrates that, when one controls for prior decision outcomes, perceived self-efficacy significantly adds to the prediction of future performance (Cervone et al., 1991; Wood & Bandura, 1989). In research on psychotherapeutic behavior change, measures of perceived self-efficacy often predict future behavior more accurately than do indices of past behavior (e.g., Bandura, Adams, & Beyer, 1977). Such predictions hold not only when predicting aggregate levels of performance but also at a "microanalytic" level, in which self-efficacy measures are used to predict behavior at the level of individual tasks (Bandura et al., 1977; Cervone, 1985). These findings are consistent with the notion that self-efficacy judgments have a causal impact on behavior.

An even stronger test of the causal role of a self-efficacy perception would be one that directly manipulates self-efficacy perceptions while holding constant all other relevant variables, such as prior experience and information about an activity. Research on human judgment under conditions of uncertainty has provided insight into ways of accomplishing this goal.

Self-Efficacy Judgment under Uncertainty

Assessing one's capabilities for performance often involves considerable uncertainty. In many settings, one cannot be sure of the precise skills that will be required, or the environmental factors that may help or impede one's performance. Such uncertainty is most apparent in novel activities. Someone who is being trained to learn a new task may have little sense of the exact challenges the task will present, or how relevant their current skills are in meeting task demands. However, even highly familiar activities can contain uncertain elements that raise questions about one's coping capabilities. Even an experienced lecturer may question his or her capabilities for the task at hand when asked to lecture on an unfamiliar topic, or in front of a potentially hostile audience.

These observations about self-efficacy judgment led us (Cervone, 1989; Cervone & Peake, 1986) to propose that judgments about one's personal efficacy may be a product of the same judgmental strategies, and subject to the same biases, as uncovered in other classes of human judgment (e.g., Kahneman, Slovic, & Tversky, 1982; Nisbett & Ross, 1980). When judging one's level of self-efficacy on an activity, individuals are considering the relation between two sets of factors: their own skills, motivation, and abilities; and the difficulties and demands of the prospective situation. There may be many relevant personal and situational factors, and much uncertainty associated with them. In natural interactions, there may be relatively little time to dwell on these self-assessments. It is precisely this type of judgment setting in which people rely on simplifying judgmental strategies, or "heuristics," that enables one to reduce complex inferential tasks to relatively simple cognitive operations. Tversky and Kahneman (1974) identified a number of such judgmental processes; a heuristic that is highly pervasive—and that also yields a solution to our issue of providing a strong test of the causal impact of self-efficacy judgment—is the process of "anchoring and adjustment" (Tversky & Kahneman, 1974).

In many situations, people make estimates by considering an initial value and subsequently adjusting this value to yield a final estimate. Initial values may come from a variety of sources: the answer to a similar problem, a relevant piece of information, a "wild guess," and so forth. For example, a student considering his or her potential performance on an SAT exam may begin by considering the level of performance achieved by a friend who has taken the test. It commonly is found that people's final estimates are "biased" in the direction of such initially considered values, or "anchor" values. In general, such a result is not surprising; many situations contain important cues that serve as viable and valid "anchors" in making estimates. However, anchoring research indicates that people's judgments are biased in the direction of initially considered values even when these anchor values are normatively inappropriate, irrelevant cues. At the extreme, anchor biases are robust even when the anchor values are literally random numbers (Tversky & Kahneman, 1974).

This impact of random cues that are devoid of any informational value suggested a novel strategy for manipulating perceived self-efficacy and for assessing the behavioral impact of self-efficacy judgments. If judgments about one's personal capabilities for performance are influenced by random anchoring cues, one can create groups of individuals with differential levels of perceived self-efficacy, yet with equivalent exposure to, experience on, and information about a given activity. Despite these groups being equivalent in these many ways, the social cognitive theory prediction is that the differential levels of perceived self-efficacy will affect future performance.

To explore the impact of anchoring biases on the formation of self-efficacy judgments and the relation between these self-judgments and subsequent behavior, we devised a simple laboratory paradigm. Because of self-efficacy theory predictions about relations between self-efficacy and coping effort on difficult activities, we examined subjects' task persistence on a challenging activity. Subjects performed a series of trials on a geometric problem-solving task in which one's aim was to trace over all the lines of a geometric figure while following certain restrictions. This task had a number of advantages. It is novel; thus, there is considerable uncertainty associated with judging one's exact performance capabilities. Success and failure on the task can be experimentally controlled; we employed numerous items that appeared only slightly more complex than items subjects had solved, yet were actually unsolvable. Subjects were given a fixed amount of time to work on this geometric task and a second alternative activity (a series of anagrams). We assessed the degree to which they persisted on the geometric task before abandoning it and switching to the alternate activity.

The anchoring manipulation was embedded in a preexperimental questionnaire. After a number of filler items, subjects responded to a question asking them whether they thought they could solve "more or less than X of the cyclical graphs." The value of "X" appeared to have been randomly generated; before subjects filled out the questionnaire, a number was pulled out of a bag filled with small index cards containing a variety of different values. The bag, of course, was rigged. The number drawn was always either a very high (High Anchor) or very low (Low Anchor) value. This number was penciled into the questionnaire item. After answering "more" or "less," subjects indicated their exact level of self-efficacy, the exact number of cyclical graphs they judged they were capable of solving. In a Control condition, no anchor value was presented. After completing the questionnaire, subjects worked on the task.

Anchoring biases powerfully affected self-efficacy judgments (Fig. 3.4). Subjects exposed to a high anchor value judged they could solve approximately 50% more of the geometric problems than did subjects exposed to a low anchor—this despite the fact that the low and high anchor values appeared to be random numbers pulled out of a bag. These differences in perceived self-efficacy generated corresponding differences in subsequent task persistence (Fig. 3.4), with high anchor subjects sticking to the task for a much longer period of time than others. Regression analyses indicated that self-efficacy perceptions fully mediated the effect of anchoring cues on behavior.

One might argue that the presentation of a single high or low anchor value— even a random one—presents a subtle social demand for high or low levels of performance. In part to address alternative explanations of the effects of an-

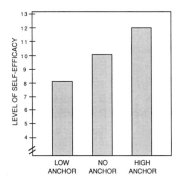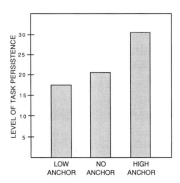

FIG. 3.4. Mean levels of perceived self-efficacy (left panel) and task persistence (right panel) as a function of exposure to apparently random high and low anchor values (Cervone & Peake, 1986). Reprinted by permission of the American Psychological Association.

choring cues, we ran a subsequent experiment that explored the possibility that anchoring biases would result from considering a set or sequence of possible outcomes in different orders (Peake & Cervone, 1989). In a preexperimental questionnaire, subjects rated their confidence in attaining five different performance levels, ranging from very low to very high levels of performance. In one condition, subjects made these ratings in an ascending order, first considering whether they would reach a low performance level. In a Descending Sequence condition, subjects made exactly the same ratings, but in an opposite order. We predicted that the value subjects considered *first* would anchor their self-efficacy estimates. Because the questionnaire items in both conditions covered the same range of outcomes, one cannot argue that they represented any differential social demands. In results that paralleled the earlier findings (Cervone & Peake, 1986), subjects in the Descending Sequence condition, who first considered the possibility of their achieving a high level of performance, showed both higher levels of perceived self-efficacy and greater subsequent persistence on the task (Peake & Cervone, 1989). Additional studies showed this sequence anchoring bias to be a general phenomenon. Across a variety of factual judgments, the order in which subjects considered various possibilities strongly affected their estimates, with judgments biased in the direction of whatever value was presented first (Peake & Cervone, 1989).

In many respects, the behavioral impact of anchor-biased self-efficacy judgments is quite surprising. Anchoring cues were presented, and perceived self-efficacy was assessed, before subjects ever had attempted the task. Subjects subsequently experienced numerous performance trials, with equivalent rates of success and failure in all experimental conditions. Given the general power of such direct, first-hand, performance feedback, one might have expected this performance information to quickly eliminate any initial group differences in perceived self-efficacy. However, the results—substantial group differences in task persistence over a large number of trials—suggest that initial efficacy judgments may have been highly perseverant (i.e., the groups may have had differing efficacy perceptions even after much equivalent experience, with these differences in self-efficacy sustaining the differences in behavior).

To address this possibility, Cervone and Palmer (1990) exposed subjects to low, intermediate, or high anchor values, assessed initial perceived self-efficacy, and then reassessed self-efficacy perceptions after subjects completed one-third, two-thirds, and an entire set of 30 of the geometric problem-solving items. Despite controlled equivalent success rates in all conditions, subjects exposed to a low anchor value persistently judged themselves to be relatively incapable of performing the task. On both of the self-efficacy reassessments, subjects who had been exposed to the apparently random low anchor value judged they could solve fewer of the remaining items than did subjects in any of the other conditions. The effects of the low anchor were evident even after the performance session had entirely concluded. When asked how well they thought they could do if, hypothetically, they were to perform the task again, low anchor subjects displayed a level of perceived self-efficacy that was significantly below their actual past performance (Fig. 3.5).

These results help to explain the earlier findings (Cervone & Peake, 1986; Peake & Cervone, 1989). Even subtle judgmental influences can strongly affect initial efficacy judgments that are made under conditions of high uncertainty. These judgmental biases have an enduring behavioral effect because people's initial perceptions of their capabilities are themselves highly persistent. This pattern of findings is consistent with social psychological research on belief perseverance. Initial beliefs can be highly resistant to change, even when the evidential basis for those beliefs is completely discredited (Anderson, Lepper, & Ross, 1980; Ross, Lepper, & Hubbard, 1975).

Anchoring biases represent a specific type of judgmental influence that arises when people begin an estimation task by considering a potential value and adjust

FIG. 3.5. Differences between past performance and perceived self-efficacy for future performance (scored such that negative values indicate self-efficacy perceptions that are lower than past attainments), as a function of initial exposure to apparently random anchor values. From Cervone, D., & Palmer, B. W. (1990). Anchoring biases and the perseverance of self-efficacy beliefs. *Cognitive Therapy and Research, 14,* 401–416. Reprinted by permission of Plenum Press.

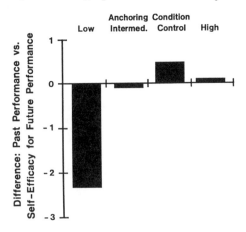

their final estimate from that value. More generally, this kind of bias arises because it is impossible for one to fully consider and integrate all the information that might be pertinent to making a complex judgment. Doing so simply exceeds one's information-processing capacities. Instead, judgments often must be based on a quick assessment of information that happens to come to mind quickly. Self-efficacy judgments, for example, largely may reflect a relatively small bit of self-knowledge, autobiographical memory, and situational information that happens to come to mind most quickly or is highly available (Tversky & Kahneman, 1973). The most cognitively available factors often may be the most important ones to consider; one's vivid memory of tumbling down a slope may indeed be quite pertinent when judging which run to attempt on one's next ski trip. However, factors other than normative importance can affect availability. An arbitrary factor or experience may lead one to focus on a particular feature of a task, or a personal strength or weakness, and thereby exert undue influence on efficacy judgments and behavior.

The role of cognitive availability in self-efficacy judgment and motivation was investigated in a study by Cervone (1989). Here, self-efficacy judgments were influenced not by having subjects consider a specific high or low level of performance, but merely by having them focus on factors that might facilitate or impede their performance. It was reasoned that focusing on potential "success" versus "failure" related factors would make them more cognitively available when subsequently judging one's capabilities for performance. In a preexperimental questionnaire, subjects were asked a number of questions about their impressions of the geometric task and experience with similar problems. Two questions served as the experimental manipulation. These items asked subjects to write brief responses describing external factors (e.g., complexity of the problems, time constraints) and personal qualities (e.g., spatial ability, difficulty in working under time pressure) that might influence their overall performance on the geometric task. In one experimental condition, these items were phrased in terms of factors that could make the task relatively easy. In another, subjects' focus was directed to factors that might make the problems difficult for them. As hypothesized, subjects who focused on personal limitations and difficult aspects of the task had the lowest judgments of their performance capabilities (Cervone, 1989). When attempting the task, these subjects also were the quickest to give up on the problems when they became difficult. Regression analyses again indicated that self-efficacy perceptions fully mediated the impact of judgmental biases on motivation.

This line of research on judgmental heuristics, self-efficacy judgment, and action (Cervone, 1989; Cervone & Palmer, 1990; Cervone & Peake, 1986; Peake & Cervone, 1989) has involved a specialized laboratory paradigm and the explicit introduction of factors designed to illustrate the role of judgmental heuristics and biases. This should not be taken to imply that such judgmental processes are rare. Numerous situations may contain salient cues that serve as anchor points in self-judgment. One's own past performance may be the most common of such cues; if so, anchoring-and-adjustment processes may be at least partly responsible for the considerable temporal stability often found in both self-perceptions and behavior (e.g., Mischel & Peake, 1982). Anchoring processes also may be at work in social situations that involve subtle indicants of ability. Langer and Benevento (1978) found that performance can be impaired by interpersonal factors such as the assignment of a social label that connotes inferiority. One effect of such a label may be to provide a low anchor. The label may bias self-efficacy judgments by leading individuals to consider the possibility of their performing relatively poorly. The availability heuristic may be relied upon in any social situation in which one must quickly assess one's capabilities to cope with a complex environment. Availability processes also may play a critical role in therapeutic interventions. Modeling therapies, including cognitive modeling procedures in which individuals envision themselves coping successfully with an activity (e.g., Hersen, Kazdin, Bellack, & Turner, 1979), may be effective in part by raising the cognitive availability of manageable aspects of a task or one's own coping skills.

CONCLUSIONS

Let us conclude by considering a somewhat broader perspective on personal and situational determinants of motivated action. The present social cognitive theory analysis of goal motivation coincides with a number of recent theoretical perspectives in highlighting a central theme, one with three parts: (a) "The self" is not a single, unitary, undifferentiated entity; instead, cognitive processes and structures related to the self are highly complex, differentiated, and multifaceted; (b) social contexts play a critical role in activating particular aspects of self-referent thinking; (c) social behavior and affect are most influenced by those aspect of self that are highly activated in a given setting. In their model of personality and social intelligence, Cantor and Kihlstrom (1987) argued that people may possess a diverse array of declarative and procedural self-knowledge and that different aspects of self-knowledge are pertinent to solving different life tasks. Markus and Wurf's (1987) model of the dynamic self-concept suggested that self-concept is highly multifaceted and that experiences are shaped by those aspects of self that are accessible at a given moment, or are part of the "working self-concept." Higgins' (1990) analysis of the mechanisms through which people assign meaning to events similarly indicated that situational cues can prime particular constructs, thus influencing the categories people use to understand and evaluate the social world and themselves. Dweck's model of motivation and personality (Dweck & Leggett, 1988; Elliott & Dweck, 1988) noted earlier, indicated that situational factors can alter the goal orientations people adopt on activities and that different goal orientations, in turn, differentially activate attributional and self-referent thinking.

Such dynamic interactions among social contexts and self-referent thinking constitute one of the most important themes in contemporary personality psychology (Cervone, 1991). Progress in understanding how individuals differ from one another in their levels of motivation and achievement, their approaches to important life tasks, and their characteristic patterns of social behavior can best be achieved by examining the reciprocal relations between the environment and the self-referent processes through which individuals understand the world, set goals for themselves, and regulate their actions.

ACKNOWLEDGMENTS

Gratitude is expressed to Jim Kelly, Mitch Rabinowitz, and Walter Scott for their comments on the manuscript.

REFERENCES

Ahrens, A. H. (1987). Theories of depression: The role of goals and the self-evaluation process. *Cognitive Therapy and Research, 11,* 665–680.

Ames, C. A. (1986). Conceptions of motivation within competitive and noncompetitive goal structures. In R. Schwarzer (Ed.), *Self-related cognitions in anxiety and motivation* (pp. 229–245). Hillsdale, NJ: Lawrence Erlbaum Associates.

Anderson, C. A., Lepper, M. R., & Ross, L. (1980). The perseverance of social theories: The role of explanation in the persistence of discredited information. *Journal of Personality and Social Psychology, 39,* 1037–1049.

Bandura, A. (1977). Self-efficacy: Toward a unifying theory of behavioral change. *Psychological Review, 84,* 191–215.

Bandura, A. (1978). The self-system in reciprocal determinism. *American Psychologist, 33,* 344–358.

Bandura, A. (1986). *Social foundations of thought and action: A social cognitive theory.* Englewood Cliffs, NJ: Prentice–Hall.

Bandura, A. (1989). Self-regulation of motivation and action through internal standards and goal systems. In L. A. Pervin (Ed.), *Goal concepts in personality and social psychology* (pp. 19–85). Hillsdale, NJ: Lawrence Erlbaum Associates.

Bandura, A., Adams, N. E., & Beyer, J. (1977). Cognitive processes mediating behavioral change. *Journal of Personality and Social Psychology, 35,* 125–139.

Bandura, A., & Cervone, D. (1983). Self-evaluative and self-efficacy mechanisms governing the motivational effects of goal systems. *Journal of Personality and Social Psychology, 45,* 1017–1028.

Bandura, A., & Cervone, D. (1986). Differential engagement of self-reactive influences in cognitive motivation. *Organizational Behavior and Human Decision Processes, 38,* 92–113.

Bandura, A., Cioffi, D., Taylor, C. B., & Brouillard, M. E. (1988). Perceived self-efficacy in coping with cognitive stressors and opioid activation. *Journal of Personality and Social Psychology, 55,* 479–488.

Bandura, A., Grusec, J. E., & Menlove, F. L. (1967). Some social determinants of self-monitoring reinforcement systems. *Journal of Personality and Social Psychology, 5,* 449–455.

Bandura, A., & Jourdan, F. J. (1991). Self-regulatory mechanisms governing the impact of social comparison on complex decision making. *Journal of Personality and Social Psychology, 60,* 941–951.

Bandura, A., & Kupers, C. J. (1964). The transmission of patterns of self-reinforcement through modeling. *Journal of Abnormal and Social Psychology, 69,* 1–9.

Bandura, A., Reese, L., & Adams, N. E. (1982). Microanalysis of action and fear arousal as a function of differential levels of perceived self-efficacy. *Journal of Personality and Social Psychology, 43,* 5–21.

Bandura, A., & Schunk, D. H. (1981). Cultivating competence, self-efficacy and intrinsic interest through proximal self-motivation. *Journal of Personality and Social Psychology, 41,* 586–598.

Bandura, A., & Simon, K. M. (1977). The role of proximal intentions in the self-regulation of refractory behavior. *Cognitive Therapy and Research, 1,* 177–193.

Bandura, A., Taylor, C. B., Williams, S. L., & Mefford, I. N., & Barchas, J. D. (1985). Catecholamine secretion as a function of perceived coping self-efficacy. *Journal of Consulting and Clinical Psychology, 53,* 406–414.

Bandura, A., & Wood, R. (1989). Effect of perceived controllability and performance standards on self-regulation of complex decision-making. *Journal of Personality and Social Psychology, 56,* 805–814.

Becker, L. J. (1978). Joint effect of feedback and goal setting on performance: A field study of residential energy conservation. *Journal of Applied Psychology, 63,* 428–433.

Betz, N. E., & Hackett, G. (1986). Applications of self-efficacy theory to understanding career choice behavior. *Journal of Social and Clinical Psychology, 4,* 279–289.

Borkovec, T. D. (1978). Self-efficacy: Cause or reflection of behavioral change? In S. Rachman (Ed.), *Advances in behaviour research and therapy* (Vol. 1, pp. 163–170). Oxford: Pergamon.

Brown, I., Jr., & Inouye, D. K. (1978). Learned helplessness through modeling: The role of perceived similarity in competence. *Journal of Personality and Social Psychology, 36,* 900–908.

Bruner, J. (1990). *Acts of meaning.* Cambridge, MA: Harvard University Press.

Campion, M. A., & Lord, R. G. (1982). A control systems conceptualization of the goal-setting and changing process. *Organization Behavior and Human Performance, 30,* 265–287.

Cantor, N., & Kihlstrom, J. F. (1987). *Personality and social intelligence.* Englewood Cliffs, NJ: Prentice-Hall.

Carver, C. S., & Scheier, M. F. (1981). *Attention and self-regulation: A control theory approach to human behavior.* New York: Springer-Verlag.

Carver, C. S., & Scheier, M. F. (1990). Principles of self-regulation: Action and emotion. In E. T. Higgins & R. M. Sorrentino (Eds.), *Motivation and cognition: Foundations of social behavior* (Vol. 2, pp. 3–52). New York: Guilford.

Cervone, D. (1985). Randomization tests to determine significance levels for microanalytic congruences between self-efficacy and behavior. *Cognitive Therapy and Research, 9,* 357–365.

Cervone, D. (1989). Effects of envisioning future activities on self-efficacy judgments and motivation: An availability heuristic interpretation. *Cognitive Therapy and Research, 13,* 247–261.

Cervone, D. (1991). The two disciplines of personality psychology. *Psychological Science, 2,* 371–377.

Cervone, D., Jiwani, N., & Wood, R. (1991). Goal-setting and the differential influence of self-regulatory processes on complex decision-making performance. *Journal of Personality and Social Psychology, 61,* 257–266.

Cervone, D., & Kopp, D. A. (1990). *Learning goals, performance goals and the differential influence of self-regulatory processes on complex decision making.* Paper presented at the Annual Convention of the Midwestern Psychological Association, Chicago.

Cervone, D., & Palmer, B. W. (1990). Anchoring biases and the perseverance of self-efficacy beliefs. *Cognitive Therapy and Research, 14,* 401–416.

Cervone, D., & Peake, P. K. (1986). Anchoring, efficacy, and action: The influence of judgmental heuristics on self-efficacy judgments and behavior. *Journal of Personality and Social Psychology, 50,* 492–501.

Cervone, D., & Williams, S. L. (in press). Social cognitive theory and personality. In G. V. Caprara

& G. L. Van Heck (Eds.), *Modern personality psychology: Critical reviews and new directions*. New York: Wiley.

Cervone, D., & Wood, R. (1991). *Goals, feedback, and the differential influence of self-regulatory processes on a complex decision task*. Unpublished manuscript, University of Illinois, Chicago.

Christensen-Szalanski, J. J. J. (1980). A further examination of the selection of problem-solving strategies: The effects of deadlines and analytic aptitudes. *Organizational Behavior and Human Performance, 25*, 107–122.

Cohen, C. E., & Ebbesen, E. B. (1979). Observational goals and schema activation: A theoretical framework for behavior perception. *Journal of Experimental Social Psychology, 15*, 305–329.

Csikszentmihalyi, M. (1990). *Flow: The psychology of optimal experience*. New York: Harper & Row.

Csikszentmihalyi, M., & LeFevre, J. (1989). Optimal experience in work and leisure. *Journal of Personality and Social Psychology, 56*, 815–822.

Dubbert, P. M., & Wilson, G. T. (1984). Goal-setting and spouse involvement in the treatment of obesity. *Behavior Research and Therapy, 22*, 227–242.

Dweck, C. S., & Leggett, E. L. (1988). A social-cognitive approach to motivation and personality. *Psychological Review, 95*, 256–273.

Earley, P. C., Connolly, T., & Ekegren, C. (1989). Goals, strategy development, and task performance: Some limits on the efficacy of goal setting. *Journal of Applied Psychology, 74*, 24–33.

Earley, P. C., Wojnaroski, P., & Prest, W. (1987). Task planning and energy expended: Exploration of how goals influence performance. *Journal of Applied Psychology, 72*, 107–114.

Elliott, E. S., & Dweck, C. S. (1988). Goals: An approach to motivation and achievement. *Journal of Personality and Social Psychology, 54*, 5–12.

Erez, M. (1977). Feedback: A necessary condition for the goal setting–performance relationship. *Journal of Applied Psychology, 62*, 624–627.

Ericsson, K. A., & Simon, H. A. (1980). Verbal reports as data. *Psychological Review, 87*, 215–251.

Festinger, L. (1942). A theoretical interpretation of shifts in level of aspiration. *Psychological Review, 49*, 235–250.

Heckhausen, H. (1967). *The anatomy of achievement motivation*. New York: Academic Press.

Hersen, M., Kazdin, A. E., Bellack, A. S., & Turner, S. M. (1979). Effects of live modeling, covert modeling, and rehearsal on assertiveness in psychiatric patients. *Behaviour Research and Therapy, 17*, 369–377.

Higgins, E. T. (1987). Self-discrepancy: A theory relating self and affect. *Psychological Review, 94*, 319–340.

Higgins, E. T. (1990). Personality, social psychology, and person–situation relations: Standards and knowledge activation as a common language. In L. A. Pervin (Ed.), *Handbook of personality: Theory and research* (pp. 301–338). New York: Guilford.

Hoffman, C., Mischel, W., & Mazze, K. (1981). The role of purpose in the organization of information about behavior: Trait-based versus goal-based categories in person cognition. *Journal of Personality and Social Psychology, 40*, 211–225.

Hsee, C. K., & Abelson, R. P. (1991). Velocity relation: Satisfaction as a function of the first derivative of outcome over time. *Journal of Personality and Social Psychology, 60*, 341–347.

Hsee, C. K., Abelson, R. P., & Salovey, P. (1991). The relative weighting of position and velocity in satisfaction. *Psychological Science, 2*, 263–266.

Huber, V. L., & Neale, M. A. (1987). Effects of self- and competitor goals in performance in an interdependent bargaining task. *Journal of Applied Psychology, 72*, 197–203.

Humphreys, M. S., & Revelle, W. (1984). Personality, motivation, and performance: A theory of the relationship between individual differences and information processing. *Psychological Review, 91*, 153–184.

Isen, A. M. (1987). Positive affect, cognitive processes, and social behavior. In L. Berkowitz (Ed.),

Advances in experimental social psychology (Vol. 20, pp. 203–253). San Diego: Academic Press.

Isen, A. M., Shalker, T. E., Clark, M., & Karp, L. (1978). Affect, accessibility of material in memory, and behavior: A cognitive loop? *Journal of Personality and Social Psychology, 36,* 1–12.

Kahneman, D., Slovic, P., & Tversky, A. (1982). *Judgment under uncertainty: Heuristics and biases* (pp. 201–208). Cambridge: Cambridge University Press.

Kahneman, D., & Tversky, A. (1982). The simulation heuristic. In D. Kahneman, P. Slovic, & A. Tversky (Eds.), *Judgment under uncertainty: Heuristics and biases* (pp. 201–208). Cambridge: Cambridge University Press.

Kanfer, F. H. (1980). Self-management methods. In F. H. Kanfer & A. P. Goldstein (Eds.), *Helping people change* (2nd ed., pp. 334–389). New York: Pergamon.

Kanfer, F. H., & Grimm, L. (1978). Freedom of choice and behavioral change. *Journal of Consulting and Clinical Psychology, 46,* 873–878.

Kanfer, F. H., & Schefft, B. K. (1987). Self-management therapy in clinical practice. In N. S. Jacobsen (Ed.), *Psychotherapists in clinical practice: Cognitive and behavioral perspectives.* New York: Guilford.

Kavanagh, D. J., & Bower, G. H. (1985). Mood and self-efficacy: Impact of joy and sadness on perceived capabilities. *Cognitive Therapy and Research, 9,* 507–525.

Kazdin, A. E. (1974). Reactive self-monitoring: The effects of response desirability, goal setting, and feedback. *Journal of Consulting and Clinical Psychology, 42,* 704–716.

Kirschenbaum, D. S. (1985). Proximity and specificity of planning: A position paper. *Cognitive Therapy and Research, 9,* 489–506.

Kirschenbaum, D. S. (1987). Self-regulatory failure: A review with clinical implications. *Clinical Psychology Review, 7,* 77–104.

Kirschenbaum, D. S., Humphrey, L. L., & Malett, S. D. (1981). Specificity of planning in adult self-control: An applied investigation. *Journal of Personality and Social Psychology, 40,* 941–950.

Kirschenbaum, D. S., Malett, S. D., Humphrey, L. L., & Tomarken, A. J. (1982). Specificity of planning and the maintenance of adult self-control: One-year follow-up of a study improvement program. *Behavior Therapy, 13,* 232–240.

Kirschenbaum, D. S., Tomarken, A. J., & Ordman, A. M. (1982). Specificity of planning and choice applied to adult self-control. *Journal of Personality and Social Psychology, 42,* 576–585.

Langer, E., & Benevento, A. (1978). Self-induced dependence. *Journal of Personality and Social Psychology, 36,* 886–893.

LaPorte, R. E., & Nath, R. (1976). Role of performance goals in prose learning. *Journal of Educational Psychology, 68,* 260–264.

Latham, G. P., & Yukl, G. A. (1976). The effects of assigned and participative goal setting on performance and job satisfaction. *Journal of Applied Psychology, 61,* 166–171.

Lee, T. W., Locke, E. A., & Latham, G. P. (1989). Goal setting theory and job performance. In L. A. Pervin (Ed.), *Goal concepts in personality and social psychology* (pp. 291–326). Hillsdale, NJ: Lawrence Erlbaum Associates.

Lepper, M. R., Sagotsky, J., & Mailer, J. (1975). Generalization and persistence of effects of exposure to self-reinforcement models. *Child Development, 46,* 618–630.

Lewin, K., Dembo, T., Festinger, L., & Sears, P. S. (1944). Level of aspiration. In J. M. Hunt (Ed.), *Personality and the behavior disorders* (Vol. 1, pp. 333–378). New York: Ronald Press.

Locke, E. A. (1968). Toward a theory of task motivation and incentives. *Organizational Behavior and Human Performance, 3,* 157–189.

Locke, E. A., & Bryan, J. F. (1967). Performance goals as determinants of level of performance and boredom. *Journal of Applied Psychology, 51,* 120–130.

Locke, E. A., Cartledge, N., & Knerr, C. S. (1970). Studies of the relationship between satisfaction, goal setting, and performance. *Organizational Behavior and Human Performance, 5,* 135–158.

Locke, E. A., Frederick, E., Lee, C., & Bobko, P. (1984). Effect of self-efficacy, goals, and task strategies on task performance. *Journal of Applied Psychology, 69,* 241–251.

Locke, E. A., & Latham, G. P. (1984). *Goal-setting: A motivational technique that works.* Englewood Cliffs, NJ: Prentice-Hall.

Locke, E. A., & Latham, G. P. (1990a). *A theory of goal setting and task performance.* Englewood Cliffs, NJ: Prentice-Hall.

Locke, E. A., & Latham, G. P. (1990b). Work motivation and satisfaction: Light at the end of the tunnel. *Psychological Science, 1,* 240–246.

Locke, E. A., Shaw, K. N., Saari, L. M., & Latham, G. P. (1981). Goal setting and task performance: 1969–1980. *Psychological Bulletin, 90,* 125–152.

Manderlink, G., & Harackiewicz, J. M. (1984). Proximal versus distal goal setting and intrinsic motivation. *Journal of Personality and Social Psychology, 47,* 918–928.

Markus, H., & Wurf, E. (1987). The dynamic self-concept: A social psychological perspective. *Annual Review of Psychology, 38,* 299–337.

Matsui, T., Okada, A., & Inoshita, O. (1983). Mechanism of feedback affecting task performance. *Organizational Behavior and Human Performance, 31,* 114–122.

Mento, A. J., Steel, R. P., & Karren, R. J. (1987). A meta-analytic study of the effects of goal setting on task performance: 1966–1984. *Organizational Behavior and Human Decision Processes, 39,* 52–83.

Miller, G. A., Galanter, E., & Pribram, K. H. (1960). *Plans and the structure of behavior.* New York: Holt Rinehart & Winston.

Mischel, W. (1973). Toward a cognitive social learning reconceptualization of personality. *Psychological Review, 80,* 252–283.

Mischel, W., & Peake, P. K. (1982). Beyond deja-vu in the search for cross-situational consistency. *Psychological Review, 89,* 730–755.

Nicholls, J. G. (1984). Achievement motivation: Conceptions of ability, subjective experience, task choice, and performance. *Psychological Review, 91,* 328–346.

Nisbett, R., & Ross, L. (1980). *Human inference: Strategies and shortcomings of social judgment.* Englewood Cliffs, NJ: Prentice-Hall.

Nisbett, R., & Wilson, T. D. (1977). Telling more than we can know: Verbal reports on mental processes. *Psychological Review, 84,* 231–259.

Payne, R. B., & Hauty, G. T. (1955). Effect of psychological feedback upon work decrement. *Journal of Experimental Psychology, 50,* 343–351.

Peake, P. K., & Cervone, D. (1989). Sequence anchoring and self-efficacy: Primacy effects in the consideration of possibilities. *Social Cognition, 7,* 31–50.

Pervin, L. A. (Ed.). (1989). *Goal concepts in personality and social psychology.* Hillsdale, NJ: Lawrence Erlbaum Associates.

Podsakoff, P. M., & Farh, J. (1989). Effects of feedback sign and credibility on goal setting and task performance. *Organizational Behavior and Human Decision Processes, 44,* 45–67.

Rehm, L. P. (1977). A self-control model of depression. *Behavior Therapy, 8,* 787–804.

Rehm, L. P. (1982). Self-management in depression. In P. Karoly & F. H. Kanfer (Eds.), *Self-management and behavior change: From theory to practice.* New York: Pergamon Press.

Rehm, L. P., & Rokke, P. (1988). Self-management therapies. In K. S. Dobson (Ed.), *Handbook of cognitive-behavioral therapies* (pp. 136–166). New York: Guilford.

Ross, L., Lepper, M. R., & Hubbard, M. (1975). Perseverance in self-perception and social perception: Biased attributional processes in the debriefing paradigm. *Journal of Personality and Social Psychology, 32,* 880–892.

Rothkopf, E. Z., & Billington, M. J. (1975). A two-factor model of the effect of goal descriptive directions on learning from text. *Journal of Educational Psychology, 67,* 692–704.

Rothkopf, E. Z., & Billington, M. J. (1979). Goal-guided learning from text: Inferring a descriptive processing model from inspection times and eye movements. *Journal of Educational Psychology, 71,* 310–327.

Russell, D., & McAuley, E. (1986). Causal attributions, causal dimensions, and affective reactions to success and failure. *Journal of Personality and Social Psychology, 50,* 1174–1185.

Sales, S. M. (1970). Some effects of role overload and role underload. *Organizational Behavior and Human Performance, 5,* 592–608.

Sarason, I. G. (1975). Anxiety and self-preoccupation. In I. G. Sarason & D. C. Spielberger (Eds.), *Stress and anxiety* (Vol. 2, pp. 27–44). Washington, DC: Hemisphere.

Sarason, I. G., Sarason, B. R., & Pierce, G. R. (1990). Anxiety, cognitive interference, and performance. *Journal of Social Behavior and Personality, 5,* 1–18.

Schunk, D. H. (1984). Self-efficacy perspective on achievement behavior. *Educational Psychologist, 19,* 48–58.

Simon, H. A., & Reed, S. (1976). Modeling strategy shifts in a problem-solving task. *Cognitive Psychology, 8,* 86–97.

Simon, K. M. (1979). Self-evaluative reactions: The role of personal valuation of the activity. *Cognitive Therapy and Research, 3,* 111–116.

Skinner, B. F. (1953). *Science and human behavior.* New York: Macmillan.

Stevenson, M. K., Kanfer, F. H., & Higgins, J. M. (1984). Effects of goal specificity and time cues on pain tolerance. *Cognitive Therapy and Research, 8,* 415–426.

Stock, J., & Cervone, D. (1990). Proximal goal-setting and self-regulatory processes. *Cognitive Therapy and Research, 14,* 483–489.

Strang, H. R., Lawrence, E. C., & Fowler, P. C. (1978). Effects of assigned goal level and knowledge of results on arithmetic computation: A laboratory study. *Journal of Applied Psychology, 63,* 29–39.

Taylor, S. E., & Brown, J. D. (1988). Illusion and well-being: A social psychological perspective on mental health. *Psychological Bulletin, 103,* 193–210.

Taylor, M. S., Locke, E. A., Lee, C., & Gist, M. E. (1984). Type A behavior and faculty research productivity: What are the mechanisms? *Organizational Behavior and Human Performance, 34,* 402–418.

Terkel, S. (1972). *Working.* New York: Pantheon.

Thomas, J. C., Jr. (1974). An analysis of behavior in the hobbits–orcs problem. *Cognitive Psychology, 6,* 257–269.

Thoresen, C. E., & Mahoney, M. J. (1974). *Behavioral self-control.* New York: Holt Rinehart & Winston.

Tubbs, M. E. (1986). Goal setting: A meta-analytic examination of the empirical evidence. *Journal of Applied Psychology, 71,* 474–483.

Tversky, A., & Kahneman, D. (1973). Availability: A heuristic for judging frequency and probability. *Cognitive Psychology, 5,* 207–232.

Tversky, A., & Kahneman, D. (1974). Judgment under uncertainty: Heuristics and biases. *Science, 185,* 1123–1131.

Watson, D. L., & Tharp, R. G. (1977). *Self-directed behavior: Self-modification for personal adjustment* (2nd ed.). Monterey, CA: Brooks/Cole.

Weiner, B. (1985). An attributional theory of achievement motivation and emotion. *Psychological Review, 92,* 548–573.

Wood, R., & Bailey, T. (1985). Some unanswered questions about goal effects: A recommended change in research methods. *Australian Journal of Management, 10,* 61–73.

Wood, R., & Bandura, A. (1989). Impact of conceptions of ability on self-regulatory mechanisms and complex decision making. *Journal of Personality and Social Psychology, 56,* 407–415.

Wood, R., Bandura, A., & Bailey, T. (1990). Mechanisms governing organizational productivity in complex decision-making environments, *Organizational Behavior and Human Decision Processes, 46,* 181–201.

Wood, R., & Locke, E. A. (1990). Goal setting and strategy effects on complex tasks. Contribution to E. A. Locke and G. P. Latham, *A theory of goal setting and task performance.* Englewood Cliffs, NJ: Prentice-Hall.

Wood, R., Mento, A. J., & Locke, E. A. (1987). Task complexity as a moderator of goal effects: A meta-analysis. *Journal of Applied Psychology, 72,* 416–425.

4 Cognitive Task Analysis as a Basis for Instructional Design

Barbara Means
SRI International

Many of the preceding chapters describe ways in which technologies can be used to implement instructional strategies drawn from cognitive principles. In this chapter, I am going to back up a bit in the process of instructional design to deal with the issue of how we determine what should be taught. Specifically, I focus on cognitive psychology approaches to the analysis of tasks for the purpose of training design. First, I briefly describe traditional approaches to task analysis for instructional design. After arguing that these approaches, although useful for many purposes, have limits when applied to cognitively demanding tasks, I discuss implications from the cognitive psychology literature for how such tasks should be analyzed. I then describe cognitive task analysis as it has been used by me and my colleagues in studies of the performance of demanding job tasks. I describe the methods and some outcomes from studies of avionics technicians and air traffic controllers. Finally, I close with a discussion of strengths and weaknesses in this approach to analyzing training requirements.

TASK ANALYSIS IN THE TRADITIONAL MOLD

A systems approach to training (generally called *instructional systems design* or, more simply, *instructional design*) dominates job training offered in the military and, for the most part, within corporate settings as well. This approach, summarized in Fig. 4.1, is conceptualized as a systematic sequence of activities beginning with the identification of the tasks that need to be trained and the analysis of those tasks, which then provides the foundation for defining instructional objectives, designing tests, and selecting instructional strategies. (See

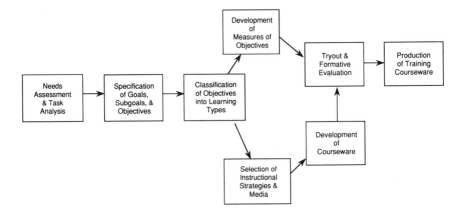

FIG. 4.1.   Stages in instructional systems development.

Briggs & Wager, 1981, or Reiguluth, 1983, for recent accounts of this process.) In traditional behavioral approaches to task analysis, the task is broken down into a series of procedural steps. The concern here is with the task as performed by experts, and the emphasis is on concrete observable actions. Typically, the instructional designer will either specify the steps him or herself on the basis of available task documentation or will interview a job incumbent who performs the task, "What do you do first? What next? What comes after that?" In this way, an algorithm for performing the task is specified, as illustrated by the example in Fig. 4.2. The analyst then proceeds to identify prerequisites for the steps in task performance. These may be subskills incorporated in task performance or information about when the task is to be performed. As Gagne (1977) described the process, the instructional designer identifies prerequisites by asking "What should the learner already know how to do or be able to recall when faced with the task of learning this new skill?"

An alternative to this rational task analysis by the instructional designer that is used in many larger scale training development efforts is to survey job incumbents or their supervisors concerning the knowledge, skills, and attitudes needed for performing various tasks ("KSAs"). Given a list of job tasks and a set of skills, knowledge elements, and attitudes, the survey respondents indicate which tasks are actually performed on the job and the KSAs of those tasks. This type of analysis provides a rationale for deciding what skills, knowledge, and attitudes should be trained for which jobs but offers less than the behavioral task analysis described previously in that it does not tell the instructional designer anything about the sequence of steps in task performance (i.e., how the skills and knowledge are used to accomplish any particular task).

The traditional behavioral approach to task analysis can be highly efficient for tasks that are deterministic enough that they *can* be specified by an algorithm,

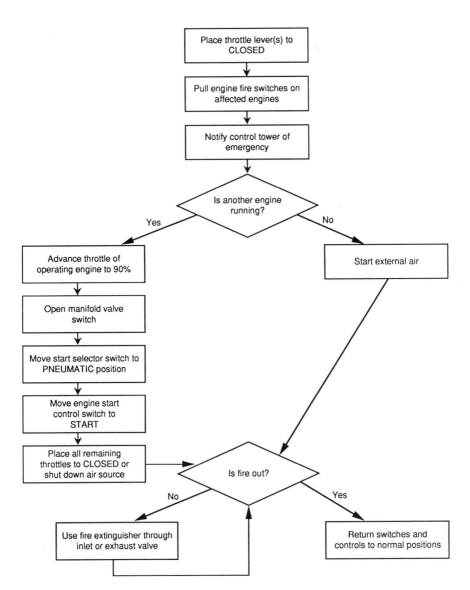

FIG. 4.2. Example of a behavioral task analysis: Extinguishing an external engine fire. Source: Aircraft Maintenance Training Development Branch (January 1990). B-52H Engine run, OJT instructor guide. Carswell AFB, TX.

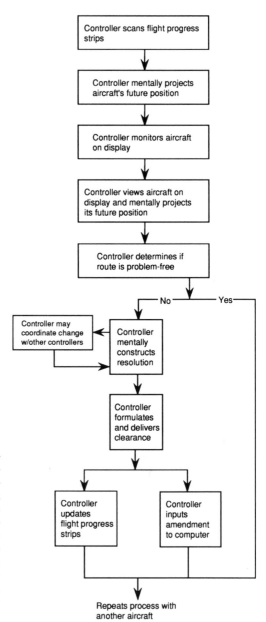

FIG. 4.3. Conventional analysis of air traffic control conflict detection and resolution. Source: Carlson, L. S., & Rhodes, L. R. (1988). A process for defining training requirements associated with new automated capabilities. In *Proceedings of the Symposium on Air Traffic Control Training for Tomorrow's Technology,* Federal Aviation Administration.

especially when the critical steps in performing the task are observable behaviors rather than cognitive operations such as hypothesis formation, judgments, or problem solving. With tasks that do not meet these criteria, however, the traditional behavioral approach to task analysis can miss the boat. An example of such a task is air traffic control (ATC). Readers experienced with some of the more complex video games may have some appreciation for what it feels like to be responsible for 15 aircraft at different altitudes moving in different directions at different speeds. Identifying when intervention is necessary (when you must tell an aircraft to change its altitude or direction in order to keep it away from other aircraft), deciding which action would be most effective, and prioritizing the multiple problems of this kind that must be handled quickly while continuing to monitor other situations is a task whose demands are primarily cognitive.

A conventional task analysis commissioned by the Federal Aviation Administration (FAA) identified the steps in air traffic control as those shown in Fig. 4.3. What is apparent from an examination of the sequence of steps is that critical processes such as mentally projecting an aircraft's future position, detecting potential conflicts, and generating and evaluating possible solutions are not really described. By itself, this analysis would tell a student nothing about how to execute these vital parts of the task and would tell an instructor nothing about how to teach them. Learning the behavioral components such as marking on flight progress strips and issuing clearances to pilots does little good if the student has not learned the processes involved in identifying which pilots need to be spoken to and determining what they must be directed to do. It is precisely in areas such as this—where tasks involve problem solving and decision making and are not algorithmic—that we encounter our most difficult training challenges and find a cognitive approach most useful.

METHODS DRAWN FROM COGNITIVE PSYCHOLOGY

The extensive cognitive psychology literature contrasting expert and novice performance in a wide variety of domains (see Chi, Glaser, & Farr, 1988, for a review) has implications for the analysis of job tasks. The research clearly demonstrates the importance of domain-specific knowledge in expert performance and, by implication, in the design of effective training. In light of this research literature, we would want someone to become deeply immersed in a domain area before developing instruction in that domain. This approach runs counter to the prevailing practice in courseware development that assumes the instructional designer can apply generalized design skills to any content and provides for relatively little exposure to the task domain. If we really want to train people toward expertise, we must understand what that means and to do so requires a great deal of knowledge about the domain. This suggests that those involved in designing instructional curricula need to spend substantial amounts of time learning the domain, and that task analysis in these fields should be a thoroughly collaborative effort in which domain experts are used extensively.

Another finding from the expert–novice literature is the importance of the way the problem is mentally represented. Research in the domain of physics, for example, shows that experts and novices categorize problems differently. Experts group together problems that illustrate the same underlying principles, whereas novices put together problems on the basis of surface features, such as mentioning the same objects (Chi, Feltovich, & Glaser, 1981). When asked to solve problems, novices quickly invoke an equation that includes both what is known (stated in the problem) and what is unknown; experts spend much more time building a qualitative understanding of the problem, often drawing diagrams before ever writing an equation (Chi, Glaser, & Rees, 1982). It is their mental representation of the problem that drives the choices made by experts.

Neither traditional behavioral task analysis, with its focus on behavioral steps (rather than the understanding of the problem that determines which steps are executed), nor survey-based job analyses, which do not even address the issue of how the task is performed, provide information about how adept performers represent problems in their domain.

Finally, the cognitive research literature describes the process whereby previously separate steps in task performance get compiled into larger and larger procedures. As these are practiced extensively, they may achieve a state of *automaticity* in which they can be executed with little or no conscious awareness. This has great advantages for task performance, because these procedures can be executed without draining limited mental resources but presents a difficulty when experts are interviewed to identify the steps in task performance. Often they have difficulty describing each step in executing the task as many steps have become fused together. Even more difficult to capture is the expert's tacit set of categories for problems in the domain (Means & Gott, 1988). Experts come to see the world through these categories without necessarily having an awareness of doing so.

An implication of this research is that experts will not be able to provide the training developer with all the knowledge or procedural steps novices need to learn on demand. Rather, an extended interaction between the expert and the training analyst is needed in which the analyst pushes the expert to consider task performance in finer and finer detail. Often, the conditions associated with use of a particular procedure are not consciously available but must be extracted by giving the expert a wide range of conditions or problems to respond to and then working jointly to elucidate the rules that are being applied.

In the remainder of this chapter, I illustrate these three characteristics of cognitive task analysis (the importance of extensive domain knowledge and the role of domain experts, the focus on how problems are mentally represented, and the need to work with concrete instances to help domain experts access knowledge that has become tacit and skills that have become automatic) by describing several specific research projects. The first study involved investigating the skills and knowledge required of electronics technicians working in Air Force jobs requiring maintenance of high-technology equipment. The second employed a somewhat different set of cognitive task analysis procedures to examine expertise in air traffic control.

COGNITIVE TASK ANALYSIS FOR AVIONICS TECHNICIANS

The commitment to using specific, realistic problems representing critical job tasks was a major driver in developing the task analysis methodology for our study of Air Force avionics technicians.[1] In these jobs, maintenance technicians work in a shop where they receive aircraft "black boxes" that have been diagnosed as faulty on the flightline. Their job is to locate the fault and either fix it (if it can be done by replacement of a circuit board) or send the part to the depot for further repair. Large computer-controlled test stations are used to evaluate the black boxes. The test station simulates the aircraft, sending signals to the black box and then receiving signals back from the box under test and comparing them to specifications. We needed a set of realistic problems representing the hard parts of the job that were to be the target for training. Because the real equipment for the job is cumbersome, expensive, and under operational demand, we realized that we would have to present problems verbally, rather than faulting actual equipment. This meant that everytime a problem was posed to a subject and he or she indicated the action he or she would like to take on the system (e.g., measure voltage at a particular point), we had to be able to tell what the result of the action would be. Thus, both developing problems and providing feedback to problem solvers were going to require a degree of domain knowledge that instructional designers would be hard pressed to develop in the time available.

In response to this situation, we developed a method for using domain experts not only as subjects but also as research collaborators. For each site at which we studied a particular job, the best performers were identified (4 to 6 individuals depending on the site). These individuals were asked to define the types of troubleshooting problems that proved to be bottlenecks even after completion of the current training program and several years of job experience. Problem types are classes of things that might go bad (e.g., "bent pin 18 on the A8 card"). After each expert generated a list of problem types that occur frequently and are

---

[1]My colleagues in designing and executing this methodology included Allan Collins, Bolt Beranek and Newman; Sherrie Gott, Air Force Human Resources Laboratory; Alan Lesgold, Learning Research and Development Center; and Chris Roth, Human Resources Research Organization. This work was supported by the U.S. Air Force, but the opinions expressed herein are those of the author and should not be construed as Air Force policy.

difficult to troubleshoot for intellectual reasons, the experts met in a group to classify the candidate problem types into increasingly general categories (e.g., data control problems). The resulting problem categories represented the difficult troubleshooting requirements for the job.

For each problem category, one domain expert was given responsibility for developing a representative problem that would be appropriate for use as a diagnostic tool or as a context for training. The expert worked with a researcher to lay out the symptoms that would first appear, alternative steps a technician might take, and what a system faulted in the hypothesized manner would do in response to each action. This process included the expert's description of how he would troubleshoot the fault and his graphic representation of the parts of the system relevant to the problem.

Once the problem was laid out and thoroughly discussed by the domain expert and the researcher, it could be administered to other technicians. We began by giving the problem to another expert technician. The expert who developed the problem described the scenario in which the initial symptoms would be noticed. The expert doing the problem solving was then asked to describe what he would do upon encountering those symptoms and why. The problem solver was allowed to consult schematics or other technical documentation (just as on the job). If he indicated that he would take a certain measurement or run an automated diagnostic test, the expert who developed the problem acted as a "system simulation," telling him what the result of that test or measurement would be. The researcher's task was to probe the problem solver for the *thinking* underlying his choice of troubleshooting actions and his interpretation of the information he received from each action.

A fairly simple problem from one of the jobs we studied can be used to illustrate the kinds of information obtained. In this job, the most difficult troubleshooting problems are those that arise because the test station itself contains a fault. The test station consists of three banks of over a dozen drawers each, with each drawer full of circuit boards. The technical documentation for the system runs to some 60 volumes. In the sample problem, the technician has come into the maintenance shop after the weekend and attempted to turn on the automated test station. When the disk is installed and the run switch turned on, the disk drive spins up and the ready light on the disk drive comes on, but the system does not boot.

Figure 4.4 shows the initial representation of the relevant components as sketched by one troubleshooter. It should be noted that this is a high-level functional model, quite unlike the schematics in the technical documentation.

For each subject attempting to solve a problem, we produced a problem-solving trace. The trace consists of units called *sequences*. The sequences are structured around the problem solver's actions, which are concrete and easily stated by informants. In system troubleshooting, there are two kinds of actions: (a) information-gathering activities, such as reading schematics, and (b) actions

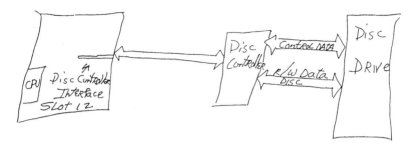

FIG. 4.4. Expert's initial problem representation.

on the system, such as running a diagnostic test. In addition to obtaining the sequence of actions (which would be just a behavioral record), we identified the *problem representation* motivating each action. We probed the troubleshooter for the reasoning, hypothesis, or goal underlying each overt action. We also record-ed the result of each action—the information gained in the case of information-gathering activities or the system's behavior, in the case of actions on the system—and the troubleshooter's interpretation of that information.

Table 4.1 displays the expert's problem-solving trace, derived from his verbal protocol, for our sample problem.

The expert's interpretation of the problem symptoms is that the computer itself is OK, but a problem exists either in the disk drive or in the interface between the computer and the disk drive. To try to distinguish between these two alternatives, he decides to try to boot the system again, this time watching the data light on the disk drive. When he does this, the data light does not come on, and the troubleshooter assumes that nothing is getting to the disk drive (and therefore that the disk drive itself can be assumed good). Thus, he has narrowed the suspect list to the disk controller, disk controller interface, and connecting cables. Because no one has been working on the station (and jiggling cables) over the weekend, he chooses to think about devices first. The disk controller has a relatively high rate of failure, and so he focuses on it. He chooses a simple check, looking at the power fault indicator inside the disk controller. Finding that it is not lit, he concludes that the problem is probably not a power fault inside the disk controller, but he wants to explore further to completely eliminate this possibility. He does this by checking the fuse and then performing voltage checks on the power supply regulator. At this point, he is thinking about power connec-tions within the disk controller, as illustrated in his second sketch (Fig. 4.5). After eliminating the disk controller as a suspect, he then goes to his alternative hypothesis, the connecting cables. Visually checking these, he finds that the read–write data cable between the disk controller and the disk drive is off.

Having recorded the problem solution as shown in the first column of Table 4.1, we can then work with our domain experts to analyze it in terms of the knowledge, skills, and strategies employed. These are shown in the second

TABLE 4.1
Sample Troubleshooting Problem Solving Record

Solution Trace	Instantiated Skill	Skill Category
Sequence 1		
PR: Computer not part of problem because it self-boots. Problem must be in disk drive or interface between it & the computer. If disk drive data light flickers on, data from the computer is getting to drive.	Knowing components involved in boot up Knowing function of disk drive data light	Device Model: Computer Interface Subsystem Device Model: Disk Drive
A: Reboot and observe data light on disk drive.		
R: Data light doesn't go on.		
I: Problem isn't in disk drive. Suspect interface between computer and disk drive (i.e., disk controller interface card, disk controller or cables).		
Sequence 2		
PR: Assume cables OK because no one has been working on the station. Suspect disk controller power because it fails fairly often.	Knowing fail rate for disk controller Knowing how power fail indicator lights function Knowing where power fail indicators are inside disk controller	Knowledge of fault probabilities (disk controller) Device Model: Fail Indicators Device Model: Disk Controller
A: Look at power fail indicators inside disk controller.		
R: Lights are not lit.		
I: Problem not likely to be power in disk controller, but could get no fault light because have 0 power.		
Sequence 3		
PR: If no power to disk controller, fail indicator lights can't light. Can check whether power coming in to disk controller at fuse.	Knowing where fuse is inside disk controller	Device Model: Disk Controller
A: Remove fuse and ohm check using DMM.	Knowing how to use DMM to check fuse	Use DMM for continuity & resistance checks
R: Near 0 ohms.		
I: Disk controller fuse OK.		

(Continued)

TABLE 4.1 (*continued*)

Solution Trace	Instantiated Skill	Skill Category
Sequence 4		
PR: Could still have no power if bad P/S regulator. Power supply regulators fail frequently.	Knowing how P/S regulator is related to power fail indicator lights	Device Model: Power Supply Regulator
A: Measure voltage at test points on power supply regulator.	Knowing disk controller P/S regulator fails often	Knowledge of fault probabilities (Power Supply Regulator)
R: ±5 and ±20 volts.		
I: Power leaving P/S regulator is OK so disk controller power must be good.	Knowing what test points on disk controller should measure	Device Model: Disk Controller
	Knowing how to measure voltages with DMM	Use DMM to test voltages
Sequence 5		
PR: Suspect cabling. Because could hear heads try to access, control data cable and cable between computer and disk controller are probably good.	Knowing that cables often slip off the disk controller	Knowledge of fault probabilities (cables)
	Knowing that if the disk drive head spins up, info is getting to disk drive from computer through the control cable	Device Models: Disk Drive and Control Cable
A: Check read/write cable between disk controller and disk drive.		
R: Cable is off at disk controller end.		
I: Fault identified.		

KEY: PR = Problem Representation
     A = Action
     R = Result
     I = Interpretation

column of the table. The troubleshooter's initial representation of the problem, for example, is based on knowledge of the components that comprise the computer–interface subsystem, and the role of each in the process of booting up the system. Thus, a great deal of device knowledge goes into his interpretation of symptoms (e.g., if the disk drive data light does not flicker on, the data signal is not getting that far). Taking another example, in Sequence 2 the troubleshooter distinguishes between device and connection problems and lets this distinction structure his troubleshooting. Another type of knowledge, base rate fault probability comes into play as he chooses between two devices (the disk controller and the disk controller interface card) for further exploration. Later sequences call upon such basic skills as using the digital multimeter (DMM) to check voltages.

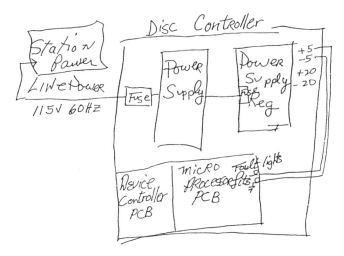

FIG. 4.5.   Expert's representation of power distribution inside the disk controller.

Whereas Column 2 describes skills and knowledge in terms specific to this problem (e.g., "knowing disk controller power supply regulator fails often"), Column 3 contains a more generic description of each (e.g., "knowledge of fault probabilities"), written in a form that is applicable across problems. These latter skill and knowledge categories, which are both broader and more generic than the statements of instantiated skills in Column 2, are useful for getting a sense of the importance of the various skill, knowledge, and strategy components within a job. To do so, we can look at the frequency with which each skill category is used across problems. Table 4.2 shows a portion of such a data summarization. By seeing the number of problems that involve a skill or knowledge category, the instructional designer can get an idea of how much weight to give it in the curriculum.

At the same time, a training or test developer may want to know how a certain skill is used within a job. By going back to the record of problem-solving sequences, the skill category can be used as an index to the portions of specific solutions in which the skill was used. The problems used as a context for collecting data on skill and knowledge requirements can be put to direct use in the development of assessment instruments (Hambleton, Gower, & Bollwark, 1988) or training materials, such as scenarios for use in an intelligent tutoring system (Frederiksen & White, 1988).

Multiple analyses of this type provide information about the kinds of knowledge about a system and its constituent devices that troubleshooters actually use and the extent to which skills, such as use of external test equipment, are important. The analyst will want to use enough problems to cover the content domain and to interview enough experts so that substantial agreement as to effective procedures emerges. Thus, the number of experts needed is dependent on the complexity of

TABLE 4.2
Matrix Showing Knowledge and Skill Requirements Across Problems

	Problem								
Skill/Knowledge/Strategy	Clock Generation	Clock/ Data	Power Supply 1	Power Supply 2	Relay	Measur. Input	Signal Condition	Wave Anal.	Bad Pins, Wiring
System & Device Knowledge									
UUT/TP/ATS Model	X			X	X			X	X
Generic Device Models									
Drawer	X	X							
Relay					X				X
Cable					X	X			X
Mechanical Fault Indicator			X						
Device Controller Card etc.	X	X							
Specific Device Models	ECP CCDP PPPS	Aux B NOISEAN	CCDP I/O	S/C	S/C MSSU	S/C SWDS	S/C MSSU IFSS		S/C
Knowledge of Fault Probabilities	CCDP	CCDP	CCDP			etc.	RF Generator		Test Package

109

the domain and the amount of variance in problem-solving approaches. Often, good agreement can be obtained with three or four experts. In some cases, twice that many may be needed to detect the dominant approach to a problem.

An alternative to using expert problem solutions as a guide for designing training would be to have those of intermediate skill levels (advanced apprentices) solve the problems. It can be argued that in complex fields their performance is a more realistic learning objective for novices. In some ways intermediate performers are easier to study, because processes are often less automatic for them, making their performance slower and more available for conscious articulation. In a world without resource constraints, I would like to see a detailed analysis of the course of skill acquisition within the domain, and this would entail detailed study of intermediate stages of proficiency as well as of full-blown expertise. If a choice must be made, however, I would argue that we need a clear picture of the ultimate objective of training, and that this can be obtained only by studying experts. In the area of system troubleshooting, for example, Tenney and Kurland (1988) found that the problem solving of intermediate troubleshooters would not provide a good model for novices. Although these technicians (with about 5 years of experience) have mastered certain procedures and can solve problems, they do not do so efficiently. Their application of procedures is stereotypic, and they avoid using technical manuals even when their own procedures are ineffective. The expert (with 10 years' experience) demonstrates a flexibility in applying procedures and a willingness to use technical documentation when needed that are important goals for training.

The previous description of the cognitive task analysis of avionics technicians illustrates both the extent to which the training designer becomes immersed in the content of the domain and the very active role played by subject matter experts. The emphasis this method places on capturing problem representations is evident from the structure of the problem-solving traces: It is the problem representation that elicits an action at each step in problem solving.

PRELIMINARY ANALYSIS OF AIR TRAFFIC CONTROL

My second example of the use of cognitive task analysis involves a task with a very different set of constraints, the high-performance domain of air traffic control. In contrast to most applications of cognitive task analysis that, like the preceding maintenance example, have concerned diagnostic tasks (either of hardware or of human physiology) where the reasoning process is deliberate and slow paced, air traffic control often must be performed under severe time pressure. Expert controllers make hundreds or even thousands of individual decisions in an hour, often with little conscious awareness of the many criteria they are using and how they are combining those criteria to arrive at a solution. Given this context, we could not expect controllers to think aloud and respond to researcher queries during the course of problem solving. To inject the kind of extensive probing routines we used with electronics troubleshooters into air traffic control would seriously distort controller performance. In coming up with an alternative method, however, we wanted to maintain our commitment to using domain experts as collaborators and using concrete problems as a context for questioning subjects about what they do, the knowledge they use to do it, and their decision processes. Our basic strategy was to videotape experts as they performed realistic air traffic control scenarios on full-scale simulators and to use the videotapes to elicit commentary from other expert controllers and retrospective protocols from our subjects.

Other aspects of our methodology were motivated by a desire to acquire evidence regarding how air traffic controllers mentally represent and organize the traffic for which they are responsible. From a practical standpoint, we were interested in the representation issue because it would provide information that would help the FAA decide whether to keep practice in traffic control without radar displays as part of their training and selection program. Controllers of the "old school" worry that new controllers are excessively dependent on the radar display and do not mentally picture air traffic in three dimensions. Controllers of the "new school" argue that the harder task of controlling traffic without a display is no longer part of the job and thus should not receive its current emphasis in training (most trainees who fail out of the program are eliminated because of difficulties with this task). From a theoretical and research orientation, we were interested in comparing chunking phenomena in air traffic control to those observed in chess (Chase & Simon, 1973), electronics (Egan & Schwartz, 1979), and physics (Chi et al., 1981).

The air route traffic control center that agreed to work with us provided (a) certified controllers with extensive experience as trainers to participate as research collaborators, (b) simulator facilities for running air traffic control scenarios, and (c) controllers to act as subjects.

The controller–collaborators worked with the research staff to select scenarios for use in this study. The selected scenarios all involved the same complex piece of air space ("sector") and a traffic quantity equal to the maximum a controller is likely to see in a typical day, as well as specific complexity factors such as questionable or intermittent radar coverage for a portion of the airspace. Through a process of peer and supervisor nominations, we obtained expert subjects who worked on the sector we had selected.

Scenarios were run using the radar simulator: The subject sat in front of a radar screen, identical to that used operationally, and viewed computer-presented radar tracks representing the various aircraft in the scenario. An adjacent flight strip bay contained the same types of flight information provided on the job. The scenario was run by one of the controller–collaborators and two assistants, working at other ATC workstations. Researchers provided instructions and audio and videotaped the subject, first as he studied the flight strip information, and then as he executed the scenario. Subjects were asked to think aloud as they studied the flight strips prior to the start of each scenario. This planning process was audiotaped as was the thinking aloud and verbal interchanges between the subject and those playing the roles of pilots and other controllers during the execution of the scenario.

After completing the scenario (which lasted between 35 and 50 minutes), the subject was asked to provide a "relief briefing" for one of the controller–collaborators, just as he would on the job. In a relief briefing, the controller turning over the sector describes what is in the sector and potential problems to which the controller coming on shift should attend.

Following the relief briefing, the subject was instructed to turn away from the radar display and was given a blank map of the sector. He was asked to sketch in all the planes that had been in the sector at the end of the scenario, indicating the call sign and/or type of aircraft. He was then asked to circle planes that went together as a group in his mind and to describe the group and explain why the planes were part of it. Following this task, the subject was given a second sector map and asked to draw in aircraft that had been involved in the three to five most critical incidents within the scenario. Again, he was asked to circle the aircraft that went together and explain why they did.

Following this initial data collection, the videotapes of the scenario execution were used in two types of review session. In the first of these, researchers reviewed the tape with the controller–collaborators to identify the major problems confronted during the scenario, alternative actions that the subject might have taken, and reasons that would support selection of one alternative or another. The second review was conducted with the subject and focused on the issues identified by the controller–collaborators. The videotape was stopped at critical points, and the subject was questioned about his plans at that time and the reasoning behind them.

The retrospective protocols gathered for a real-time high-performance task (such as air traffic control) are more vulnerable than the concurrent protocol methods used in less time-sensitive domains (such as avionics troubleshooting). Because the subjects' reports of the reasoning underlying their actions are provided retrospectively, there is greater concern about the reports' validity (Ericsson & Simon, 1984). It is difficult for subjects not to be influenced by their knowledge of what happened later in the scenario.

Although troublesome, this difficulty in pinning down the reasons behind every action with complete confidence is not really crippling when data across multiple subjects and problems are being combined to produce a set of training objectives; that is, we do not really need to know the reason for every single act in every single scenario if we can specify the knowledge that is used in making decisions, the skills that are required, and the strategies that are used to direct and orchestrate the performance.

Some Sample Findings

Retrospective Verbal Protocols.   As in the studies of electronics troubleshooters, detailed examination of the controller subject protocols can be used to identify the skills and knowledge controllers use. Table 4.3 shows a series of excerpts

TABLE 4.3
Excerpts from Controller's Retrospective Protocol

[Elapsed Time = 10:38. LN93 has just re-requested a direct route to GNV.]

1	E: Do you have any plan now for approaches?
2	S: Yeah. That's why I let the Lifegaurd go back direct Gainesville
3	with no questions. November 59 Papa's going to be first. November 59
4	Papa within 3 miles is going to be started down to 3000. 2000 [unintelligible]
5	E: What about AeroCoach 4?
6	S: AeroCoach 4 . . . I'll take him to the VOR, turn him out to the west, se-
7	quence him behind 59 Papa because if you'll look at AeroCoach 4, he's al-
8	ready a little bit slower than November 59 Papa.
9	E: So at this point, you're thinking 59 Papa's going to go first . . .
10	S: 59 Papa's going to go first, AeroCoach will swing right in behind
11	him . . .

[Elapsed Time = 10:40.]

12	S: Just looking at the strips and trying to see where everybody else
13	was going to fit, I knew I was going to have to spin those two and I
14	looked up at Taylor, I've got the 5 and the 11 up there. They're also
15	going to be a factor so they're going to have to be cleared to hold.
16	Just a simple 360 is not going to do it.
17	E: So you already have the plan now . . .
18	S: If they need 10 miles between them that's all I can do. There's
19	not enough speed differential to just sit there and zigzag them and I
20	didn't have the time with the approaches I was going to have to
21	sequence down below.

[Elapsed Time = 10:41. After giving N437 an altitude of 3000.]

22	E: Tell us about the approach sequence.
23	S: OK. For the moment, I've got, I've still got November 59 Papa's
24	going to be #1; and in my mind I've already made plans for AeroCoach 4
25	to hit the VOR and track westbound, maybe even slightly northwestbound
26	and go behind November 59 Papa, #2. And depending on how it worked
27	out with November 437 and the Lifeguard, if it wouldn't delay the
28	Lifeguard, November 437 was going to be second, I mean third. But I
29	looked at that and I said "Nah, there's no way that Cessna 182's going
30	to beat that Lifeguard in" so I just cleared him to draft to hold
31	north.

(Continued)

TABLE 4.3 *(continued)*

[Elapsed Time = 10:43. After directing AeroCoach 4 to descend & maintain 2000, turn left & take heading of 330.]

32	E: This is what confused me.
33	S: I dumped the AeroCoach so low so fast?
34	E: Right. Especially when you're planning to have 59 Papa come in,
35	who's still at 6000. Is that ordinary?
36	S: For me, that's not out of the ordinary. The lower I get him, the
37	slower he's going to go. He'll fit right into the sequence behind 59
38	Papa.

[Elapsed Time = 10:45. After directing Lifeguard 93 to descend and maintain 7000.]

39	E: I got the air security and the Lifeguard problem pretty much
40	solved. And I'm still keeping Lifeguard up a little bit, so he can keep
41	trucking for the airport 'cause if I delay it too much, Delta's going to
42	be a problem.

from the scenario review with one of our subjects. At this point in the scenario, there is an emergency flight (Lifegaurd) from the northwest seeking to land at the same airport as five other aircraft, at various altitudes and headings. The controller must figure out how to sequence these flights for arrival and resolve an impending conflict between two aircraft at the same altitude. He must also deal with a set of planes in another part of his sector that have to be put into a 10-mile in-trail sequence as requested by the Jacksonville terminal control facility.

Table 4.4 shows some of the skills and knowledge apparent in the controller's explanation of his actions. His strategy of giving a lower altitude to the aircraft he wants to land after the Lifeguard flight, for example, (lines 33–37) reflects his knowledge of aircraft operating principles (at a lower altitude the plane will have to go slower). Another segment (lines 12–21) reveals that his choice of control strategy is based in part on a consideration of the cognitive load that other tasks will place on him. Because he is going to be busy in another part of the sector, he chooses a strategy that will require him to issue one command rather than a whole series of instructions to pilots.

The entries in Table 4.4 are actually examples of what I referred to in the electronics technician example as skill and knowledge "categories." A cognitive task analysis also yields a more detailed breakdown of the specific skills and knowledge required within each category. For example, in this scenario, the specific aircraft-operating characteristics that the controller must know include the speed of a Cessna 182 compared to that of an air ambulance. We have found that both the detailed and the more abstract (knowledge category) levels of description are useful in specifying training needs (Means & Roth, 1988).

TABLE 4.4
Sample of Skills and Knowledge
Used by Expert Subjects

Knowledge
• Separation standards • Priorities • Aircraft operating characteristics

Skills
• Estimating arrival times • Directing attention • Issuing holding patterns

Metacognitive Functions
• Assessing cognitive load • Selecting operations that minimize load

Traffic Drawing and Grouping. Given a blank sector map at the end of the scenario, controllers recalled 86% of the aircraft in their sector. False positive reports were generally either aircraft that had been in the sector but left before termination of the scenario or aircraft that were scheduled to come in but had not yet arrived. The occurrence of the latter type of error suggests that expert controllers mentally "look ahead" and start thinking about an aircraft, based on the flight strip information, before its track ever appears on the radar display.

The order in which aircraft were drawn on the sector map was consistent with the way in which the aircraft were subsequently grouped in 42 of 43 cases. Thus, as in other studies of expertise, there is evidence of chunking. Moreover, both the pattern of inclusion and controllers' rationales for their groupings suggest that controllers mentally organize air traffic on the basis of potential conflicts and

TABLE 4.5
Groupings Used by Controllers in Drawing Air Traffic

	Controller			
	1	*2*	*3*	*Total*
Arrivals	2	1	2	5
Arrivals with overflight	1	0	0	1
Crossings over a fix	0	2	0	2
Crossings not over a fix	0	0	1	1
Head-on pair	0	1	0	1
MOA operation	1	1	1	3
10-mile in trail	1	1	1	3
Total number of groupings	5	6	5	16

required control actions rather than physical proximity on the radar display. There were 17 cases in which an aircraft was not grouped with the aircraft physically closest to it on the display. This result supports the argument that controllers' mental representations are not merely mental analogs of the two dimensions represented spatially on the radar display.

Subjects' rationales for their groupings in the immediate traffic drawing task (in which subjects were not directed to draw traffic in terms of "events") are shown in Table 4.5. The groupings have obvious links to required control actions (e.g., 10 miles in trail), and there was very high consistency across controllers in the types of groupings used. Thus, their organization is not too idiosyncratic for use in training. The fact that there was no case in which an aircraft with logical membership in a group (e.g., an arrival into GNV) was not recalled if the group was recalled provides further evidence that expert controllers think about the traffic in their sectors in terms of well-organized chunks.

SUMMARY OF IMPLICATIONS FOR AIR TRAFFIC CONTROL

This method for examining a high-performance task provided a wealth of detail about how air traffic control is performed. Table 4.4 illustrates the kind of information about task requirements that is gleaned from a detailed analysis of expert performance. The results of the traffic drawing and grouping task suggest that good controllers construct a mental representation of the air traffic in their sector that is not isomorphic to the physical representation on the radar screen. It was clear also that what appears to the uninitiated as chaos on the radar display is actually a small number of well-organized chunks for the experienced controller. This organization is one of the factors keeping task demands within limits. Another is the controller's sensitivity to increasing mental workload and his consideration of this issue in selecting control strategies. A related metacognitive skill we observed was concern with potential future memory problems, such as forgetting a lower altitude aircraft while descending one at a higher altitude or confusing two planes with similar call signs. Although considerable more data collection and analysis would be required, we believe that a cognitive task analysis approach can be used to obtain the information needed to model expert performance, and that the model could then be used explicitly in designing instruction.

DISCUSSION

Having argued for the utility of cognitive task analysis as a basis for designing instruction, I feel obligated to note the drawbacks and pitfalls that we have encountered. One problem stems from the fact that real-world problem solving is ill structured: There are multiple ways to define the problem and multiple satisfactory ways to solve it. Although some ways are better than others, many are more or less equivalent, and there is not one "correct" approach. Moreover, given a sequence of problem-solving actions, there are multiple feasible explanations for why those actions should be taken.

It is desirable to obtain problem solutions from enough experts to get a sense of the most frequently used approach to a problem, but rational analysis, empirical measures of efficiency, or the opinion of a "superexpert" may be used also in selecting a particular approach to incorporate in training. It is also appropriate to make sure the training acknowledges the fact that there are different approaches to problem solution, even if one particular expert solution is selected for demonstration purposes.

A second limitation apparent from the preceding illustrations is that this kind of work requires researchers to immerse themselves in the technical detail of a subject domain that is generally far removed from their own training. This requirement is supported, but not eliminated, by the active participation of domain experts as collaborators. A related issue is the fact that a cognitive task analysis provides massive quantities of data. Developing meaningful categories and codifying the data require a tremendous effort not only on the conceptual level but also in terms of the sheer amount of meticulous labor required. Part of this effort entails discriminating between what is idiosyncratic or site specific and what is general enough to be included in a nationwide training program. The work is complicated also by the fact that the project team will be constantly gaining new insights into the task domain, leading to an evolution of conceptual categories and the need to revise the painstaking work executed previously.

This problem is mitigated to some extent, however, by the fact that additional effort at the stage of task analysis can result in savings in the amount of domain knowledge that instructional designers must acquire during the stage of developing training materials. In more conventional instructional development projects, many of the details of how tasks are performed do not come to light until someone is actually trying to write training exercises. With a cognitive task analysis, this effort is shifted up front, and the training development team becomes much more knowledgeable about the job tasks before making a final selection of instructional objectives. In addition, the specific problems and performance details uncovered in the task analysis can be used in training and testing.

Nevertheless, a cognitive approach to task analysis generally requires more detailed study and hence greater time and expense than do more traditional approaches. The reader may well ask, "Is it worth it?" Perhaps the best way to answer this question is to contrast the kind of information provided in Tables 4.1 and 4.4 with the output of a more conventional analysis shown in Fig. 4.3. If the task analysis is really going to guide the development of high-quality instruction, the kinds of information provided in Table 4.1—specifics concerning what needs to be learned and a demonstration of how it is used in performing the task—are vital. Too often, we teach students facts or procedures without ever explaining how they are going to be used to accomplish any practical task. When we provide a fully procedural blueprint, of the kind shown in Fig. 4.3, there is a tendency to spell out what to do without ever explaining why it should be done that way. The result is usually acquisition of a "brittle" procedure, one that works as long as the task can be performed in an absolutely routine fashion but "breaks" whenever the environment or task constraints change. I would argue not that cognitive task analysis is required in every training situation, but that it is a powerful methodology that can significantly improve the quality of the instruction designed for cognitively complex tasks that must be performed flexibly and well.

ACKNOWLEDGMENTS

This research was supported by contracts to the Human Resources Research Organization from the U.S. Air Force and the Federal Aviation Administration. My collaborators on this work included Chris Roth, Human Resources Research Organization, and Mark Schlager, now at SRI International.

REFERENCES

Briggs, L. J., & Wager, W. (1981). *Handbook of procedures for instructional design* (2nd ed.). Englewood Cliffs, NJ: Educational Technology Publications.

Chase, W. G., & Simon, H. A. (1973). The mind's eye in chess. In W. G. Chase (Ed.), *Visual information processing* (pp. 215–281). New York: Academic Press.

Chi, M. T. H., Feltovich, P. J., & Glaser, R. (1981). Categorization and representation of physics problems by experts and novices. *Cognitive Science, 5,* 121–152.

Chi, M. T. H., Glaser, R., & Farr, M. J. (Eds.). (1988). *The nature of expertise.* Hillsdale, NJ: Lawrence Erlbaum Associates.

Chi, M. T. H., Glaser, R., & Rees, E. (1982). Expertise in problem solving. In R. Sternberg (Ed.), *Advances in the psychology of human intelligence* (Vol. 1, pp. 17–76). Hillsdale, NJ: Lawrence Erlbaum Associates.

Egan, D. E., & Schwartz, B. J. (1979). Chunking in recall of symbolic drawings. *Memory and Cognition, 7,* 149–158.

Ericsson, K. A., & Simon, H. A. (1984). *Protocol analysis.* Cambridge, MA: MIT Press.

Frederiksen, J. R., & White, B. Y. (1988). *Restoring lost apprenticeships.* Paper presented at the annual meeting of the American Educational Research Association, New Orleans.

Gagne, R. M. (1977). *The conditions of learning* (3rd ed.). New York: Holt Rinehart & Winston.

Hambleton, R. K., Gower, C., & Bollwark, J. (1988). *Developing measures of cognitive skills.* Paper presented at the annual meeting of the American Psychological Association, Atlanta.

Means, B., & Gott, S. P. (1988). Cognitive task analysis as a basis for tutor development: Articulating abstract knowledge representations. In J. Psotka, L. D. Massey, & S. A. Mutter (Eds.), *Intelligent tutoring systems: Lessons learned* (pp. 35–57). Hillsdale, NJ: Lawrence Erlbaum Associates.

Means, B., & Roth, C. (1988). *Some outcomes of a cognitive analysis of troubleshooting.* Paper presented at the annual meeting of the American Psychological Association, Atlanta.

Reiguluth, C. M. (Ed.). (1983). *Instructional-design theories and models: An overview of their current status.* Hillsdale, NJ: Lawrence Erlbaum Associates.

Tenney, Y. J., & Kurland, L. C. (1988). The development of troubleshooting expertise in radar mechanics. In J. Psotka, L. D. Massey, & S. A. Mutter (Eds.), *Intelligent tutoring systems: Lessons learned* (pp. 59–83). Hillsdale, NJ: Lawrence Erlbaum Associates.

5 Learning by Problem Solving in a Coached Apprenticeship System

Gareth Gabrys
Arlene Weiner
Alan Lesgold
Learning Research and Development Center
University of Pittsburgh

LEARNING BY SOLVING PROBLEMS

How do people learn to solve new kinds of problems? During the past two decades, an important body of psychological knowledge has developed in response to this question. As this knowledge has developed, the hope has grown among instructional psychologists and educators that it can be used to improve people's problem solving and people's learning in general. Learning by solving problems might overcome several limitations often present in knowledge acquired from conventional schooling: *incomplete knowledge* that is overly general or the brittle product of rote learning; *inert knowledge* that cannot be used when it is needed; *inflexible knowledge* that cannot be applied to new but similar situations. Learning from problem solving (Tuma & Reif, 1980) has been proposed as a method for fostering fluently applicable skill. In an influential version of learning by problem solving, learners receive the guidance of structured problem-solving experiences but still must discover, through practice, how to apply their knowledge to new problem instances. Problem solving in a variety of forms has been associated especially with the pedagogy of mathematics and of science, but some educational psychologists now advocate that even such school subjects as history should be learned through problem solving (e.g., The Cognition and Technology Group at Vanderbilt, 1990; Collins, 1991). An even more appealing area for learning by doing problem solving is in technical training, the instruction of practical problem-solving skills. Yet, ironically, practical job training in recent years has tended to become more classroom based and more separated from "doing."

119

We are convinced that under the right conditions practical, flexible problem solving can be learned by doing, that is, by engaging in complex problem-solving tasks. One of us has led the successful development of a computer-based environment for learning "by doing" (Katz & Lesgold, 1991, in press; Lajoie & Lesgold, 1990; Lesgold, in press; Lesgold, Eggan, Katz, & Rao, in press; Lesgold, Lajoie, Bunzo, & Eggan, 1992). The system teaches technicians to diagnose failures of very complex electronic systems.[1] In this chapter we look briefly at other methods of instruction; we then examine the cognitive theory that undergirds the training, some possible limitations on such training, and how such limitations might be dealt with; we then turn to the example of the "Sherlock" computer-based systems; and we conclude with a summary of the implications for learning problem solving "by doing" in general.

The Promise of Learning by Problem Solving.   It is expected that the student who learns through problem solving will retain more, because problem solving engages the student's active, generative, cognitive processes; that the knowledge acquired will be useful, rather than "inert," because the conditions of possible use would be similar to the conditions of learning; and that the knowledge might be flexible, adaptable to similar new situations, because in the course of problem solving the learner has built up knowledge of the set of alternative possibilities in the problem area.

Despite the considerable enthusiasm for learning by problem solving and its central role in cognitive theories of skill acquisition, there are now signs that it may suffer the same fate as discovery learning. Discovery learning was proposed as a way of fostering active and applicable learning (Shulman & Keislar, 1966). Discovery learning took various forms but generally placed emphasis on learners' active construction of knowledge rather than on their passive reception of instruction. It received much early attention, but its efficacy was not supported by empirical work (Hermann, 1969). As with discovery learning, there is little clear-cut evidence that knowledge acquired through problem solving is superior to knowledge acquired through direct instruction. Additionally, the efficacy of learning by problem solving has come under fire from researchers interested in learning from worked examples (e.g., Sweller, 1988). Sweller, indeed, claims that the demands of the problem-solving process make learning by problem solving less efficient that other instructional methods.

---

[1]The Sherlock II intelligent coached practice system for avionics troubleshooting was developed by a team that has included (either currently or in the recent past) Marilyn Bunzo, Richard Eastman, Gary Eggan, Maria Gordin, Linda Greenberg, Edward Hughes, Sandra Katz, Susanne Lajoie, Alan Lesgold, Thomas McGinnis, Dan Peters, Rudi Prabowo, Govinda Rao, and Rose Rosenfeld. The work we report was supported by contracts with the Human Resources Division, Armstrong Laboratories, United States Air Force. We benefited from the advice of numerous colleagues in that work and also from that of Air Force collaborators, notably Sherrie Gott.

Inert Knowledge and Inflexible Knowledge.   It is increasingly evident that knowledge is context bound: retrievable and usable only in contexts that somehow remind a person of the contexts in which the knowledge was acquired or has been exercised. All too often, the only context in which school knowledge is exercised is in verbal recall on tests. When problems are encountered in the real world, then, it is not surprising that principles learned in the classroom do not come to mind. For example, Caramazza, McCloskey, and Green (1981) asked students to predict what would happen to the motion of a ball acting as a pendulum bob when the string suspending it was cut. They found that a large proportion of subjects who had completed a high school or college physics course nevertheless predicted incorrectly. Presumably, in the experimental situation the subjects did not call up the knowledge of physical laws that they had been taught. Specifically, they confused the path the bob had been following prior to the cut with its velocity at the instant of the cut.

Further, the schooled knowledge that is available for recall frequently consists of rigid algorithmic knowledge that differs from the rapid adaptable skill seen in expert performance. To illustrate, consider problems like the following:[2]

> *You need to order tiles to cover the floor of a hallway 5' × 8'.*
> *How many 6" × 6" tiles will you need?*   (1)

School has probably trained the readers of this chapter to deal with this problem almost automatically. The solver is probably hardly conscious of having planned a multistep procedure: *To find the number of 6" × 6" tiles needed, I'll first find the area in square feet, then find out how many tiles are needed per square foot. Finally, I'll multiple the two results.* Such a plan is a goal structure for solving the problem, with the subgoals of finding the area in square feet and finding a factor that gives the number of tiles needed per square foot. Most likely, we immediately identified the problem as an "area" problem dressed in the clothing of a realistic context and consequently "ran" a well-learned procedure—an algorithm—for calculating area.

In contrast to the first problem, we may go astray in the course of solving the following problem, whose goal structure is not so obvious:

> *You need to order broadloom carpeting to cover the floor of a*
> *hallway 5' × 8'. The carpeting is sold for $15 per running foot*
> *for 6' widths, $22 per running foot for 8' widths, and $30 per*
> *running foot for 12' widths. What is the lowest cost you can pay*
> *for the amount you need?*   (2)

---

[2]The carpeting problems are invented, rather than empirical. We use them as simplified surrogates for such highly complex and knowledge-rich problems as that of a garment designer who has to consider pattern matching and minimize waste for thousands of pieces, or a cost estimator estimating how much a machine shop should bid on a job requiring expensive materials.

If we simply engage the problem as a standard school area problem, a number of errors can occur. First, we may not know how to proceed, because the wording is so different. Or, we may proceed but in a very inefficient manner. What is likely to occur in such a situation is a *breakdown* (a term from Heidegger; see Ehn, 1988) of a rote-learned way of interacting with the world (in this case the world of school word problems). Whether we can handle this breakdown depends on the extent to which we understand why our school-learned procedure works the way it does and also understand enough to develop variations better suited to this special case of carpet installation.

In any case, our solution probably will not be as efficient as that of a carpet layer, who is experienced in cutting and laying carpet. The carpet layer's expert knowledge will constrain the approach to the problem. Because our hypothetical expert deals physically with cutting and waste, and because carpeting comes in only a few standard widths, the expert probably will note immediately that cutting 5 feet of 8-foot-wide carpeting leaves no waste, whereas 8 feet of 6-foot-wide carpeting would. The problem for this expert, then, is not a generic area problem at all but rather a problem of carving out areas from carpet rolls. In many cases, the goal of problem-solving learning, then, can be seen as the development of more refined capabilities for interacting with a task in a particular domain, along with the conceptual knowledge needed to stretch these capabilities in the face of breakdowns (i.e., when problem situations are slightly different from what we expect; see Clancey, 1991).

Comparison with Other Instructional Methods

Any global comparison of instructional methods across all skills and conditions is hardly likely to be informative. How useful an instructional method will be depends greatly on the nature of the target skill, the competence of the learner, the desired performance outcome, and the demands of the learning process. Most methods that have been proposed are valuable for some learning requirements. The important question is: What is the nature of their boundary conditions? Here we look briefly at several methods that have been recommended for learning complex skills.

Direct Instruction. The most common institutionalized means of acquiring a skill is direct instruction. Directly telling someone how to solve a problem is the most efficient means of conveying a solution procedure or strategy, provided that the person can understand what you are saying and that no transfer is expected (e.g., Biederman & Shiffrar, 1987). However, there are important limitations on direct instruction. A verbal description of a problem solution commonly under-specifies both the conditions in which the solution applies and the procedure itself. Also, a verbal description depends on the learner having knowledge of the referents described in the instruction. Explaining procedures for troubleshooting a power supply will be of little value to someone who has never seen one and has no experience with the components of which it is composed. Sometimes, too, verbal instructions are a substitute for understanding a problem. It is much easier to follow a recipe than to understand the reasons behind a specific course of action, but when even small changes in the problem situation arise (e.g., wanting to make a double recipe of a cake), understanding may be needed in order to adapt the recipe (what are the constraints of pan sizes and baking times that will produce a properly baked cake). For many tasks, a sufficient level of shared understanding is likely throughout the population (e.g., using a telephone), but in many other situations it is not (e.g., computing the stress on a bridge span).

Current instructional practices are quite vulnerable to these limitations. Instruction is often provided in a classroom, outside the problem-solving context, and knowledge is assessed by testing the ability to state rules rather than the ability to perform appropriate actions in various contexts. Knowledge acquired through direct instruction is not always inert, of course; a functional knowledge of the problem domain may confer the ability to apply it. Kieras and Bovair (1984) showed that providing subjects with instruction about the functions of a control panel enabled them to learn an operating procedure more quickly and use it more flexibly than subjects not given the information. The functional information supports inference about the operating procedure, according to Kieras and Bovair, and hence superior learning.

Didactic, verbal presentation of information is also more likely to be helpful when the instructor and trainee share referents, and when the instructional context maps onto the context of application. Those who share a good deal of common ground speak in "restricted code" that may be unintelligible to outsiders (Bernstein, 1962). An expert practitioner may attempt to elaborate to provide adequate specification yet still impose a heavy burden of adaptation on the uninitiated. This is because the everyday performances of a community of practice occur with minimal reflection on the process by its members. Such reflections are triggered by breakdowns of ongoing activity, but seldom by the activities themselves (see Ehn, 1988, and his discussions of neo-Heideggerian ideas). Restricted code is efficient within a community of practice, particularly where there is a context of objects to point to. Wenger's (1990) study of insurance claims processors shows the extremes of highly contextualized and decontextualized verbal instruction. Trainees received formal courses on how to process claims. These courses, however, were not wholly effective. Among other things, they generally consisted of verbal instruction in algorithmic procedures. The reasons behind the procedures, when revealed, were often meaningful in terms of actuarial decisions but not in the context of the work that claims processors do, nor in the terms they might use in handling calls from customers. In contrast, one worker would often ask another for advice while working on a problem. Here, there is every reason to believe that the information acquired is as applicable as knowledge constructed entirely from experience. Peer advice is most likely to have shared meanings or lead to negotiation of meaning—the meanings of terms used are entailed by the task at hand. This is very different from lectures on solving problems, for which there is often no assurance that the meanings of terms used are shared between teacher and student.

On the other hand, the peer advice may not include sufficient attention to broader corporate goals. Providing multiple local and global contexts for problem-solving instruction is not always straightforward. The context of the problem to be solved may be different for different people. For example, because shared knowledge is not necessarily common knowledge, peer-provided information still was insufficient to enable Wenger's claims processors to handle customer complaints. A customer thinks in terms other than the boxes on a processor's display screen. Explanations that say "I took Lines A and J and added them to get the total on Line M" do not explain to a customer why the same claim will be paid in some circumstances and not in others.

Between the extremes of abstract lectures and on-the-job peer advice is a range of other forms of instruction. For example, Wenger's workers sometimes received instructional memoranda. These described changes mandated by their superiors to procedures that were familiar to them. Such memoranda are more likely to change performance if they are grounded in categories of experience that recipients have already formed, and if they discuss alterations to tasks that can readily be understood within the context of prior experience. For example, a memorandum concerning a choice that is already part of a worker's problem-solving experience will likely be understood and thus be effective instruction. So, if part of processing a claim is to attach Form A or Form B depending on circumstances, then a new instruction that women under 40 now get Form B will likely be effective (for processing the claim, but probably not for explaining to a customer why a claim was or was not paid). On the other hand, verbal instructions that require completely transforming the approach to the task are likely to be much less effective.

Observing a Model.   In traditional apprenticeship settings, an important part of learning was modelling. An expert would carry out a skilled performance in front of a trainee, possibly selecting the performance to be especially revealing of the target knowledge on which the demonstration focused and possibly commenting on the reasons for various actions. Demonstrations of problem solving permit the learner to think ahead a step. Thus, they afford a kind of sheltered practice opportunity, in which the trainee attempts to predict what the expert will do next—provided that the trainee knows to do this. Models can reinforce this process by "thinking aloud," considering and rejecting alternatives that are wrong but tempting, and directly illustrating impasses and means for resolving them. Collins, Brown, and Newman (1989) gave examples of successful learning of cognitive skills by observation of a problem-solving process. What is being demonstrated in successful modelling is not just an algorithm but also the heuristics necessary to attack a problem. In some versions of this method, the students are encouraged to participate in and to imitate the master's procedures, and they gradually take over the active role while the master provides diminishing support.

Studying Examples.   Another method of acquiring problem-solving knowledge is from studying a worked example. The method of studying worked examples is currently championed by Sweller (Sweller, Chandler, Tierney, & Cooper, 1990), who has argued that extensive study of worked examples is a more efficient means of developing knowledge of problem solving than practice at problem solving without specific prior instruction in how to proceed. Sweller and colleagues have demonstrated the advantages of studying worked examples in several experiments. Sweller and Cooper (1985; Cooper & Sweller, 1987), for example, found that students who combined problem solving with the study of worked examples learned several types of math procedures more quickly than students who only solved problems. Similar results have been observed by Sweller et al. (1990), Tarmizi and Sweller (1988), and Ward and Sweller (1990).

There are some questions, however, as to the flexibility of the knowledge acquired from studying examples. In one experiment, Sweller and Cooper (1985) observed that students who studied worked examples in addition to problem solving performed better on similar test problems than students who only solved problems, but they performed worse on dissimilar test problems. Cooper and Sweller (1987) were able to obtain better transfer for the worked examples group on dissimilar problems, but only by simplifying the task and providing more examples to study. They argue that students of worked examples quickly learned how to solve the kinds of problems they recognized as similar to the worked examples, but that they did not recognize the dissimilar problems as requiring the same kind of solution. Sweller argued that the cognitive load imposed by the problem-solving process interferes with the kinds of reflective thinking needed to articulate clear generalizations of the problem-specific knowledge that is acquired. For dissimilar problems, extensive practice is required to automatize problem-solving operators before any improvement can be observed. This is not because automation of thinking is required to solve dissimilar problems, but rather because it frees up cognitive capacity during practice, allowing the trainee to reflect on what he or she is learning and perhaps to discover appropriate generalizations. If transfer is an aim of instruction, and more examples must be studied in order to effect transfer, the comparative efficiency imputed to the study of worked examples is reduced. This formulation suggests that some mixture of worked example study, during which reflection is possible, and actual problem-solving practice, during which new ideas can be tested, would work best, and that is in fact the paradigm Sweller used in his studies.

Another potential problem with the study of worked examples is lack of meaningfulness. The study of worked examples may facilitate quick learning of a solution procedure for problems similar to the examples, but the learner will acquire meaningful knowledge only by integrating his conceptual knowledge with the example while studying it. Although Zhu and Simon (1987) observed that students can learn meaningfully through studying worked examples, some students who study worked examples tend to treat them as recipes to follow rather than engaging in meaningful learning. Chi, Bassok, and colleagues (Chi & Bassok, 1989; Chi, Bassok, Lewis, Reimann, & Glaser, 1989) have observed that students vary in their tendency to integrate their conceptual knowledge with the procedure they induce from an example. They observed that some students traced through an example, explaining each step to themselves in terms of the domain concepts they had acquired. Less successful students, in contrast, spent only a minimal amount of time studying an example but later, when confronted with a similar problem, tried to use it as a recipe. Paradoxically, Cooper and Sweller (1987) observed that low ability students were the ones who benefited most from studying worked examples in their experiments. High ability students appear to learn just as well from problem solving as from studying worked examples. Presumably, they have sufficient cognitive capacity to reflect on their ongoing problem solving. A tentative conclusion is that more successful learning from problem solving can be mediated by strategy, by greater cognitive processing capacity, or possibly by superior domain knowledge (see also Lesgold & Perfetti, 1978).

Discovery Learning.   Discovery learning is a term used to describe situations in which a student is permitted to explore a task domain freely. The idea is that by experimentation he or she can come to understand the domain. Everyday experience suggests that this might work for some students in some situations. For example, most children who use Nintendo™ games learn via discovery, sometimes conducting extensive experimentation to discover relationships between their context-specific actions and outcomes of those actions. A primary criticism of discovery learning is that learners may not engage in all the aspects of the target skill they will need for the full range of situations in which the skill will be used. One reason is that learners may not know the character of the task domain well enough to figure out what besides a specific case they need to understand. Providing learners with an adequate mix of problems to solve provides such guidance and hence may have advantages over free exploration. This was shown in a recent study by Charney, Reder, and Kusbit (1990). They compared subjects learning to operate a computer spreadsheet program by means of free discovery, problem solving, or tutorial training that provided exact commands to enter. On later test problems, subjects were able to use commands learned by problem solving more quickly and with fewer errors than commands learned by following a tutorial or through free exploration. Although subjects in the free-exploration group practiced applying commands, they did not try all the variations in the commands and consequently failed to discover important functions. (The market for booklets of hints for Nintendo™ games suggests that this incompleteness also arises in that realm.) Charney et al. proposed that successful discovery learning requires the ability to pose goals for oneself. Learners who are more familiar with a domain and able to pose goals may learn better from free discovery than learners unfamiliar with a domain. For new learners, then, problem solving appears to provide better training than discovery learning construed as free exploration. Of course, mixes of the approaches may be possible that are better than any one pure approach.

The Theory of Learning by Problem Solving

During the last decade, research on problem solving, expertise, and skill acquisition has greatly advanced our understanding of how people learn during problem solving (see Chi & Bjork, 1991, and VanLehn, 1989, for recent reviews). The analysis of problem solving as a *search* through a *problem space*[3] for a successful sequence of problem-solving actions, or *operators,* is a framework for much of this research. Within this framework, detailed studies of people learning to solve puzzle-like problems have provided information on the specific processes of learning by problem solving (e.g., Anzai & Simon, 1979; Kotovsky, Hayes, & Simon, 1985). Work on expertise has provided valuable information about changes in problem-solving processes that occur with increased knowledge and experience (Chi, Glaser, & Rees, 1982; Larkin, 1983; Voss, Greene, Post, & Penner, 1983). Both lines of research have distinguished between *algorithmic* procedures, (specific solution paths) that always entail the same result if they are executed correctly, and *heuristics,* rules that guide search but do not guarantee a result.

Another cornerstone of cognitive psychology is the finding that human cognition operates with fundamental limits on how much it can keep in mind, the *resource limits* of "working memory." Theories of skill acquisition (Anderson, 1983a; Newell, 1990; Schneider & Detweiler, 1987), although they focus primarily on increasing the speed and reliability of already acquired skills, have also provided some insight into how cognitive resource load can be reduced, so that new knowledge can be acquired during problem solving.

An important and robust finding of the information-processing approach to expertise is that it is usually characterized by "strong methods"—problem-solving methods specific to a domain—rather than by general "weak methods" that might be useful generally across all domains. In order to study how people solve new problems, researchers frequently minimize the possibility of using "strong methods" based on prior knowledge by presenting "toy" problems. For

---

[3]A problem space is a graphical representation whose nodes represent states during problem solution and whose links represent specific problem-solving actions. A correct solution is a path in that graph from the node representing initial problem state to the node representing the solution state.

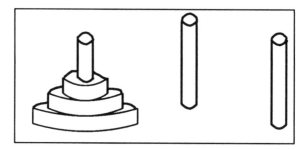

FIG. 5.1.   Tower of Hanoi Puzzle.

toy problems, the solver's problem representation generally contains little information beyond what is given in the problem presentation. For example, there have been extensive studies of people attempting to solve "Tower of Hanoi" problems. In this class of problems (see Fig. 5.1), there are usually three vertical pegs. In the initial state of the problem, one peg holds a graduated set of disks or rings in order of size, with the largest at the bottom. The other two pegs are empty. The usual goal is to move all the disks on the first peg to the third peg, so that they are again in smallest-to-largest order, moving one disk at a time from one peg to another, but never placing a larger disk atop a smaller disk. The Tower of Hanoi problem has been to the study of problem solving what the fruit fly has been to genetics, a standard problem-solving task readily reproducible and solvable in a conveniently small amount of time. Rich contributions to knowledge about how people learn to solve novel problems have been made by studies of people telling what they are thinking while they solve Tower of Hanoi problems and similar problems. The process of learning to solve a problem or class of problems successfully has been analyzed as having three main phases: constructing an appropriate *problem representation, automatization of operators,* and *chunking* (e.g., Anzai & Simon, 1979).

Problem Representation.   Confronted with a problem, the problem solver constructs an initial understanding, encoding the problem in a mental *problem representation.* How the problem is represented may determine whether the solution process is successful. The "insight" problems extensively studied by Gestalt psychologists (cf. Köhler, 1969) were characteristically problems in which changing the representation of a problem—reseeing it—leads to an almost instantaneous solution: an "aha!" experience. A more practical finding is that expert problem solving often is characterized by getting the best initial representation of problems rather than by searching for different solution sequences (Larkin, 1983). Our carpet layer represented Problem (2) in domain-specific terms—how many linear feet of various carpet widths will suffice—and thus reached a solution in a minimum number of steps. Even where a good representation does not enable "reading off" a solution, problem representations are critical. They provide cues for the mental search for problem-solving actions. Remembering former cases that seem analogous provides both positive indexing—what pops up—and negative constraints—what is excluded because it probably won't work—on any search for possible actions. One characteristic of developing expertise in a field is developing a useful indexing system: a "knowledge structure" that classifies situations in a way that is useful for solving problems in that field. For example, Chi et al. (1982) showed that more expert physics students index problems differently from less expert ones. Students who had taken only one course in physics classified problems on the basis of surface features of their presentation, like whether they involved pulleys or inclined planes. The more expert graduate students of physics, classified the same problems on the basis of the physical laws required to solve them. Thus, the experts' representations of the problems included information about the problem solution.

Characteristics of the problem presentation can greatly affect the difficulty of problem solving and therefore affect learning. Kotovsky et al. (1985) presented people with "isomorphs" of the Tower of Hanoi problems. Isomorphs are problems that are different in their surface presentation but can be represented with the same underlying problem space: Their solutions require the same sequence of operations. Kotovsky et al. asked subjects to solve problems in which three monsters of different size held different-size globes. In some presentations, the experimenter asked the solver to move globes from one monster to another; in other isomorphic presentations the solver was asked to shrink or expand stationary globes. Kotovsky et al. reported several factors in the presentations that affected how quickly subjects solved isomorphs. One factor was how easy it was to imagine the "moves." Problems that can be solved by imagining "moving" objects from place to place are easier to solve than structurally similar problems in which the surface presentation require imagining changes in the objects' size or type.

Another factor that affects problem-solving difficulty is whether the problem situation is plausible. It is easier to solve a problem that presents large acrobats supporting smaller acrobats than one in which the smaller ones hold up the larger. Perhaps location changes and implausible problems require more working memory than spatial changes and plausible problems. Thus, characteristics of a problem presentation may affect problem-solving difficulty through the amount of mental workload they require, and part of expertise is knowing how to find an efficient representation. For this reason, in the Sherlock technical training work (discussed later), novice technicians are supported in their problem solving by presenting an expert's abstract representation (based on functional relations) overlaid on the physical configuration of the complex device that confronts them.

Automatization of Operators.   In all cognitive theories of skill acquisition, practice is central. Problem solving can impose a considerable load on working memory, and various theories agree that practice reduces mental workload. Pre-

cisely how practice accomplishes this is described differently by different theories. All theories, however, must account for two general phenomena: the reduction in demand for conscious attention, and the compounding of actions into
larger action sequences. Theoretical descriptions of the second phenomenon are
discussed in the next section. This section describes how Anderson's (1983a,
1983b) ACT* theory and Schneider's CAP2 theory (Schneider & Detweiler,
1987) analyze the role of practice in producing a reduction in deliberate attention
and in the generalization and discrimination of procedural knowledge.

In Anderson's ACT* theory, the process of learning a skill consists in part of
building productions, rules that ensure that a particular action will be produced
rapidly and reliably whenever a certain condition exists. In the following rule,
the "if" clause is the condition and the "then" clause is the action.

*IF your goal is to subtract one number from another, and the top number in the
column is smaller than the bottom number THEN add 10 to the top number in the
column and subtract 1 from the top number in the column to the left.*

In ACT* theory, the effect of practice is to strengthen the condition-action bind-
ing. The greater the strength associated with a production, the less time will be
required for conflict resolution, that is, to decide whether this production or
another one with a similar condition will fire. As strength increases, the production eventually fires automatically without conflict resolution.

A different account of automatization, known as priority learning, is given by
Schneider's CAP2 model (Schneider & Detweiler, 1987). This is a connectionist
model. Knowledge is represented as vectors of 1s and 0s that are transmitted
between different processors (e.g., visual and motor processors). Associative
learning takes place when a transmitted vector (e.g., a condition pattern) becomes associated with a new vector (e.g., an action pattern) within the connection weights of a module. Initially, this module will transmit the new vector only
when the condition is received *and* deliberate attention signals the module to
transmit its information. However, with practice, the module learns that when it
receives certain patterns that have a high priority associated with them, it should
transmit its information without being told to. At this point, the module is
operating automatically and requires no conscious attention.

In addition to reducing cognitive load, strengthening and priority learning
enable the generalization and discrimination of procedural knowledge. One possible effect of practice is that a learner engages in an inductive process that
generalizes the features of the condition of applicability that are relevant and
discriminates them from those that are irrelevant. In this view, when the learner
applies an operator successfully in a given context, he or she learns to produce
the action in response to the exact condition then prevailing. However, because
contexts are never identical from one occasion to the next, part of the learning
process is to come to know which contextual features are critical and which are

irrelevant to deciding to apply the operator. This generalization or induction process requires a sample of occasions in which the operator was applied successfully, and it may even require some experiences of failure. The study of worked examples has not included sufficient attention to factors that might influence the extent and accuracy of generalization and discrimination.

Even when performance is successful, the connection between a condition and a successful action may not be noticed every time (i.e., memory for a particular experience in which a particular operator was used in a particular context is not certain). Practice might provide both increased certainty that specific context-operator pairings are noticed and generalization of such pairings over highly similar contexts. A particularly interesting effect of practice was that reported by Mandler (1968). Mandler studied negative transfer—giving a previously learned response in a new task that is superficially similar to the original training task but requires a different response. Up to a point, the better the original response had been learned, the more negative transfer took place. But beyond that point, very good learning in the original task resulted in less negative transfer. It has been suggested that "learning to learn" may be responsible for this relationship (Druckman & Bjork, 1991).

Chunking.   The second way that practice reduces the cognitive load of problem solving is to link actions that consistently follow one another in achieving some goal so that deliberate attention is not required to perform each one. The process of building such macro-operators is referred to as "chunking" in Newell's (1990; Laird, Newell, & Rosenbloom, 1987) SOAR model and as "composition" in Anderson's (1983a, 1983b) ACT* model.

Newell, in his SOAR theory, sees this chunking of productions as *the* essential process in learning: "Chunking is learning from experience" (p. 185). In his theory, chunking collects separate problem-solving actions into a procedure for solving a goal. Chunking also associates the procedure with the problem situation in which it applies. It is impasse driven; that is, chunking takes place when a successful action follows a problem-solving impasse. When SOAR reaches an impasse, it searches for a possible action, using generic "weak" methods. Actions that resolve an impasse are chunked into a single production, and there are also specific rules for deciding on the conditions for that production. The mechanism for composing larger procedures in Anderson's ACT* model is composition. Productions that tend to occur close together in time are detected and composed into a single production that combines their individual conditions and actions. In both SOAR and ACT*, the effect is to reduce the complexity of search for an appropriate response by replacing searches with their results, replacing cognitive activity with perceptual activity. Thus cognition is replaced by recognition. Ideally, once a familiar problem situation is recognized, a bundle of actions can be retrieved that will solve the problem optimally.

Although the theories of skill acquisition account well for the mechanisms of chunking and composition, they tend to oversimplify the process of determining *which* problem states become associated with solution procedures. The models assume that when the learner confronts a task he or she knows how to set subgoals that will move toward accomplishment of the task. This subgoal-setting knowledge is presumed to come either from instruction or from cognitive activity driven by knowledge failures (i.e., impasses). In addition, however, at least two other sources of subgoals must be considered. One source is the tendency of the learner to remember certain *state configurations*. Some problem states may be easier to notice and recall. A second source of subgoals is the pattern of the solution sequence. Solution steps may form natural spatial or motor patterns. A chunk based on such a pattern may be more likely to be associated with the achievement of the state that is produced as a result of executing it (e.g., arpeggios in music, components of common chords played in sequence, are both perceptual units and action units for a musician). Chunking mechanisms based only on the detection of sequential co-occurrence or knowledge failures do not explain the occurrence of such subprocedures (an arpeggio has emergent perceptual properties and is not merely a common note sequence). However, a theory that includes mechanisms based on configural salience or detection of sequential patterns requires a great deal more complexity. One possibility is that configural properties of situations and tasks have sufficient stereotypy that they are likely to lead to stereotypic plans, or goal structures, for problem solving. Association of chunks with a pending subgoal would, in fact, fit quite nicely within a theory like SOAR.

The critical role of practice, then, is to chunk, or compose procedures, and also to establish the conditions under which the chunked procedures are to be run. During problem solving, the solver is associating possible solution steps together into a solution procedure, and also associating the procedure with the context of its use. There are some conditions that facilitate these processes. First, the solver must have some steps available for chunking and some weak methods to search for them. Second, there must be sufficient cognitive resources to run the processes. The learning environment can support this process in a number of ways. For example, it can render more obvious associations that would be hard to notice, or it can provide "external memory" to reduce the cognitive load.

Current Issues in Learning by Problem Solving

We next consider three issues that arise from a critical review of learning from problem solving. The first is how learning by problem solving is to be accomplished: Do the learning processes that operate during problem solving operate automatically or do they require deliberate attention? Empirical findings on this question are currently at odds with the theoretical models of skill acquisition we have just sketched. The second issue bears on whether, except for toy problems, learning by problem solving is efficacious. Sweller and his colleagues (1988;

Sweller et al., 1990) flash a caution light for advocates of learning by problem solving, arguing that the cognitive load of problem solving competes with the learning process. The final issue is whether problem solving results in superior knowledge; more flexible, that is, transferable. Learning by problem solving will be favored over other approaches if it can be shown to result in more useful knowledge being learned more efficiently and more universally.

The Importance of Intentionality.   Models of skill acquisition, such as ACT* and SOAR, have treated chunking as occurring implicitly, without intention. In this view, practice leads ineluctably to the composition of productions and their generalization or discrimination. Recent research on human learning, however, has raised questions about the effectiveness of implicit, or incidental, learning and has suggested a much larger role for intentional learning processes, such as hypothesis testing. The two positions may not be incompatible. Even if the chunking process is automatic, it may still be influenced by the distribution of attention over different features (or different components of working memory). Alternatively, the role of intentional processing may go beyond feature activation.

For example, Anderson's original ACT* theory described the general learning mechanism as automatic (Anderson, 1983a). In that model, the processes of discrimination and generalization were presumed to take place without conscious intention. However, Anderson (1983b) later proposed instead that a conscious strategic process is responsible for the learning of productions. Lewis and Anderson (1985) go even further in supporting active hypothesis testing as a means for learning operators. Their results suggest that the association of problem-solving operators with problem features is facilitated by requiring solvers to make explicit verbal statements and therefore to test hypotheses. This does not mean that no automatic learning occurs, but rather that conscious processes generate opportunities for important knowledge to be "chunked"; that is, learning works best when the learner is part teacher, shaping the situations encountered by a relatively automatic chunking mechanism.

VanLehn (1991) recently provided additional evidence that explicit hypothesis testing is critical to learning by doing. VanLehn reanalyzed Anzai and Simon's (1979) protocol of a subject repeatedly solving the Tower of Hanoi problem, developing increasingly sophisticated strategies in the course of problem solving. VanLehn observed that the subject's change in strategy could be traced to several specific learning events during the course of problem solving. Many of these events constituted "big impasses" of which the subject was consciously aware and about which she often commented, as opposed to the "little impasses" that represent the more continual level of activity in the Soar scheme (Laird et al., 1987). Additionally, after her second solution attempt, the subject engaged in explicit hypothesis testing, solving one, two, and three disk versions of the Tower of Hanoi problem without any prompting from the experimenter.

Cognitive Load. Although theories of learning by problem solving implicitly recognize the resource demands imposed by problem solving, cognitive resource limitations have not been the focus of studies of problem solving. In recent years, however, Sweller and colleagues (Owen & Sweller, 1985; Sweller, 1988; Sweller et al., 1990) have argued that problem solving may impose such a heavy cognitive workload as to impair learning. In particular, they argued that in problem solving inductive learning processes must compete for resources with means–ends analysis, a strategy commonly used in dealing with a new problem. Means–ends analysis is a "weak method" that the solver uses to work toward a goal that he or she does not know how to achieve directly. The solver sets intermediate goals (subgoals) intended to decrease the distance between the current state and the goal and works toward those. Thus, for example, a solver confronted with the Tower of Hanoi problem has two choices of initial move: Put the smallest ring on the destination peg or on the remaining empty peg that is not the destination peg. She or he may set a subgoal of getting the maximum number of rings on the destination peg, looking ahead a move or two, and so may begin by placing the smallest ring on the intermediate peg, with the subgoal of transferring the second ring to the destination peg and so getting two rings to the destination. In this case, the solver needs to remember the ultimate goal, the subgoal, the problem constraints, and the preceding state of the problem. In the Tower of Hanoi problem, the physical state of the equipment helps the solver recall the problem state and the goal, but in other types of problems such support is not available. Sweller and colleagues argue that a greater emphasis should be given to instructional methods that impose less of a workload, such as the study of worked examples.

As evidence for their claim that means–ends analysis impairs learning, Sweller and colleagues have shown on various tasks that providing subjects with a specific goal can impair learning as compared with providing subjects with a nonspecific goal. Sweller asserted that subjects given a specific goal use means–ends analysis to solve the problem, whereas subjects given a nonspecific goal cannot use means–ends analysis. Owen and Sweller (1985), for example, provided two groups of subjects with two-triangle trigonometry problems. One group was asked to find the length of a specific side, which required satisfying a subgoal (solving for the length of the side shared by the two triangles). The other group was given the nonspecific goal of calculating the length of as many sides of a triangle as possible. They found that subjects given the nonspecific goal performed more accurately on similar test problems than subjects asked to calculate the length of a specific side. The subjects given the specific goal, they argued, were forced to use additional working memory resources to maintain the subgoal and thus had less capacity available for learning. It is difficult to evaluate this claim. However, because the nonspecific goal subjects solved for more sides, their improved accuracy may have resulted from additional practice.

Sweller (1988) replicated the Owen and Sweller experiment, controlling for amount of practice and including a secondary task as a measure of workload. If problem solving with a specific goal requires more cognitive resources than problem solving with a nonspecific goal, one might expect that subjects given the specific goal would show a greater performance tradeoff with the secondary task (which was to recall the previous problem). Sweller found that the two groups did not differ in time to solve the problem, number of errors, or on time to recall the previous problem (the secondary task) but did find that the groups differed in the number and type of errors they made on the secondary task. Sweller argued that this difference was due to the greater working memory load imposed by means–ends analysis.

Sweller's research has brought into focus the difficulty, only tacitly acknowledged by theories of skill acquisition, that problem-solving processes and intentional inductive learning processes may compete with each other for limited working memory resources. Note that these results do not directly demonstrate that decreased working memory during problem solving impairs learning—we still have two partial results from the two different studies. Further, even if the demands of problem solving are shown to compete with efficient learning, perhaps acquiring knowledge through problem solving has advantages, such as resulting in transferable knowledge that can offset the inefficiency of learning under high workload conditions.

Transferability. As mentioned previously, many instructional researchers believe that knowledge acquired through problem solving is more useful, because it is more transferable, than knowledge acquired through direct instruction. There are two main reasons for this belief. First, learning during problem solving can match the conditions of learning to the conditions of application. This is important because the transfer of skill has been shown to depend heavily on the correspondence between the context of training and the context of use. Second, learning during problem solving may preserve a trace of alternate paths and strategies encountered in a training problem and so may be useful in the case of a similar problem that requires a somewhat different solution.

Research on transfer of training (see Gick & Holyoak, 1987, for a review) has found that, in general, not much transfer occurs altogether. Transfer usually is found only when the exact conditions of training are reproduced in the target situation. Learning in the context of solving a problem can match the conditions of learning to the conditions of use, thus producing greater transfer. Unfortunately, the same argument works in the opposite direction. It is also possible that providing more problem context can reduce transfer. If a learner associates incidental features of the problem situation with a solution procedure, that procedure may be represented in too specific a manner to transfer easily to a new situation. Wright and Shea (1991), for example, recently found that the speed of simple choice reactions can be influenced by incidental features of the training context. One solution to this problem is to have learners solve problems that vary incidental features but consistently maintain relevant features. Variability of training has been recommended as a means of facilitating transfer, even where variability impairs initial learning (Druckman & Bjork, 1991).

One way to resolve the apparent conflict arising from these results might be to seek principles for deciding exactly how much similarity and how much variability problem features must have for optimal transfer. However, we may simply not do very well at identifying the features that might be relevant to such an approach. Understanding what a person notices, or could have noticed, in a complex real-world situation is extremely difficult. This is particularly true in predicting the behavior of beginners. Domain experts can articulate some of the features that are relevant to problem solution. However, their very expertise tends to make them blind to features that may correlate partially with critical features but not be relevant. Surface features and "distracting" elements of the environment are influential in determining what novices learn from problem-solving activity (Lewis & Anderson, 1985). Novices are sometimes sensitive to superficial features that experts overlook (Chi et al., 1982; Greeno, 1989). To the extent that they are not relevant beyond the environments of initial learning, these distractor features may not support transfer at all.

The painful news in all of this is that the minimal principles we have for predicting transfer of problem-solving training are probably applicable only when the training is based on deep expert knowledge as well as a keen sense for what is salient, or even moderately apparent, to students at different stages of learning. The "situated learning" movement has made this problem the organizing point for a different approach, one emphasizing learning as necessarily embedded and therefore to be pursued in the context of real work (Brown, Collins, & Duguid, 1989; Wenger, 1990). Advocates of situated learning emphasize that work that someone needs to have done imparts authenticity. Authenticity is usually discussed for other reasons, but it also relates to motivation. Internal features of a situation, that is, the state of the learner, may be as critical for transfer as external ones. One difference, then, between school problem solving and real-life problem solving is the motivation for performance.

A further reason to expect greater transfer from learning by problem solving than from other instructional methods is that, in addition to learning the solution procedure, the learner may also acquire a trace of the reasoning process that constructed the solution. During problem solving, the solver may explore paths that do not lead to the goal, achieve partial solutions, and use strategies later discarded. The trace may contain information about alternative paths that may prove useful for achieving other goals within the same domain. In the case where the learner has engaged in domain-specific reasoning to construct the solution, the trace constitutes an explanation of the procedure's applicability (Chi et al., 1989; DeJong & Mooney, 1986). Even where the solver has used general methods that do not reflect knowledge of the particular domain, it is possible that the trace itself can be used to find a solution. Carbonell (1986) has proposed that similarities between the ways problems are solved can be the basis for noticing that one has solved a similar problem in the past.

Despite these reasons for expecting that knowledge acquired through problem solving gives greater transfer, research that has looked for transfer of problem-solving procedures has had disappointing results. Recent experiments by McDaniel and Schlager (1990), however, suggest that learning by problem solving may confer an advantage in learning domain specific *strategies*. They argue that exploratory activity in a problem-solving task domain has a positive effect *if* the learner discovers procedures for generating novel solution strategies specific to the domain. For example, the learner might transfer strategies for deciding what kind of already learned procedures should be used in a specific new kind of problem. This exploratory form of problem-solving learning should have positive effects on transfer, then, only in cases where situations prompt the discovery of a strategy relevant to the particular cases one will later encounter. Note further that executing the steps of a transferable strategy does not guarantee that the strategy has been "discovered" in a form sufficiently general to be applied to new tasks.

McDaniel and Schlager (1990) presented two experiments consistent with this interpretation. Most interesting in their studies is the case where discovery learners (i.e., those not given complete instructions) used an ineffective strategy on the training problem that was a helpful approach to a transfer problem. These particular learners in fact used, on the transfer task, knowledge from a "mistake" that occurred during the course of their discovery learning. Given that expertise in many real-world domains does not involve finding a single optimal solution but rather in solving many different kinds of problems in the same domain, the acquisition of knowledge of other paths of the problem space and knowledge of domain-specific strategies are important advantages for learning by problem solving. If people can learn from their mistakes during problem solving as well as from their ultimate successes, this increases the likelihood that problem-solving practice will pay off—provided that the mix of problems "covers" the domain (i.e., that it generates the right mix of learning and "mistakes").

Lessons for the Design of Learning

The research we have reviewed here provides important new information about learning about problem solving. First, it appears that learning by problem solving depends more on intentional learning strategies than was previously thought. Models of skill acquisition have previously described learning as implicit. The work by Lewis and Anderson (1985) and VanLehn (1991) suggests that explicit hypothesis testing may be an important part of learning during problem solving. Second, it now appears that problem solving's large demand on working memory may actually impair learning compared with other instructional methods

(Sweller, 1988). Overtaxing memory may impair the function of inductive learning processes such as hypothesis testing. Sweller (1988) has argued that use of means–ends analysis is sufficient to overtax working memory and impair learning, but it is also clear that people can, given the right circumstances, learn useful procedures from problem solving. The importance of any impairment, then, must be weighed against any potential benefits of learning from solving problems. Druckman and Bjork (1991) stated: "A learner . . . should be challenged [by training manipulations that] may impair training performance, [which] not only help the learner to process the learning task more deeply, but also suggest appropriate processes for transfer" (p. 49).

Finally, if there are advantages to learning by problem solving, they are likely to be in the use of domain-specific strategies rather than in the transfer of specific procedures. Direct instruction and worked examples are more efficient means of conveying a specific problem-solving procedure, so any advantage from problem solving is likely to result from "bad" paths visited during problem solving that may become valuable for future problems, or in the acquisition of strategies for solving problems in a specific domain. Of course, there are other issues in the design of instructional approaches that may favor learning by doing generally, including building of confidence in attacking novel situations and the development of the skills needed to learn from doing (just as there are skills needed to learn from examples).

SUPPORTING LEARNING BY PROBLEM SOLVING FOR COMPLEX SKILL TRAINING

Coached Apprenticeship Systems

We turn to a practical application of accumulated knowledge of learning by problem solving: how to support the learning of complex skills by problem solving in a computerized practice environment. Two promising means of support are inducing intentional learning and reducing cognitive load. We discuss ways of accomplishing this in an intelligent training system for electronic troubleshooting skills.

For the past several years, Lesgold and colleagues (the Sherlock project, see Footnote 1) have been working to create computer-based coached practice environments that provide learners with opportunities to engage in complex problem solving. They have described these systems as *coached apprenticeship systems,* reflecting the philosophy of creating apprenticeship opportunities for complex skills that might otherwise go untaught or unpracticed. In the Sherlock approach, the learner practices a complex problem-solving skill by attempting to solve realistic complex problems like those he or she will soon encounter on the job. The computer environment supplies graphical presentations that represent experts' mental models of the devices encountered in the domain and provides intelligent coaching upon request, about expert heuristics and procedures. Although the Sherlock approach incorporates several different instructional techniques (e.g., observing the example provided by expert modelling, problem solving, exploration), it places a major emphasis on engaging in problem solving in the actual context of a skill's use. In addition to the potential benefits of learning from problem solving, placing the learner in the work context provides a rationale for acquiring a skill as well as social support from other learners of varying expertise. The system was designed for a literal apprenticeship, in that it is a "shop" environment with real connection to the trainees' livelihood.

The first version of this coached apprenticeship system was Sherlock I (Katz & Lesgold, 1991, in press; Lajoie & Lesgold, 1990; Lesgold, in press; Lesgold et al., in press; Lesgold et al., 1992). Sherlock I was developed to aid in the training of aviation electronics ("avionics") technicians faced not only with the problem of diagnosing failures in navigation components of complex aircraft, but also potentially with failures of the complex diagnostic equipment. Sherlock I provided trainees with opportunities to solve difficult problems whose goal is to find the cause of failure of electronic test equipment containing several cubic meters of densely packed printed circuit cards. Test equipment faults occur only infrequently on the job and can be extremely difficult to find. Sherlock I enabled trainees to practice locating faults in an abstracted simulation of the test station with the aid of an intelligent coach. The presentation was designed to make essential problem features salient by emphasizing the functional relations of the components. Practice on the Sherlock I system was free from some of the distractions of actual testing procedures (e.g., the physical problems and the time involved in accessing a deeply buried component in order to test it) and the potential stress of having to troubleshoot under extreme time pressure. Therefore the memory of problem-solving actions could be maintained during the time it took to solve extended problems, and also between problems. Probably all these factors contribute to observations that trainees in field tests could achieve a level of skill in 20 to 25 hours on Sherlock that would normally take 4 years of on-the-job training (according to independent Air Force evaluations).

In the Sherlock I system, trainees solved problems of increasing difficulty under the guidance of a generally nonintrusive coach. When a trainee reached an impasse in solving a problem, he or she could ask the coach for advice. The specificity of the advice given by Sherlock varied with the trainee's estimated ability and insistence. A student estimated to be capable of resolving an impasse would only be given a summary of prior actions and general encouragement, whereas a student not expected to be able to resolve the impasse would be given more specific advice on which component to test next and why. Generally, assistance was offered only when requested.[4] Only in situations when a trainee

---

[4]It was necessary to tell trainees that using the coach was ok ("real men and women ask for help" was the approach we took).

was about to make a potentially fatal or damaging error would Sherlock intrude on the trainee's problem solving.

One weakness in the training given by Sherlock I, however, was a lack of opportunity for learning by reflection. Trainees were expected to learn during their problem-solving episodes. If learning is impaired under high workload problem solving, as Sweller suggests, trainees may not have been achieving their full learning potential. Also, they may not have received adequate support for the work of learning (as opposed to the actual problem-solving process). These weaknesses are addressed in Sherlock II, a system just now being completed. Sherlock II was designed to promote intentional learning strategies that build on problem solving and to avoid working memory limitations that can arise in the midst of problem solving.

Intentional Learning Strategies: Looking Back and Looking Forward

Sherlock II encourages intentional learning strategies by providing episodes in which learners are expected to compare their own recent performance with expert performance. We expect they will adjust their subsequent performance to be more like the expert's. Such adjustment requires the use of two processes: reflection and planning. After attempting to solve a problem, a learner reflects on what he or she did and how it compares to what an expert does. Then, the learner plans how to change his or her performance to make it more like the expert's. It is worthwhile to discuss these two processes in more detail.

Reflection. When a learner explicitly reviews actions taken during problem solving, an opportunity is created for noticing patterns in the solution, desirable subgoals and procedure chunks. Simon (1980) has emphasized the importance of reflection in his characterization of learning by problem solving as a process of studying a self-generated worked example. Although there are some similarities between reflecting on one's own problem solution and the study of a worked example, there are also important differences. In problem solving, the learner has engaged in problem solving and gained a familiarity with the problem-solving choices at each step. This enables the learner to be aware of the choices available and to attend to the reasons why one action was selected over another. This trace of generative problem solving is likely to make learning by reflection more productive than learning from a worked example.

Planning. A complement to reflecting on problem solving is to plan problem-solving moves before attempting a solution. When planning is used this way, it can be viewed as a form of hypothesis testing. A learner can generate a problem solution and then test whether it solves the problem or subproblem. Learning from planning is closely related to the ability to form explanations. Artificial-intelligence models of planning incorporate explanation as a means of learning to avoid repeating past failures. Planning models with learning components (e.g., Hammond, 1986; Sussman, 1975) have emphasized the importance of explanation in the construction and testing of plans. CHEF (Hammond, 1986), for example, builds plans for meals. When a plan fails, CHEF attempts to explain why the plan failed and saves this information to prevent making the same mistake when constructing a new plan. In human learning, Chi et al. (1989) have suggested that forming explanations is an important means of integrating conceptual and procedural information.

The drawback in this process is that planning constructs a solution procedure without the benefit of feedback on each problem-solving move. If one has enough knowledge to predict the effects of problem-solving actions on the task environment, the loss of feedback costs little. For concrete problems, such as the Tower of Hanoi, such knowledge is usually available at the outset of the problem, and the physical presentation provides an external aid to memory. People have extensive experience with manipulating physical objects and can easily represent the effect of moving a small ring from one peg to another. For some other domains, common knowledge is sufficient for planning. But for many complex domains, planning knowledge must be specially learned. Knowledge about the effects of actions must be acquired before planning is possible.

Although reflection and planning can be used independently, the two strategies naturally complement each other. In situations where a leaner has more than one opportunity to solve a problem, a cycle of reflection and planning can lead to effective learning. For example, a learner may begin by attempting a solution to a problem, then reflect on the attempt and construct an explanation for what went wrong. Then, the learner can construct a plan on the basis of the explanation and attempt the problem again. If the plan succeeds, the learner has both learned a solution procedure and associated it with the problem-solving context in a meaningful way—in terms of an explanation. Combining reflection and planning also creates the opportunity for reproducing a failure, which can often be more informative than a correct solution.

Intentional Learning and Cognitive Load

In the first section of this chapter we described the concern that some researchers have raised over the possibility that cognitive load impairs learning by problem solving. According to these researchers, learning is impaired by the excessive working memory requirements of some problem-solving strategies, such as means–ends analysis. We do not believe that cognitive overloading is necessarily a concern for intentional learning. During planning, generating a problem solution, maintaining a changing mental representation of the problem, and keeping track of the plan steps place a great demand on working memory. But executing the completed plan requires only minimal working memory resources, for monitoring. Remaining resources can be dedicated to explaining why the plan succeeds or fails. Reflection, in contrast, may place a large demand on working memory, which must maintain the trace of the solution path throughout problem solving. However, the intentional nature of the strategy appears to be important. As Reed and Johnsen (1977) observed, immediate recall of a solution path is quite good under intentional learning conditions as compared with both implicit learning conditions and delayed recall. Thus, reflection and planning in the context of explicit problems may not entail cognitive overloading in the way that implicit learning under means–ends analysis appears to, especially if reflection builds on just-experienced problem-solving situations. Of course, we do not yet have good boundary conditions for these results. Tasks involving speeded performance or extreme complexity may suffer more from working memory overload problems and consequently from poor learning by doing.

In particular, when solution paths are very long and complicated, learning by reflection may be limited by the learner's ability to remember the path. In such cases, this memory requirement can easily be eliminated by the use of external memory (e.g., paper and pen, computer) to keep track of moves and then redisplay them after the problem-solving episode. Collins and Brown (1988) have discussed several ways that a computer can be used to foster reflection. These include demonstration of a target skill, replay of the learner's performance, abstracted replay of the solution process, and spatial reification (providing a concrete representation of an abstract process or concept). These techniques can also be combined. For example, a computer could replay a learner's problem-solving choices (literally or abstractly) and simultaneously compare it with a demonstration of an expert's performance, enabling the learner to observe how his or her own performance deviates from an expert's. Sherlock II supports reflection by an abstracted replay of the trainee's performance and an expert's.

Supporting Learning in Sherlock II

In Sherlock II, intentional learning strategies are supported by means of a two-phase learning by doing process. In the first phase, trainees attempt to find a solution to a complex fault diagnosis problem with the aid of an intelligent coach. Following solution of the problem, the trainees enter a phase we term *reflective follow-up*. In this phase, the trainees can replay their problem solutions step by step. At each step, they can obtain a description of the problem state and an evaluation of their choice of action. Additionally, the trainees can obtain an explanation of what an expert would have done at that point in the problem. Not only does this enable the trainees to compare their performance with the expert's, it also reduces the cognitive load of remembering their own performance while observing the expert's. We believe that these system features will improve the effectiveness of learning from problem solving.

Orienting the Learner's Attention.   During problem solving a learner may fail to notice important aspects of the problem structure. In Sherlock II, the learner's attention is oriented to important problem state information by the use of an abstracted interactive display. While looking for a fault, a trainee needs to think of the electronic equipment in terms of what its components do and how they are connected in the situation of the current configuration, which changes with the specific test step being run. The abstraction of the display enables the trainee to deal with the equipment at a functional level rather than only at a physical level. Sherlock II's display is also interactive. By selecting a component with a mouse, the user can obtain a description of what the component does. The display also uses color to orient the trainee to the relevant aspects of the problem and reduces the cognitive load of maintaining component status in memory.[5]

Reinstating the Problem Context.   One potential drawback of learning by reflection following problem solving is the need to remember the solution path. In Sherlock II, this memory requirement is eliminated. As each step is replayed during the reflection period, the system provides a summary of the important pieces of information the user has established by previous tests and the problem-solving actions the user has taken. The summary serves as a reminder to the trainee of the problem context in which decision was made. Preserving awareness of the problem context is an important aspect of acquiring knowledge structures that support transfer, because it helps assure that appropriate conditions are learned from artificial practice situations. In addition to the summary, Sherlock II provides an evaluation of each action. Efficient and productive actions are marked with a green check mark. The trainee can also ask why a statement was marked as productive or as not optimally productive.

Expert Comparison.   In addition to reflecting on his or her own problem-solving behavior, a trainee can compare his or her performance to that of an expert. At each step in the trainee's replay, the system can explain what an expert would have done. This description is provided in terms of the overall goal structure, the specific actions taken, and what information was learned from performing the action. Providing an explanation at these levels is an attempt to make the expert's reasoning process more transparent to the trainee. As Brown (1990) has argued, an essential aspect of supporting apprenticeship learning is to let the learner observe the decision process behind the expert's choice of

---

[5]An interesting aside must be offered concerning these displays. To some extent, learning to construct representations corresponding to such displays is the transferable skill we hope to teach. Consequently, we will likely end up requiring trainees to construct their own displays using simple interface tools and then have Sherlock critique them, rather than simply having Sherlock draw the appropriate pictures right away.

action. While keeping the information load bearable, learning by doing systems need to find ways for students to look inside the expert to see what choices had to be made, why they were made as they were, and what the overall goal structure for expert performances might be.

CONCLUSIONS

Our view is that learning by doing is an effective method for acquiring problem-solving skills provided that certain important conditions are fulfilled. First, to the extent that expert performance involves explicit planning or implicit knowledge of a strategy (i.e., a problem solving plan), it is helpful to make that plan's structure apparent and for students to practice developing those portions that must be tuned to specific situations. Second, the situation in which learning by doing takes place needs to support intentional consideration of the context in which choices are made and actions performed. Third, the task situation should support realistic levels of planning and of reflections on plans and how they are working out. Fourth, overload problems can be avoided by designing environments to act as external memories that keep the information most useful to productive activity readily available and that can "replay" past activity. Fifth, modeling of high-quality performance by an expert (human or machine) can be a useful adjunct to learning by doing, especially if there is support available for comparing expert performance to one's own performance and for articulating differences between the two.

REFERENCES

Anderson, J. R. (1983a). *The architecture of cognition*. Cambridge, MA: Harvard University Press.
Anderson, J. R. (1983b). Knowledge compilation: The general learning mechanism. *Proceedings of the International Machine Learning Workshop* (pp. 203–212). Monticello, IL.
Anzai, Y., & Simon, H. A. (1979). The theory of learning by doing. *Psychological Review, 86,* 124–140.
Bernstein, B. (1962). Social class, linguistic codes, and grammatical elements. *Language and speech, 5,* 221–240.
Biederman, I., & Shiffrar, M. M. (1987). Sexing day-old chicks: A case study and expert systems analysis of a difficult perceptual-learning task. *Journal of Experimental Psychology: Learning, Memory, and Cognition, 13,* 640–645.
Brown, J. S. (1990). Toward a new epistemology for learning. In C. Frasson & G. Gauthier (Eds.), *Intelligent tutoring systems: At the crossroad of artificial intelligence and education* (pp. 266–282). Norwood, NJ: Ablex.
Brown, J. S., Collins, A., & Duguid, P. (1989). Situated cognition and the culture of learning. *Educational Researcher, 18,* 32–41.
Caramazza, A., McCloskey, M., & Green, B. (1981). Naive beliefs in "sophisticated" subjects: Misconceptions about trajectories of objects. *Cognition, 9,* 117–123.
Carbonell, J. G. (1986). Derivational analogy: A theory of reconstructive problem solving and

expertise acquisition. In R. S. Michalski, J. G. Carbonell, & T. M. Mitchell (Eds.), *Machine learning: An artificial intelligence approach* (Vol. II, pp. 371–392). Los Altos, CA: Morgan Kaufmann.

Charney, D., Reder, L., & Kusbit, G. W. (1990). Goal setting and procedure selection in acquiring computer skills: A comparison of tutorials, problem solving, and learner exploration. *Cognition and Instruction, 7*, 323–342.

Chi, M. T. H., & Bassok, M. (1989). Learning from examples via self-explanations. In L. B. Resnick (Ed.), *Knowing, learning, and instruction: Essays in honor of Robert Glaser* (pp. 251–282). Hillsdale, NJ: Lawrence Erlbaum Associates.

Chi, M. T. H., Bassok, M., Lewis, M. W., Reimann, P., & Glaser, R. (1989). Self-explanations: How students study and use examples in learning to solve problems. *Cognitive Science, 13,* 145–182.

Chi, M. T. H., & Bjork, R. A. (1991). Modeling expertise. Anonymous chapter in D. Druckman & R. A. Bjork (Eds.), *In the mind's eye: Enhancing human performance* (pp. 57–79). Committee on Techniques for the Enhancement of Human Performance, Commission on Behavioral and Social Sciences and Education, National Research Council, Washington, DC: National Academy Press.

Chi, M. T. H., Glaser, R., & Rees, E. (1982). Expertise in problem solving. In R. J. Sternberg (Ed.), *Advances in the psychology of human intelligence* (Vol. 1, pp. 7–75). Hillsdale, NJ: Lawrence Erlbaum Associates.

Clancey, W. (1991). Review of Rosenfield's "The invention of memory." *Artificial Intelligence, 50,* 241–284.

The Cognition and Technology Group at Vanderbilt (1990). Anchored instruction and its relation to situated cognition. *Educational Researcher, 19*(6), 2–10.

Collins, A. (1991). Cognitive apprenticeship and instructional technology. In L. Idol & B. F. Jones (Eds.), *Educational values and cognitive instruction: Implications for reform* (pp. 121–138). Hillsdale, NJ: Lawrence Erlbaum Associates.

Collins, A., & Brown, J. S. (1988). The computer as a tool for learning through reflection. In H. Mandl & A. Lesgold (Eds.), *Learning issues for intelligent tutoring systems* (pp. 1–18). New York: Springer.

Collins, A., Brown, J. S., & Newman, S. (1989). Cognitive apprenticeship: Teaching the craft of reading, writing, and mathematics. In L. B. Resnick (Ed.), *Knowing, learning, and instruction: Essays in honor of Robert Glaser* (pp. 453–494). Hillsdale, NJ: Lawrence Erlbaum Associates.

Cooper, G., & Sweller, J. (1987). Effects of schema acquisition and rule automation on mathematical problem-solving transfer. *Journal of Educational Psychology, 79,* 347–362.

DeJong, G., & Mooney, R. (1986). Explanation-based learning: An alternative view. *Machine Learning, 1,* 145–176.

Druckman, D., & Bjork, R. A. (Eds.). (1991). *In the mind's eye: Enhancing human performance.* Committee on Techniques for the Enhancement of Human Performance, Commission on Behavioral and Social Sciences and Education, National Research Council. Washington, DC: National Academy Press.

Ehn, P. (1988). *Work-oriented design of computer artifacts.* Stockholm: Arbetslivscentrum.

Gick, M. L., & Holyoak, K. J. (1987). The cognitive basis of knowledge transfer. In S. M. Cormier & J. D. Hagman (Eds.), *Transfer of learning* (pp. 9–46). New York: Academic Press.

Greeno, J. (1989). Situations, mental models, and generative knowledge. In D. Klahr & K. Kotovosky (Eds.), *Complex information processing: The impact of Herbert A. Simon* (pp. 285–318). Hillsdale, NJ: Lawrence Erlbaum Associates.

Hammond, K. J. (1986). CHEF: A model of case-based planning. *Proceedings* AAAI-86, Vol. 1 (pp. 267–271). Los Altos, CA: Morgan-Kaufmann.

Hermann, G. (1969). Learning by discovery: A critical review of studies. *Journal of Experimental Education, 38,* 58–72.

Katz, S., & Lesgold, A. (1991). Modeling the student in Sherlock II. In J. Kay & A. Quilici (Eds.), *Proceedings of the IJCAI-91 Workshop W.4: Agent modelling for intelligent interaction* (pp. 93–127). Sydney, Australia.

Katz, S., & Lesgold, A. (in press). The role of the tutor in computer-based collaborative learning situations. In S. Lajoie & S. Derry (Eds.), *Computers as cognitive tools.* Hillsdale, NJ: Lawrence Erlbaum Associates.

Kieras, D. E., & Bovair, S. (1984). The role of a mental model in learning to operate a device. *Cognitive Science, 8,* 255–273.

Köhler, W. (1969). *The task of Gestalt psychology.* Princeton, NJ: Princeton University Press.

Kotovsky, K., Hayes, J. R., & Simon, H. A. (1985). Why are some problems hard? Evidence from Tower of Hanoi. *Cognitive Psychology, 17,* 248–294.

Laird, J. E., Newell, A., & Rosenbloom, P. S. (1987). SOAR: An architecture for general intelligence. *Artificial Intelligence, 33,* 1–64.

Lajoie, S., & Lesgold, A. (1990). Apprenticeship training in the workplace: Computer coached practice environment as a new form of apprenticeship. *Machine-Mediated Learning, 3,* 7–28.

Larkin, J. (1983). The role of problem representation in physics. In D. Gentner & A. L. Stevens (Eds.), *Mental models* (pp. 75–98). Hillsdale, NJ: Lawrence Erlbaum Associates.

Lesgold, A. (in press). Assessment of intelligent training systems: Sherlock as an example. In E. Baker & H. O'Neil, Jr. (Eds.), *Technology assessment: Estimating the future* (tentative title). Hillsdale, NJ: Lawrence Erlbaum Associates.

Lesgold, A., Eggan, G., Katz, S., & Rao, G. (in press). Possibilities for assessment using computer-based apprenticeship environments. In W. Regian & V. Shute (Eds.), *Cognitive approaches to automated instruction.* Hillsdale, NJ: Lawrence Erlbaum Associates.

Lesgold, A. M., Lajoie, S. P. Bunzo, M., & Eggan, G. (1992). SHERLOCK: A coached practice environment for an electronics troubleshooting job. In J. Larkin, R. Chabay, & C. Scheftic (Eds.), *Computer assisted instruction and intelligent tutoring systems: Shared goals and complementary approaches* (pp. 201–238). Hillsdale, NJ: Lawrence Erlbaum Associates.

Lesgold, A. M., & Perfetti, C. A. (1978). Interactive processes in reading comprehension. *Discourse Processes, 1,* 323–336.

Lewis, M. W., & Anderson, J. R. (1985). Discrimination of operator schemata in problem solving: Learning from examples. *Cognitive Psychology, 17,* 26–65.

Mandler, G. (1968). Association and organization: Facts, fancies, and theories. In T. R. Dixon & D. L. Horton (Eds.), *Verbal behavior and general behavior theory.* Englewood Cliffs, NJ: Prentice-Hall.

McDaniel, M. A., & Schlager, M. S. (1990). Discovery learning and transfer of problem-solving skills. *Cognition and Instruction, 7,* 129–159.

Newell, A. (1990). *Unified theories of cognition.* Cambridge, MA: Harvard University Press.

Owen, E., & Sweller, J. (1985). What do students learn while solving mathematics problems? *Journal of Educational Psychology, 77,* 272–284.

Reed, S. K., & Johnsen, J. A. (1977). Memory for problem solutions. In G. H. Bower (Ed.), *The psychology of learning and motivation* (Vol. 11, pp. 161–201). New York: Academic Press.

Schneider, W., & Detweiler, M. (1987). A connectionist/control architecture for working memory. In G. H. Bower (Ed.), *The psychology of learning and motivation* (Vol. 21, pp. 53–119). New York: Academic Press.

Shulman, L., & Keislar, E. (Eds.). (1966). *Learning by discovery: A critical appraisal.* Chicago: Rand McNally.

Simon, H. A. (1980). Problem solving and education. In D. T. Tuma & F. Reif (Eds.), *Problem solving and education: Issues in teaching and research* (pp. 81–96). Hillsdale, NJ: Lawrence Erlbaum Associates.

Sussman, G. J. (1975). *A computer model of skill acquisition.* New York: American Elsevier.

Sweller, J. (1988). Cognitive load during problem solving: Effects on learning. *Cognitive Science, 12,* 257–285.

Sweller, J., Chandler, P., Tierney, P., & Cooper, M. (1990). Cognitive load as a factor in the structuring of technical material. *Journal of Experimental Psychology: General, 119,* 176–192.

Sweller, J., & Cooper, G. A. (1985). The use of worked examples as a substitute for problem solving in learning algebra. *Cognition and Instruction, 2,* 59–89.

Tarmizi, R. A., & Sweller, J. (1988). Guidance during mathematical problem solving. *Journal of Educational Psychology, 80,* 424–436.

Tuma, D. T., & Reif, F. (1980). *Problem solving and education: Issues in teaching and research.* Hillsdale, NJ: Lawrence Erlbaum Associates.

VanLehn, K. (1989). Problem solving and cognitive skill acquisition. In M. I. Posner (Ed.), *Foundations of cognitive science* (pp. 527–579). Cambridge, MA: MIT Press.

VanLehn, K. (1991). Rule acquisition events in the discovery of problem-solving strategies. *Cognitive Science, 15,* 1–47.

Voss, J. F., Greene, T. R., Post, T. A., & Penner, B. C. (1983). Problem-solving skill in the social sciences. In G. Bower (Ed.), *The psychology of learning and motivation* (Vol. 17, pp. 165–213). New York: Academic Press.

Ward, M., & Sweller, J. (1990). Structuring effective worked examples. *Cognition and Instruction, 7,* 1–39.

Wenger, E. (1990). *Toward a theory of cultural transparency: Elements of a social discourse of the visible and the invisible.* Unpublished doctoral dissertation, Department of Information and Computer Science, The University of California, Irvine.

Wright, D. L., & Shea, C. H. (1991). Contextual dependencies in motor skills. *Memory & Cognition, 19,* 361–370.

Zhu, X., & Simon, H. A. (1987). Learning mathematics from examples and by doing. *Cognition and Instruction, 4,* 137–166.

6 Question Asking During Tutoring and in the Design of Educational Software

Arthur C. Graesser
Natalie K. Person
John Huber
Memphis State University

Question asking has had a rather controversial status in the fields of cognitive science and education. At the optimistic end of the continuum, question asking is allegedly at the heart of active learning, creativity, curiosity, and deep comprehension (Collins, Brown, & Larkin, 1980; Markman, 1985; Olson, Duffy, & Mack, 1985; Schank, 1986; Sternberg, 1987). The ideal learner is absorbed in processes of formulating good questions and answering these questions while comprehending text, comprehending events in the world, writing, problem solving, and making decisions. Researchers have discussed several methods of teaching students to generate good questions, such as the inquiry learning method (Collins, 1985, 1988), the Socratic method (Collins & Stevens, 1982), and the reciprocal training method (Palinscar & Brown, 1984). Some of these methods of training students to ask good questions have produced remarkable improvements in comprehension (King, 1989; Palinscar & Brown, 1984), particularly for poor students.

The other end of the continuum presents a more pessimistic picture. Student-generated questions are both infrequent and unsophisticated in classroom settings (Dillon, 1988; Flammer, 1981; Kerry, 1987). Less than 3% of classroom questions are asked by students. Nearly all these questions are shallow questions that address explicit material, as opposed to sophisticated questions that involve inferences, application, synthesis, and evaluation. A person may need to master a substantial amount of knowledge about a topic before good questions emerge (Miyake & Norman, 1979). It is widely recognized that there are costs to posing questions in a classroom setting. Students are humiliated for revealing their lack of knowledge or for interrupting the teacher. Teachers frequently have trouble understanding student questions so they end up dismissing the questions or answering the wrong questions (Coombs & Alty, 1980). Unfortunately, teachers are poor role models for generating good questions; only 4% of teacher questions are higher level questions (Kerry, 1987). Very few teachers are sophisticated Socratic tutors who ask carefully planned sequences of thought-provoking questions that expose students' misconceptions and contradictions.

Given that students and tutors are normally poor question generators, perhaps intelligent tutoring systems on computers might provide a foundation for more effective inquiry. Intelligent tutoring systems (ITS) have imported models in artificial intelligence that formally specify the knowledge representations, problem-solving methods, reasoning heuristics, question-answering procedures, and cognitive mechanisms that underlie effective teaching (Anderson, Boyle, & Reiser, 1985; Sleeman & Brown, 1982; Wenger, 1987). A typical ITS keeps track of the knowledge that a particular student has about the topic and identifies the student's misconceptions. The ITS formulates problems, questions, answers to questions, and explanatory feedback that corrects the student's knowledge gaps and misconceptions. The student who learns from an ITS technology presumably would be exposed to good questions and answers to questions during the tutorial interaction.

One serious bottleneck in the ITS enterprise is that there are serious limitations in modern human–computer interfaces. An ideal interface would minimize communication barriers between computer systems and human users (Card, Moran, & Newell, 1983; Norman & Draper, 1986). In a system with no barriers, the user would have a natural conversation with the computer in order to get the computer to accomplish a variety of useful tasks. Unfortunately, the existing computer systems in artificial intelligence have not advanced to the point where smooth quick dialogues occur between computers and people. Natural language comprehension and production are extremely difficult (if not impossible) for computer systems to accomplish (Winograd & Flores, 1986). Human–computer interfaces can be designed in a manner that minimizes reliance on the computer interpreting or producing lengthy text in natural language. However, these systems are typically too complicated to learn and use.

Successful communication between a computer and user would require a "mixed initiative dialogue" (Robertson & Zachary, 1990). In a mixed initiative dialogue, both the computer and the user can ask questions, answer questions, issue requests, give advice, and perform other speech acts. Most computer systems do not have the capability of a mixed initiative dialogue. In computer-centered dialogues, the computer asks all the questions and the user supplies the answers. In user-centered dialogues, the user asks the questions whereas the computer supplies the answers. A computer system is clearly more flexible and powerful to the extent that the conversation can be controlled by either the user or the computer. Such a system would be capable of accommodating computer questions, user answers, user questions, and computer answers.

Mixed initiative dialogues have been designed for sophisticated systems in artificial intelligence, such as expert systems (Buchanan & Shortliffe, 1984), intelligent tutoring systems (Sleeman & Brown, 1982; Wenger, 1987), and natural language comprehension systems (Allen, 1983; Bruce, 1982; Schank, 1986). However, the dialogue capabilities in these systems are very primitive because the systems handle a small subset of questions and answers. Moreover, the scope of the most successful systems cover very restricted semantic domains (e.g., train schedules, airline reservations, bacterial infections) rather than general databases (e.g., an encyclopedia). These research efforts have uncovered many of the challenges in designing an impressive and useful mixed initiative dialogue facility.

There have been frequent attempts in computer science and artificial intelligence to make the process of question asking easier for the user (Lang, Graesser, Dumais, & Kilman, in press). The earliest formats for asking questions involved rigid query languages in which the words and syntax of the questions needed to be entered in a precise manner. Rigid query languages are difficult to learn and use, however, so they are avoided in contemporary interface designs. A "structured query language" (SQL) was developed to make the commands and queries similar to English, but the expressions were still cryptic, difficult to learn, and awkward for nonprogrammers. Systems have been designed with special facilities that fall somewhere between the extremes of a rigid query language and natural language: Query by Example (Zloof, 1975), the RABBIT system's "retrieval by reformulation" (Williams, 1984), Texas Instruments menu-driven natural language interface (Tennant, 1987), the ASK TOM system (Schank, Ferguson, Birnbaum, Barger, & Greising, 1991), and the Point and Query (P&Q) interface (Graesser, Langston, & Lang, 1991; Lang et al., in press). For example, in the P&Q interface, the user simply points to a word, phrase, or picture element on the computer screen and then points to a question that is relevant to that element. In principle, it is possible to design a mixed initiative dialogue facility that is fairly easy to use and that does not require the computer to interpret natural language.

The designer of a mixed initiative dialogue facility would benefit from a psychological theory of question asking that is grounded in empirical data. Such a theory would identify the mechanisms that trigger questions when individuals ask questions in naturalistic environments. The theory would identify the types of questions that are asked in the context of specific knowledge domains. In particular applications, the designer could collect data from people who use the system and analyze what questions they ask.

There are two general goals that we hope to accomplish in this chapter. First, we document the types of questions and question generation mechanisms that occur in the context of a normal tutoring session between adults. We analyzed the questions that tutors and students asked in 30 tutoring sessions. The tutoring sessions covered six difficult topics in a research methods course, such as operational definitions, interactions, factorial designs, and hypothesis testing. Each question was analyzed on three dimensions that were identified in a question categorization scheme proposed by Graesser, Person, and Huber (in press):

(a) degree of specification, (b) question category, and (c) question generation mechanism. Regarding our second goal, we speculate on how the design of intelligent tutoring systems might accommodate the results of these analyses. We ultimately argue that the constraints of computer technology, effective pedagogy, and natural conversation are sometimes incompatible and that question-asking facilities on computers need to optimally juggle these sets of constraints.

A THEORETICAL ANALYSIS OF QUESTIONS

Our analysis of questions was based on a theoretical scheme reported by Graesser et al. (in press). This GPH scheme acknowledges the distinction between an *interrogative* expression and an *inquiry*. An interrogative expression would end in a question mark (?) if it were captured in print. An inquiry is any speech act in which the speaker is genuinely seeking new information from the listener (van der Meij, 1987); it is defined conceptually rather than syntactically. For example, all the following expressions are inquiries:

> What is a *t*-test? (interrogative)
> Tell me what a *t*-test is. (command)
> I don't understand what a *t*-test is. (assertion)

Just as inquiries are not always interrogative expressions, interrogative expressions are not always inquiries. For example, "Why is this a dependent variable?" is an inquiry, whereas "Why don't you copy this graph on the board?" is a request. A *question* is defined as an interrogative expression, an inquiry, or both.

The GPH scheme categorizes each question on three dimensions: degree of specification, question category, and question generation mechanism. These dimensions are briefly described in this section (see Graesser et al., in press, for a more thorough description of this analysis of questions).

Degree of Specification

Questions vary in the degree to which the linguistic content specifies the information being sought. Questions with high specification have words or phrases that refer to elements of the desired information and the relevant background information within which the desired information is embedded. Questions with low specification have few words or phrases; the dialogue context is needed for the answerer to "fill in" the missing information. The following examples illustrate how a question can be posed with high, medium, versus low specification:

> What are the variables in the factorial design in experiment 2? (high specification)
> What are the variables? (medium specification)
> What about these? (low specification)

A question is frequently misinterpreted when the question has low specification and the answerer does not understand the dialogue context.

Question Category

Table 6.1 lists the 18 question categories in the GPH scheme. Each category is identified on the basis of semantic, conceptual, and pragmatic criteria rather than lexical and syntactic criteria; that is, each question stem (e.g., why, how) does not have its own category because most stems are polysemous. For example, a *how* stem exists in a causal antecedent question (e.g., How did the experiment fail?), an instrumental-procedural question (How do you present the stimulus on each trial?), and a quantification question (How many levels are on this variable?). The fact that the question categories are defined on the basis of meaning rather than form is consistent with computational theories of question answering in artificial intelligence (Lehnert, 1978; Schank & Abelson, 1977; Souther, Acker, Lester, & Porter, 1989).

Two theories provided most of the categories in the GPH scheme. D'Andrade and Wish (1985) identified eight major speech act categories that can handle virtually all speech acts in conversations: question (interrogatives), assertion, request–directive, reaction, expressive evaluation, commitment, and declaration. The GPH scheme includes questions, assertions, and requests–directives because these were the only categories that involved interrogatives and inquiries. Questions are segregated into subcategories. Most of these subcategories were extracted from Lehnert's (1978) taxonomy, which was motivated by a computational theory of question answering (called QUALM) that handles questions in the context of narrative text. Additional categories in the GPH scheme were identified by Graesser et al. (in press) when they analyzed questions that occur in a diverse corpus of tutoring sessions.

TABLE 6.1
Question Categories in Graesser, Person, and Huber (in press) Scheme

Question Category	Abstract Specification	Example
Short Answer		
Verification	Is a fact true? Did an event occur?	Is the answer five?
Disjunctive	Is X or Y the case? Is X, Y, or Z the case?	Is gender or female the variable?
Concept completion	Who? What? What is the referent of a noun argument slot?	Who ran this experiment?
Feature specification	What qualitative attributes does entity X have?	What are the properties of a bar graph?
Quantification	What is the value of a quantitative variable? How many?	How many degrees of freedom are on this variable?

(Continued)

TABLE 6.1 (*continued*)

Question Category	Abstract Specification	Example
Long Answer		
Definition	What does X mean?	What is a *t*-test?
Example	What is an example label or instance of the category?	What is an example of a factorial design?
Comparison	How is X similar to Y? How is X different from Y?	What is the difference between a *t*-test and an *f*-test?
Interpretation	What concept or claim can be inferred from a static or active pattern of data?	What is happening in this graph?
Causal antecedent	What state or event causally led to an event or state?	How did this experiment fail?
Causal consequence	What are the consequences of an event or state?	What happens when this level decreases?
Goal orientation	What are the motives or goals behind an agent's action?	Why did you put decision latency on the y-axis?
Instrumental/procedural	What instrument or plan allows an agent to accomplish a goal?	How do you present the stimulus on each trial?
Enablement	What object or resource allows an agent to perform an action?	What device allows you to measure stress?
Expectational	Why did some expected event not occur?	Why isn't there an interaction?
Judgmental	What value does the answerer place on an idea or advice?	What do you think of this operational definition?
Assertion	The speaker makes a statement indicating he lacks knowledge or does not understand an idea.	I don't understand main effects.
Request/Directive	The speaker wants the listener to perform an action.	Would you add those numbers together?

According to Table 6.1, questions are segregated into "short-answer" questions and "long-answer" questions. The answers to short-answer questions are normally answered in a single word or short phrase. Long-answer questions invite lengthy replies of a sentence or several sentences. Compared to short-answer questions, the long-answer questions impose a burden on the answerer to supply lengthy coherent answers.

A particular question may be assigned to more than one question category in Table 6.1. One frequent amalgamation occurs when a verification question is combined with another category. For example, the question "Are there three levels on the variable?" is an amalgamation of a quantification question (i.e., How many levels are on the variable?) and a verification question (i.e., a question that invites a YES–NO answer). Given that hybrid questions exist, the question category dimension can be treated as a polythetic categorization scheme in addition to a monothetic scheme. In a monothetic scheme, any given question is assigned to one and only one category; in a polythetic scheme, a question can be assigned to several categories (Stokal, 1974).

Question Generation Mechanisms

The GPH scheme has 21 mechanisms that trigger questions. These 21 mechanisms, which are listed in Table 6.2, are clustered into four categories: (a) correction of knowledge deficits, (b) monitoring common ground, (c) social coordination of action, and (d) control of conversation and attention. Some of these question generation mechanisms have been identified in computer models of question generation, problem solving, and reasoning (Kass, in press; Klahr & Dunbar, 1988; Laird, Rosenbloom, & Newell, 1987; Schank, 1986), in theories of natural language comprehension and conversation (Clark & Schaefer, 1989), and in theories of learning (Collins, 1988; Palinscar & Brown, 1984; Sleeman & Brown, 1982). However, some of the categories were discovered empirically when Graesser et al. (in press) analyzed a large corpus of tutoring sessions.

The descriptions of the 21 question generation mechanisms in Table 6.2 should be adequate for the purposes of this chapter. Those categories in the correction of knowledge deficit cluster occur when the questioner discovers that his or her knowledge base is incomplete or in error. An answer to the question is expected to rectify the knowledge deficit. Those mechanisms in the *monitoring common ground* cluster address the common ground (i.e., shared knowledge) between the questioner and answerer (Clark & Schaefer, 1989). Speech participants constantly introduce, update, and verify knowledge in the common ground; they often do this by asking questions. Whereas common ground knowledge is shared by questioner and answerer, questioner-knowledge is in the knowledge base of only the questioner, and answerer-knowledge is in the knowledge base of only the answerer. In a tutoring session, the tutor tries to augment the common ground knowledge about the topic and to identify what knowledge the student

TABLE 6.2
Question Generation Mechanisms in Graesser, Person, and Huber
(in press) Scheme

Correction of Knowledge Deficits
    Obstacle in planning and problem solving
    Gap in knowledge
    Glitch in explanation/Contradiction
    Decision among equally attractive alternatives
Monitoring Common Ground
    Estimation or establishment of common ground
    Confirmation of a belief
    Comprehension gauging (global comprehension)
    Questioner's assessment of answerer's knowledge
    Questioner's attempt to have answerer generate an inference
Social Coordination of Action
    Indirect request
    Indirect advice
    Gain permission
    Offer
    Negotiation
Control of Conversation or Attention
    Rhetorical questions
    Gripe
    Reply to summons
    Change speaker
    Focus on agent's actions
    Greeting

---

has. Questions in the *social coordination of action* cluster are generated in order to manipulate people or to coordinate actions within a group of people, as discussed in speech act theories (Austin, 1962; D'Andrade & Wish, 1985; Gibbs & Mueller, 1988; Searle, 1969). Finally, questions in the *control of conversation and attention* cluster are asked in order to initiate, terminate, or monitor the flow of conversation among speech participants. Some, but not all, of these questions invite replies.

Constraints of Technology, Pedagogy, and Natural Conversation

We argued earlier that the success of an intelligent tutoring system depends in part on its questioning facilities. If the ITS had a mixed initiative dialogue, the designer would need to be concerned with four categories of speech acts: computer–tutor questions, user–learner questions, computer–tutor answers, and user–learner answers.

    There are three interacting systems that impose constraints on the questions that can be asked in an intelligent tutoring system. *Technological constraints* include limitations in existing computer technology. In particular, the repertoire of questions that the computer can handle is limited by the fact that it is very difficult for computers to produce and interpret natural language. *Pedagogical constraints* are imposed by ideal teaching strategies that are implemented in tutoring and classroom environments. According to some philosophies of education, for example, it is inappropriate for the teacher or computer to impose excessive control by asking all the questions (Dillon, 1988). The *constraints of natural conversation* reflect general characteristics of dialogue and communication in normal conversations (in this case, tutoring sessions). A tutoring system would probably not succeed if its questioning facilities were incompatible with the normal patterns of conversation.

As it turns out, the constraints imposed by technology, pedagogy, and natural conversation are sometimes incompatible from the perspective of the design of question-asking facilities. This became obvious when we analyzed questions on degree of specification, question category, and question generation mechanisms.

Degree of Specification.   Consider the contrast between questions with a low versus a high degree of specification. Questions with a high degree of specification are easiest for computers to handle, so technological constraints yield the prediction of high > low. Regarding computer (tutor) questions, such questions are generated by question generation algorithms and databases that have a rich, if not complete, specification of the problem under consideration. Extra computational work is needed to delete elliptically various linguistic elements in the question. This explains why it is frequently difficult for a user to interpret computer-generated questions; there are so many "irrelevant" elements and parameters specified on the screen that it is difficult for the user to search and decipher what the computer's question is. Extra computations would be needed to filter out the background content and to focus on those elements that are closely tied to the intended question. Regarding user-generated questions, it is also easiest for computer systems to handle high rather than low specification questions. It is difficult for computers to infer intended questions from sparse linguistic input because computers have difficulties comprehending language, generating knowledge-based inferences, and interpreting the dialogue context.

High specification questions would be preferred over low specification questions in the context of pedagogical constraints. When questions are highly specified by either the computer or the student, there is a higher likelihood that the intended questions are correctly interpreted and a lower density of misconceptions. Good teachers attempt to articulate a question both completely and precisely. Good teachers encourage students to model this style of posing questions.

We needed to collect data in order to determine whether low or high specification questions occur most frequently in naturalistic tutoring sessions. If high specification questions are very prevalent in normal tutoring sessions, then the constraints of technology, pedagogy, and conversation would be perfectly compatible; we would consistently integrate high specification questions into the design of question-asking facilities. On the other hand, if high specification questions are rare in normal tutoring sessions, then we would need to design a question-asking interface (for student questions) that minimizes the incompatibility among technology, pedagogy, and conversation. Perhaps a special interface would need to be designed for student questions. For example, such a design might begin with a low specification question and embellish the question incrementally (via extended computer–human dialogue) until a high specification question is achieved. In fact, there are some question-asking facilities that capitalize on the incremental nature of posing a question (Deerwester, Dumais, Landauer, Furnas, & Harshman, 1990; Dumais, 1988; Williams, 1984).

Question Categories.   Consider the contrast between short-answer questions and long-answer questions. Computers are clearly best equipped to handle short-answer questions. This is because it is difficult for computers to produce and comprehend natural language. When the student asks a long-answer question, the computer would have trouble producing an answer that involves connected discourse; when the computer asks a long-answer question, the computer would not be able to interpret a paragraph of information that the student enters as an answer. Technological constraints clearly produce a preference for short-answer questions over long-answer questions.

In contrast to the technological constraints, the pedagogical constraints dictate a preference for long-answer questions over short-answer questions (Dillon, 1988; Kerry, 1987). Long-answer questions are more sophisticated and require the answerer to engage in more active cognitive processing (e.g., the integration, organization, and synthesis of knowledge). When a student is asked a long-answer question, the lengthy answer requires more active participation and exposes more of the student's misconceptions. When the teacher is asked a long-answer question, the teacher presents material that is well organized and logically sound. Short-answer questions (by teacher and student) create a learning experience that is comparatively choppy and disconnected.

Once again, data need to be collected in order to assess whether short- versus long-answer questions are most prevalent in normal tutoring sessions. If long-answer questions prevail, then more effort is needed to advance the computer technology that accommodate lengthy answers. If short-answer questions prevail, then we might want to design computer interfaces that promote active organized thinking processes by issuing and receiving a series of short-answer questions.

Question Generation Mechanisms.   Technologically, it is more difficult to design computer systems with mixed initiative dialogues than systems in which only the computer asks questions or only the student asks questions. In contrast, there is a preference for mixed initiative dialogues from the perspective of pedagogy (Palinscar & Brown, 1984). Data need to be collected in order to estimate the prevalence of student questions and tutor questions in normal tutoring sessions.

We mentioned earlier that student questions are very rare in classroom settings. This would suggest that students are not active, inquisitive, creative learners who accurately self-regulate their knowledge about a topic. If students ask a low frequency of questions and their questions are rarely in the category of "correction of knowledge deficit" (see Table 6.2), then it may be a futile exercise to design an intelligent tutoring system with a mixed initiative dialogue. Instead, a system with computer-generated questions would be adequate. On the other hand, if questions are more frequent in tutoring sessions (as opposed to classroom settings) and the density of knowledge deficit questions is high, then there would be a greater incentive to build an interface with mixed initiative dialogue. Alternatively, the human–computer interface would need to be designed in a manner that teaches students how to ask good questions about a topic they know very little about.

COLLECTION OF DATA IN 30 TUTORING SESSIONS ON RESEARCH METHODS

We have argued that there is a need to analyze the questions that individuals ask in natural tutoring sessions and to assess whether these questions are compatible with the constraints of technology and pedagogy. The present study investigated the questions generated by students and tutors in 30 tutoring sessions on research methods. The findings from this study should provide some guidance for designing question-asking facilities in intelligent tutoring systems. We would not be surprised if our findings would apply to other types of computer systems, such as expert systems, intelligent decision support systems, and text retrieval systems.

We adopted the GPH scheme (Graesser et al., in press) when we analyzed the student questions and tutor questions; that is, we analyzed each question on the dimensions of degree of specification, question category, and question generation mechanism. These analyses provided descriptive data on the types of questions generated in tutorial sessions. The analyses permitted us to compare the constraints of natural conversation with those of technology and pedagogy. On the basis of these empirical data, we can offer informed recommendations and speculations on what question-asking facilities would be feasible on computer systems.

Students and Tutors

The 30 tutoring sessions included 3 different tutors and 18 undergraduate students enrolled in a psychology course on research methods at Memphis State University. Participation in the tutoring sessions was a course requirement. Each of the 18 students was randomly assigned to 2 tutoring topics, with a different tutor for each of the two topics; this yielded a total of 36 possible sessions. Data from 6 of the 36 tutoring sessions was eliminated either because the student failed to arrive at the session or because the quality of the videotaped session did not permit accurate transcription. The tutors were graduate students at Memphis State University who had previously received an A in either an undergraduate or graduate level course on research methods. Each tutor was paid $500 for tutoring students in 12 tutoring sessions.

Learning Materials

The instructor selected 6 topics that are normally troublesome for the students in the research methods course. These topics were: (a) variables, (b) graphs, (c) inferential statistics, (d) the generation of a design from a hypothesis, (e) factorial designs, and (f) interactions. Each topic had 3 or 4 subtopics that further embellished the material. For example, the subtopics for the tutoring session on variables were: operational definitions, types of scales, and values of variables. An index card was prepared for each topic that included the main topic and the 3 or 4 subtopics.

Both the students and the tutors were required to read specific pages in a research methods text entitled *Methods in behavioral research* (Cozby, 1989). The material assigned to each topic had a mean of 14 pages. If a student failed to read the required material, the tutoring session was postponed to a later date. The assigned reading material served as a common ground between the tutors and the students. Moreover, the tutoring sessions were coordinated with the lecture material; the topic in each tutoring session was covered in a lecture within 1 week prior to the tutoring session. Therefore, the students were given substantial opportunities to study the material before they started a tutoring session.

Equipment and Setting for Tutorial Sessions

The room used for the tutoring session was equipped with a video camera, a television set, a marker board, colored markers, a table, two chairs, and the textbook in the course. The television screen was covered with a blanket during the entire tutoring session. The video camera was positioned at an angle that captured the student and the entire marker board. Therefore, the transcripts of the tutoring sessions included both spoken utterances and messages on the marker board.

Procedure of Tutoring Session

The student entered the tutoring room and sat in view of the video camera. The tutor gave the student the topic index card and asked the student to read it aloud. The tutoring session proceeded and lasted approximately 45 minutes. The tutors were told that they should make every attempt to facilitate a highly interactive session and to resist the temptation of simply lecturing to the student. Otherwise, the tutors were free to follow any format they wished during the tutoring session. The tutoring sessions spanned an 8-week period during the course. The topics that covered the first 3 of the 8 weeks were variables, graphs, and statistics, respectively. A 2-week break followed these 3 weeks of tutoring sessions. The remaining three topics were covered in the 3 weeks following the break: generation of a design from a hypothesis, factorial designs, and finally interactions.

Transcriptions of the Tutoring Sessions

The transcribers were instructed to prepare very complete and detailed transcriptions of each tutoring session. They transcribed the entire tutoring sessions verbatim, including all "ums," "ahs," word fragments, broken sentences, and pauses. The transcribers included figures and messages that individuals wrote on the marker board. Each written transcription was verified for accuracy before it was coded and analyzed.

Coding of Transcripts

The second and third authors segmented each of the protocols into speech acts. Once these speech acts were identified, another pair of judges was trained to identify the questions (interrogatives and inquiries) in the tutoring protocols. These judges achieved extremely high reliability scores in deciding whether or not a speech act was a question (Cronbach's $\alpha = .96$).

Another pair of judges was trained to categorize each question on degree of specification. The values were low, medium, and high, as discussed earlier. These judges scored practice tutoring sessions and were retrained until they achieved a satisfactory degree of reliability (i.e., a Cronbach's α of .70 on two protocols). Once this threshold of reliability was reached, each judge scored approximately half the questions on degree of specification. A spot sample reliability score was .94.

Another pair of judges was trained to score each question on the dimension of question category. In a monothetic classification task, the judges assigned each of the questions to 1 of the 18 categories in Table 6.1. In a few cases, they had difficulties in classification because questions were sometimes amalgamations of two categories. The most frequent amalgamation by far included questions that combined the verification category with one of the other categories, as discussed earlier (e.g., "Do you see why this experiment has a problem?"). In these cases, the judges were instructed to give the verification category lower priority than the other categories. In a similar fashion, the assertion and request–directive categories were given lower priority than the other categories in the monothetic classification scheme. The judges scored practice tutoring sessions and were retrained until they achieved a .70 reliability score on two protocols. Each judge scored approximately one half of the questions among the 30 tutoring sessions. A spot sample reliability score was .95.

In addition to the monothetic classification, the same two judges completed a polythetic classification on the question categories; that is, they assigned each question to one or more categories in addition to their first choice alternative (from the monothetic scheme). They also indicated whether their first-choice category was a satisfactory choice or whether the additional categories were needed for each question. Therefore, each question could be assigned to several question categories instead of only one. In the final analysis of the polythetic scheme, we included all categories that were first choices and all additional categories that the judges believed were needed for a question. Nevertheless, the analyses from the polythetic classification scheme were very similar to those of the monothetic classification scheme. Therefore, we report data from the monothetic analyses in the next section.

Two additional judges scored the questions on question generation mechanisms (see Table 6.2), following the same procedure as that described previously for question categories. A spot sample reliability score was .81 in the monothetic classification scheme. A polythetic classification scheme was performed as well, but data from the polythetic scheme are not reported in this chapter because they were quite redundant with the analyses using the monothetic scheme.

ANALYSIS OF TUTORING SESSIONS AND IMPLICATIONS FOR THE DESIGN OF COMPUTERIZED QUESTION-ASKING FACILITIES

This section reports the results of our analysis of questions in the tutoring sessions. Each question was analyzed on three dimensions: degree of specification, question category, and question generation mechanism. For each of these dimensions, we discuss the results in the context of technological, pedagogical, and conversational constraints. On the basis of these constraints, we offer recommendations and speculations on the types of question-asking facilities that would be feasible in intelligent tutoring systems.

Overall Number of Questions by Students and Tutors

For each of the 30 tutoring sessions, we scored the number of tutor questions and student questions. In statistical tests that compared scores of students and tutors, we treated this "questioner" variable as a between-groups variable; that is, the unit of analysis (i.e., case) was considered a tutor–student combination rather than an individual student or a particular tutor. Questioner (tutor vs. student) was treated as a between-subjects variable so statistical tests were very conservative. In contrast, variables that examined differences between categories of questions (e.g., high, medium, vs. low specifications) are treated as within-subjects variables. We also performed follow-up analyses using nonparametric statistics (i.e., sign tests, chi-square tests, Mann-Whitney ANOVA by ranks) instead of parametric statistics. However, the nonparametric statistics are not reported here because the results from these analyses were perfectly compatible with those from the parametric statistical analyses.

There were significantly more questions generated by tutors than by students, F (1, 58), $= 69.90$, $p < .05$. The mean frequencies of tutor questions versus student questions (per tutoring session) were 95.2 and 21.3, respectively. Therefore, 82% of the questions were asked by tutors and 18% were asked by students. The rate of student questions was high for these tutoring sessions involving college students, compared to studies of questioning behavior in classrooms. In classrooms, less than 3% of the questions are asked by students (Kerry, 1987). The 18% figure in the present study is significantly higher than the 3% figure from the previous classroom studies.

There are several possible explanations for the fact that there was a high percentage of student questions in this study. One possible explanation is that tutoring sessions are inherently more interactive than classroom settings. Another explanation is that our tutors followed our instructions to stimulate interactive tutoring sessions. Yet another possible explanation is that the students in this study were well prepared; student questions should be positively correlated with level of understanding (Miyake & Norman, 1979). The present study was not designed to test among these alternatives. The important implication, from the standpoint of this study, is that the students were not entirely passive recipients of the tutor's training regime.

Degree of Specification

There were significant differences in frequencies among low, medium, and high specification questions. For students, the mean frequencies of low, medium, versus high specification questions per session were 5.7, 15.2, versus .4, respectively, $F(2, 58) = 65.11$, $p < .05$. The high specification questions did not significantly differ from 0 in the case of students. Regarding tutor questions, the frequencies of low, medium, versus high specification questions were 42.3, 50.3, versus 2.6, respectively, $F(2, 58) = 39.10$, $p < .05$. High specification questions were extremely rare both for tutors and for students (less than 3% of the questions).

The fact that high specification questions are extremely rare has important implications for the design of question-asking facilities in computers. According to one solution to this conversational constraint, question-asking facilities should permit the user to pose a question in an incremental fashion; that is, there should be a computer–user dialogue that accumulates elements, parameters, and context-sensitive features of a fully specified question. For example, the RABBITT interface (Williams, 1984) contains a "retrieval of reformulation" method of posing the question. The user first enters an initial set of question attributes. Based on this information, the computer embellishes the question with additional attributes and options that are plausible inferences. The user verifies the additional attributes and selects among the options; this content sometimes reminds the user of yet additional attributes. Eventually, a fully specified question evolves.

An alternative solution would be to adopt the "Point and Query" (P&Q) interface (Graesser et al., 1991; Lang et al., in press) or the interface on Schank's ASK TOM system (Schank et al., 1991). The user of a P&Q system first points to a content element and then points to one of a small set of questions that are relevant to the content element. The computer quickly presents either a preformulated answer to the question or an answer that is constructed in a more intelligent manner. Graesser has developed and tested a model for human question answering (called QUEST) that successfully accounts for answers that adults give to a broad diversity of questions (i.e., most of the question categories in Table 6.1; Graesser & Clark, 1985; Graesser & Franklin, 1990; Graesser & Hemphill, 1991; Graesser, Lang, & Roberts, 1991; Graesser, Robertson, & Anderson, 1981). It is easy to pose questions on a P&Q interface; the user simply points to a content element and then to a question. Each question is fully specified so the process of the user specifying a question is circumvented. The P&Q is a feasible solution when there are small or manageable numbers of alternative questions that can be handled by the system. On the other hand, it would be impractical when there is a very large number of relevant questions.

Question Category

Table 6.1 presents the 18 question categories. We found that a substantial proportion of these questions were verification questions, both for tutors and for students (51%). Verification questions place the least burden on the answerer because the answerer merely answers YES or NO. Of course, answerers are often more cooperative and helpful by providing more lengthy answers that justify the YES–NO answers or that correct misconceptions that are presupposed by the question (Kaplan, 1983). Compared to other question categories, however, verification questions place the least burden on the answerer.

Aside from verification questions, the question categories that were most prevalent were concept completion questions (14%), instrumental–procedural questions (13%), and interpretation questions (12%). Here are some examples of these question categories:

Which variable is the independent variable? (concept completion)
How do you compute a *t*-test? (instrumental procedural)
What does this pattern of data mean? (interpretation)

The other question categories in Table 6.1 were considerably less frequent (7% or lower, averaging over student and tutor questions).

As discussed earlier, technological constraints would favor short-answer questions over long-answer questions, whereas pedagogical constraints would favor long-answer questions over short-answer questions. We performed some analyses to assess the constraints of conversation. For each of the 30 tutoring sessions, we computed the proportion of questions that invited long answers versus short answers, following the classification scheme in Table 6.1. Note that there are many more categories of long-answer than short-answer questions. For student questions, the proportion scores were significantly higher for short- than long-answer questions: .64 versus .36, respectively; the same trend held for tutor questions: .61 versus .39.

The preceding data indicate that conversational constraints are compatible with technology, but incompatible with pedagogy. Long-answer questions are problematic for computers because it is difficult for computers to comprehend or to produce lengthy answers. However, long-answer questions are desired pedagogically because they encourage integration and organization (Collins, 1988; Dillon, 1988; Kerry, 1987; Palinscar & Brown, 1984). In conversation, long-answer questions place a greater burden on the answerer than do short-answer questions, so they are less prevalent. Although tutors should encourage the students to provide lengthy descriptions and explanations, the tutors' percentage of long-answer questions was no different than that of students (39% vs. 36%, respectively). It appears that tutors succumb to the constraints of natural conversation rather than good pedagogy.

In an analysis of 44 tutoring sessions, Person (1990) reported that the distribution of question categories varied significantly among students. However, the categories of student questions were not affected by differences among tutors, even though the tutors had quite different tutoring styles. This suggests that it might be difficult to modify the profile of student questions by changes in the computerized question-asking facilities in intelligent tutoring systems. Students may need extensive exposure to good questions before they learn how to modify their question-asking strategies.

Given that short-answer questions are most feasible in the design of question-asking facilities, we would recommend intelligent tutoring systems that formulate sequences of short-answer questions that are judiciously selected to optimize learning. Such questions would expose the student's misconceptions or would be at the frontier of the student's knowledge base (i.e., not too difficult and not too easy; Collins, 1988; Palinscar & Brown, 1984; Sleeman & Brown, 1982; Vygotsky, 1978; Wenger, 1987). On the basis of the student's short answers, the computer would subsequently estimate the student's knowledge and diagnose the student's misconceptions. The computer would provide explanatory feedback that expands the student's knowledge base and repairs the student's misconceptions by presenting short, preformulated messages. This design of an intelligent tutoring system would minimize the need for the computer to generate and interpret lengthy novel text; yet it would promote learning at a deep level.

Question Generation Mechanisms

Table 6.2 lists the question generation mechanisms in the GPH scheme. The most frequent mechanism underlying student questions was "confirmation of a belief" (54%). These questions occur when the student wants to verify that the tutor's belief about some fact is the same as that of the student's. The following example illustrates this questioning mechanism:

> STUDENT: So the next topic is a factorial design. Isn't that when there are many independent variables?

In this example, the student asks the question in order to confirm that his or her definition of a factorial design is on the mark. The fact that over half of the student questions were in this category suggests that the students did take some active control in estimating their level of knowledge. The students both assert their belief (i.e., A factorial design has many independent variables) and then inquire whether the belief is correct (i.e., Is that belief true or false?). This is a more active posture than simply asking the tutor to define factorial design (i.e., "What is a factorial design?").

One third of the student questions were in the general cluster of "correction of knowledge deficits." These question generation mechanisms are triggered when the student identifies a gap, contradiction, anomaly, obstacle, or uncertainty in his or her knowledge base. For example, the following question involves a "glitch in an explanation" because there is an anomalous element in a problem; the student asks the tutor a question in search for an explanation.

> STUDENT: You do the *t*-tests by computing the numbers in different stages. Here are the scores in the two groups. That's fine. But how did this "$p <$ .05" get here?

The fact that a hefty proportion of the students' questions were in the "correction of knowledge deficit" cluster is consistent with the claim that students do actively monitor their knowledge rather than passively receive information from the tutor.

The tutors' question generation mechanisms were substantially different than those of the students. The tutors typically asked questions that evaluated the student's level of knowledge. The two most frequent categories of tutor questions were in the common ground category and accounted for 74% of their questions: "comprehension gauging" and "questioner's assessment of the answerer's knowledge." When tutors ask comprehension gauging questions, they inquire about the student's global level of understanding (i.e., "Do you understand?"). Questions in the other category focus on particular information (e.g., "Do you understand why a Type I error might have occurred here?").

Although the tutors asked substantially more questions than the students, the students asked most of the questions in the "correction of knowledge deficit" cluster. We computed the frequency of tutor questions and student questions in this category for each of the 30 tutoring sessions. The mean frequency of questions in this category was significantly higher for the students than the tutors, 6.9 versus 1.6, respectively, $F(58) = 18.84$, $p < .05$. Whereas 33% of the students' questions were in this category, only 2% of the tutors' questions were in this category. Once again, students indeed monitor and try to correct their own knowledge deficits.

The most prevalent cluster of questioning mechanisms for both tutor and student involved the monitoring of common ground. The mean frequencies of questions that involved these mechanisms were significantly higher for tutors than for students, 79.7 versus 12.5, respectively, $F(58) = 47.89$, $p < .05$. The percentage of student questions in the "common ground" cluster was 60%, whereas the percentage was 84% for tutor questions. Tutors clearly spend most of their efforts trying to find out what the student knows and testing the student's knowledge. In contrast, students spent most of their time asking questions to verify that their knowledge was compatible with that of the tutors.

The tutors took more control over the tutoring sessions because their frequency of questions was substantially higher in the final two clusters of mechanisms than that of the students. Regarding the "social coordination of action," the frequency scores were significantly higher for tutors than for students, 8.5 versus .9, respectively, $F(58) = 21.90$, $p < .05$. Regarding "control of conversation and attention," the frequencies were higher for tutors than students, 5.1 versus .6, $F(58) = 29.92$, $p < .05$. The percentage scores were consistent with these frequency scores; 14% of the tutor questions were in these two categories, whereas only 7% of the student questions were in these categories.

Our analysis of the question generation mechanisms supports the feasibility of a mixed initiative dialogue facility in intelligent tutoring systems. We originally feared that students would rarely ask questions and that the few questions they asked would not penetrate important deficits in their knowledge. Had this been the case, a computer-centered question-asking facility would have been adequate. However, our fears were based on research on student questioning in classroom settings (Dillon, 1988; Kerry, 1987) rather than in tutoring sessions. The tutoring setting is apparently quite different, at least for college students who had ample time to study the material. Our analysis of the questions in the present study indicate that students are not entirely passive recipients of the tutor's material. They ask questions, approximately one question every 2 minutes. Most of their questions address either deficits in their knowledge or beliefs that need confirmation. To some extent, the students did regulate the course of their knowledge acquisition.

On the other hand, there do appear to be limits to the students' inquisitiveness. The students did not vigorously ask dozens of questions per minute and impatiently wait for answers. They did not identify a large set of gaps and contradictions in their knowledge base and subsequently ask questions to rectify all these deficits. They occasionally identified problems in their comprehension of the material but were not exhaustive self-regulators of their knowledge base.

Although students did take some control over the tutoring session by asking questions, a substantial responsibility fell on the shoulders of the tutor in guiding the tutoring session. The tutors asked the vast majority of the questions. The tutors frequently "grilled" students on subtopics and gauged their level of understanding. The typical tutor strategy was to identify the student's deficits and then to supply relevant information that fills in the missing information. The tutors rarely took an indirect approach, such as the Socratic method (Collins, 1985; Collins & Stevens, 1982). According to the Socratic method, the tutor asks carefully planned sequences of thought-provoking questions that reveal the students' misconceptions and contradictions; the students are expected to discover their own deficits in knowledge as they answer these well-crafted questions. The Socratic method was not very prevalent in the present study because very few tutor questions were in the category "questioner's attempt to have answerer generate an inference" (3%). The Socratic method is very difficult for the typical tutor to apply because it requires a sophisticated understanding of the student's knowledge and a mechanism for asking clever questions. Highly trained tutors and intelligent tutoring systems are needed to successfully implement the Socratic method. This would require a very intelligent computer system that is capable of accurately identifying deficits in the student's knowledge base.

SUMMARY

The designer of question-asking facilities in intelligent tutoring systems and other forms of educational software should recognize the constraints that are imposed by technology, pedagogy, and natural conversation. In this chapter we have identified many of these constraints and have reported data on questions that are asked in tutoring sessions. These analyses support the following general claims:

1. Whereas technological and pedagogical constraints favor high specification questions over low specification questions, high specification questions are rarely generated by students. Therefore, computerized question-asking facilities need to circumvent this bottleneck in some fashion, such as a Point & Query interface or the ability to pose a question in a distributed, incremental fashion.

2. Whereas pedagogical constraints favor long-answer questions over short-answer questions, it is beyond the capability of computer technology to produce

and interpret lengthy answers that are novel (as opposed to answers that are stereotypical and preformulated). Moreover, both students and tutors tend to favor short-answer questions over long-answer questions. Therefore, tutoring systems may need to be designed around short-answer questions. The computer might guide the tutoring session by asking a judiciously selected sequence of short-answer questions. These questions should have a high likelihood of diagnosing the student's knowledge deficits and misconceptions.

3. It is feasible to design an intelligent tutoring system with a mixed initiative dialogue in which both the student and the tutor ask and answer questions. Our worry was that students would not be sufficiently inquisitive to ask questions that address their own knowledge deficits. This study revealed, however, that students in tutoring sessions do ask a modest amount of questions that address their knowledge deficits. In turn, human tutors ask a high frequency of questions that diagnose the student's level of knowledge.

The interface that provides the mixed initiative dialogue needs to be designed in a manner that encourages curiosity in the student and that implements more sophisticated pedagogical strategies on the part of the computer. This recommendation is based on two of the findings in our analysis of tutoring sessions. First, students are moderately curious to the extent that they ask questions that arise from their knowledge deficits and that confirm beliefs that they already have; however, they ask only a moderate number of questions, which did not come close to covering the total space of their knowledge deficits. Second, the tutors rarely apply sophisticated pedagogical strategies, such as the Socratic method or the reciprocal training method. Instead, they resort to grilling students on subtopics and to presenting information that fills perceived gaps in the student's knowledge base.

ACKNOWLEDGMENTS

This research was funded by grants awarded to the first author by the office of Naval Research (N00014-88-K-0110 and N00014-90-J-1492). We thank Angela McGlaun, Mark Langston, Brenda Johnson, and John White for assisting us in data analysis and coding.

REFERENCES

Allen, J. (1983). Recognizing intentions from natural language utterances. In M. Brady & R. C. Berwick (Eds.), *Computational models of discourse* (pp. 27–105). Cambridge, MA: MIT Press.
Anderson, J. R., Boyle, C. F., & Reiser, B. J. (1985). Intelligent tutoring systems. *Science, 228*, 456–462.
Austin, J. L. (1962). *How to do things with words.* Oxford: Oxford University Press.

Bruce, B. C. (1982). Natural communication between person and computer. In W. G. Lehnert & M. H. Ringle (Eds.), *Strategies for natural language processing* (pp. 55–88). Hillsdale, NJ: Lawrence Erlbaum Associates.

Buchanan, B. G., & Shortliffe, E. H. (Eds.). (1984). *Rule-based expert systems.* Menlo Park, CA: Addison–Wesley.

Card, S. K., Moran, T. P., & Newell, A. (Eds.). (1983). *The psychology of human–computer interaction.* Hillsdale, NJ: Lawrence Erlbaum Associates.

Clark, H. H., & Schaefer, E. F. (1989). Contributing to discourse. *Cognitive Science, 13,* 259–294.

Collins, A. (1985). Teaching and reasoning skills. In S. F. Chipman, J. W. Segal, & R. Glaser (Eds.), *Thinking and learning skills* (*Vol. 2,* pp. 579–586). Hillsdale, NJ: Lawrence Erlbaum Associates.

Collins, A. (1988). Different goals of inquiry teaching. *Questioning Exchange, 2,* 259–294.

Collins, A., Brown, J. S., & Larkin, K. M. (1980). Inference in text understanding. In R. J. Spiro, B. C. Bruce, & W. F. Brewer (Eds.), *Theoretical issues in reading comprehension* (pp. 385–407). Hillsdale, NJ: Lawrence Erlbaum Associates.

Collins, A., & Stevens, A. (1982). Goals and strategies of inquiry teachers. In R. Glaser (Ed.), *Advances in instructional psychology* (*Vol. 2,* pp. 65–119). Hillsdale, NJ: Lawrence Erlbaum Associates.

Coombs, M. H., & Alty, J. L. (1980). Face-to-face guidance of university computer users-II: Characterizing advisory interactions. *International Journal of Man–Machine Studies, 12,* 407–429.

Cozby, P. (1989). *Methods in behavioral research* (3rd ed.). Mountain View, CA: Mayfield.

D'Andrade, R. G., & Wish, M. (1985). Speech act theory in quantitative research on interpersonal behavior. *Discourse Processes, 8,* 229–259.

Deerwester, S., Dumais, S. T., Landauer, T. K., Furnas, G. W., & Harshman, R. A. (1990). Indexing by latent semantic analysis. *Journal of the Society for Information Science, 141*(6), 391–407.

Dillon, J. T. (1988). *Questioning and teaching: A manual practice.* New York: Teachers College Press.

Dumais, S. T. (1988). Textual information retrieval. In M. Helander (Ed.), *Handbook of human–computer interaction* (pp. 673–727). New York: North–Holland.

Flammer, A. (1981). Towards a theory of question asking. *Psychological Research, 43,* 407–420.

Gibbs, R. W., & Mueller, R. A. G. (1988). Conversational sequences and preferences for indirect speech acts. *Discourse Processes, 11,* 101–116.

Graesser, A. C., & Clark, L. F. (1985). *Structures and procedures of implicit knowledge.* Norwood, NJ: Ablex.

Graesser, A. C., & Franklin, S. P. (1990). QUEST: A cognitive model of question answering. *Discourse Processes, 13*(3), 279–304.

Graesser, A. C., & Hemphill, D. (1991). Question answering in the context of scientific mechanisms. *Journal of Memory and Language, 30*(2), 186–209.

Graesser, A. C., Lang, K. L., & Roberts, R. M. (1991). Question answering in the context of stories. *Journal of Experimental Psychology: General, 120*(3), 254–277.

Graesser, A. C., Langston, M. C., & Lang, K. L. (1991). Designing educational software around questioning. In the *Proceedings of the 1991 International Conference on the Learning Sciences* (pp. 204–210). Charlottesville, VA: Association for the Advancement of Computing in Education.

Graesser, A. C., Person, N. K., & Huber, J. D. (in press). Mechanisms that generate questions. In T. Lauer, E. Peacock, & A. C. Graesser (Eds.), *Questions and information systems.* Hillsdale, NJ: Lawrence Erlbaum Associates.

Graesser, A. C., Robertson, S. P., & Anderson, P. A. (1981). Incorporating inferences in narrative representations: A study of how and why. *Cognitive Psychology, 13,* 1–26.

Kaplan, S. J. (1983). Cooperative response from a portable natural language system. In M. Brady & R. C. Berwick (Eds.), *Computational models of discourse.* Cambridge, MA: MIT Press.

Kass, A. (in press). Question asking, artificial intelligence, and human creativity. In T. Lauer, E. Peacock, & A. C. Graesser (Eds.), *Questions and information systems*. Hillsdale, NJ: Lawrence Erlbaum Associates.

Kerry, T. (1987). Classroom questions in England. *Questioning Exchange, 1*(1), 32–33.

King, A. (1989). Effects of self-questioning training on college students' comprehension of lectures. *Contemporary educational psychology, 14,* 366–381.

Klahr, D., & Dunbar, K. (1988). Dual search space during scientific reasoning. *Cognitive science, 12*(1), 1–48.

Laird, J., Rosenbloom, P. S., & Newell, A. (1987). SOAR: An architecture for general intelligence. *Artificial Intelligence, 33*(1), 1–64.

Lang, K. L., Graesser, A. C., Dumais, S. T., & Kilman, D. (in press). Question asking in human–computer interface. In T. Lauer, E. Peacock, & A. C. Graesser (Eds.), *Questions and information systems*. Hillsdale, NJ: Lawrence Erlbaum Associates.

Lehnert, W. G. (1978). *The process of question answering*. Hillsdale, NJ: Lawrence Erlbaum Associates.

Markman, E. M. (1985). Comprehension-monitoring: Developmental and educational issues. In S. F. Chipman, J. W. Segal, & R. Glaser (Eds.), *Thinking and learning skills (Vol. 2,* pp. 275–291). Hillsdale, NJ: Lawrence Erlbaum Associates.

Miyake, N., & Norman, D. A. (1979). To ask a question one must know enough to know what is not known. *Journal of Verbal Learning and Verbal Behavior, 18,* 357–364.

Norman, D., & Draper, S. (1986). *User-centered system design-new perspectives on human–computer interaction*. Hillsdale, NJ: Lawrence Erlbaum Associates.

Olson, G. M., Duffy, S. A., & Mack, R. L. (1985). Question asking as a component of text comprehension. In A. C. Graesser & J. B. Black (Eds.), *The psychology of questions* (pp. 219–226). Hillsdale, NJ: Lawrence Erlbaum Associates.

Palinscar, A. S., & Brown, A. L. (1984). Reciprocal teaching of comprehension-fostering and comprehension-monitoring activities. *Cognition and Instruction, 1*(2), 117–175.

Person, N. K. (1990). *The documentation of questioning mechanisms and types of questions in tutoring protocols*. Unpublished master's thesis, Memphis State University, Memphis, TN.

Robertson, S. P., & Zachary, W. W. (1990). Conclusion: Outlines of a field of cooperative systems. In S. Robertson, W. Zachary, & J. Black (Eds.), *Cognition, computing, and cooperation* (pp. 399–414). Norwood, NJ: Ablex.

Schank, R. C. (1986). *Explanation patterns: Understanding mechanically and creatively.* Hillsdale, NJ: Lawrence Erlbaum Associates.

Schank, R., & Abelson, R. P. (1977). *Scripts, plans, goals, and understanding: An inquiry into human knowledge structures*. Hillsdale, NJ: Lawrence Erlbaum Associates.

Schank, R., Ferguson, W., Birnbaum, L., Barger, J., & Greising, M. (1991). ASK TOM: An experimental interface for video case libraries. *Proceedings of the 13th Annual Conference of the Cognitive Science Society* (pp. 570–575). Hillsdale, NJ: Lawrence Erlbaum Associates.

Searle, J. R. (1969). *Speech acts*. London: Cambridge University Press.

Sleeman, D. H., & Brown, J. S. (Eds.). (1982). *Intelligent tutoring systems*. New York: Academic Press.

Souther, A., Acker, L., Lester, J., & Porter, B. (1989). Using view types to generate explanations in intelligent tutoring systems. *Proceedings of the 11th Annual Conference of the Cognitive Science Society* (pp. 123–130). Hillsdale, NJ: Lawrence Erlbaum Associates.

Sternberg, R. J. (1987). Questioning and intelligence. *Questioning Exchange, 1,* 11–13.

Stokal, R. R. (1974). Classification. *Science, 185,* 115–123.

Tennant, H. R. (1987). Menu-based natural language. In S. C. Eckroth & D. Eckroth (Eds.), *Encyclopedia of artificial intelligence* (pp. 594–597). New York: Wiley.

van der Meij, H. (1987). Assumptions of information-seeking questions. *Questioning Exchange, 1,* 111–117.

Vygotsky, L. S. (1978). *Mind in society.* Cambridge, MA: MIT Press.

Wenger, E. (1987). *Artificial intelligence and tutoring systems*. Los Altos, CA: Morgan Kaufman.

Williams, M. D. (1984). What makes RABBIT run? *International Journal of Man–Machine Studies, 21*, 333–352.

Winograd, T., & Flores, C. F. (1986). *Understanding computers and cognition*. Norwood, NJ: Ablex.

Zloof, M. M. (1975). Query by example. *Proceedings of the National Computer Conference, 44*, 431–438. Arlington, VA: AFIPS Press.

7

Inserting Context into our Thinking About Thinking: Implications for a Theory of Everyday Intelligent Behavior

Stephen J. Ceci
Ana I. Ruiz
Cornell University

The concept of "general intelligence" has fascinated researchers for the entire century. Many may imagine that this concept has fallen into disrepute as a result of the numerous methodological and conceptual attacks by those who have demonstrated that measures of general intelligence fall short of capturing the totality of an individual's cognitive functioning. However, measures of general intelligence are alive and thriving in the psychometric community. Despite the conceptual and methodological criticisms that have been made against it, general intelligence is still alleged to be the best predictor of many real-world achievements.

In fact, the superior predictiveness of general intelligence has been a cardinal tenet of those in the psychometric community, who have touted it as the single best predictor of an individual's academic, social, and occupational success that is currently available. In short, ability is seen as synonymous with a score on a test of general cognitive ability.

The best known and most validated measure of general cognitive ability is the IQ test. There have been thousands of "validity generalization" studies demonstrating that IQ scores predict school, work, and social success better than does any other measure, including motivation, scores on specific cognitive ability tests (e.g., spatial reasoning, verbal fluency, mechanical aptitude), or relevant background experience. It is not that psychometric researchers dispute the existence or importance of specific cognitive abilities, motivation, or background experience; it is merely that they believe that the single most important predictor of success is a measure of general ability (i.e., an IQ score or one of its many statistical surrogates; e.g., SAT, GATB, ASVAB).

Linda Gottfredson (1986) summarized much of the validity literature in her meta-analysis on the link between work and IQ, concluding:

General cognitive ability (IQ) not only predicts job performance moderately well, but it also predicts performance better than does any other worker attribute. It predicts performance equally well for blacks, Hispanics, and whites . . . and 'on the job' performance is linearly related to general intelligence. On the average, increasingly higher IQ levels are associated with increasingly better job performance . . It appears that more extensive training or experience in relevant job skills can temporarily render less intelligent workers equally productive as more intelligent but less experienced workers, but that the latter will outperform the former within a few years, if not much sooner, depending on the complexity of the job . . . There is no evidence that less g-loaded traits (e.g., motivation) can compensate for differences in (general) intelligence. (p. 395)

Thus, according to the psychometricians, measures of general intelligence are a valuable means of predicting worker efficiency, and the national economy would save upwards of $180 billion per year if all workers were assigned to their jobs on the basis of their scores on a test of general intelligence, and the city of Philadelphia would lose $170 million over a 10-year period if it selected its municipal workers by a random method instead of using its test of general intelligence (Hunter, 1983, 1986; Hunter & Hunter, 1984; Hunter & Schmidt, 1982; Hunter, Schmidt, & Rauschenberger, 1984). In short, many believe that the best way to fit people to jobs is simply to use their IQ scores.

In this chapter we attempt to show that one's position on the validity of general intelligence has important consequences for the direction of applied cognitive research on learning and development. After briefly discussing the statistical support for the notion of general intelligence, we attempt to show that there are compelling reasons—both ones having to do with scientific philosophy and ones having to do with empirical findings—that militate against the notion of general intelligence, and in favor of the position that there exist multiple, statistically independent cognitive "muscles" that are influenced by the context in which they develop. We conclude by arguing that the strategy that will give applied cognitive research its greatest practical leverage is one that takes into consideration the differing ecologies of the organism and how these affect the way cognition unfolds.

SOME STATISTICAL PRELIMINARIES IN THE CONSTRUCT VALIDATION OF GENERAL INTELLIGENCE, OR g

General Intelligence, or g.

There are a few things that need to be known about IQ if we are to jettison the concept of general intelligence, and we presume that very few critics actually do know these things. It is important to bear these "facts" in mind if one is to criticize IQ as a measure of general intelligence because they make the job of doing so more difficult. This is not to say that it cannot be done; but it does mean that an informed criticism of general intelligence must bear these facts in mind.

First, by general intelligence is meant a singular mental (or biological) force that to some extent determines how well we do on all types of cognitive tasks and thus is responsible for correlations in performance across seemingly divergent tasks like vocabulary, digit memory, mathematics, and spatial reasoning. Various theorists have posited different underlying sources of general intelligence, or g. For example, researchers working at a more biological level of analysis view g as the result of the signal-to-noise ratio in the nervous system's coding of sensory information. This is the mechanism that regulates how much information can be picked up from one's environment and encoded. Neurophysiologists have suggested that the nervous systems of individuals with high IQs behave more efficiently than the nervous systems with low IQs. For instance, if subjects are told to merely listen to auditory clicks that are delivered through a headphone, and the clicks are either presented randomly or orderly, it has been found that the electrical activity of the brain of high IQ persons responds more to the randomly presented clicks than to the orderly sequences of clicks. This does not appear to be true of persons with lower IQs (Schafer, 1987); thus their evoked potentials show greater activity during periods of relatively redundant information. Because some researchers have suggested that a test's g-loading (i.e., the extent to which it measures general intelligence) is a reflection of the number or centrality of the neural processes required for its successful completion (Jensen, 1980), it is assumed that the central nervous system's style or rate of responding to information in the environment determines its processing efficiency. Therefore, individuals who do well on vocabulary will also tend to do well on spatial reasoning, mathematics, memory, and so on, because the same nervous system that enabled them to learn lots of information in one domain (e.g., verbal) will also have enabled them to learn lots of information in other domains (e.g., they will have learned more about the optical flow and contours of their spatial environment).

In contrast to this physiological approach to conceptualizing general intelligence or g, those who work at a more cognitive level of analysis view g as the result of attentional and/or metacognitive mechanisms that play a role in virtually all tasks (see Ceci, 1990a, 1990b, for review of various positions). If one has poor attentional regulation, they will do poorly on all tasks that require attention, which is virtually all cognitive tasks. The same is true of metacognitive insights; if one has poor insights into the inner workings of their cognitive system, this should inhibit their performance on virtually all tasks, because it is hard to imagine a single task that does not require some level of metacognitive awareness for its successful completion (Sternberg, 1985).

Therefore, no matter whether one chooses a cognitive or a neurophysiological level of analysis, the fundamental empirical phenomenon of cross-task correlation is the same; that is, it is usually the case that individuals who score well above average on one test (e.g., vocabulary) score above average on other tests, too (e.g., math, spatial reasoning, memory); and those who score well below average on one test tend to score below average on others.

This empirical observation of cross-task correlation has led researchers to posit an underlying factor that is alleged to be involved in virtually all cognitive performances. This perspective does not deny that other more specific cognitive abilities are also involved in performance (e.g., a specific spatial ability, a specific memory ability, or a specific verbal ability), but it does claim that all tasks require some of this underlying factor, g, for their performance. In order to see why this claim is made, it is necessary to consider the way g is determined from an individual's test scores.

Deriving g.   The traditional way that g was assessed was to analyze subjects' scores on a variety of tests and compute some measure of the average correlation among the tests. The first to do this was the statistician Charles Spearman (Spearman, 1904), who observed that scores on cognitive tests like math, vocabulary, and mechanical aptitude tended to be positively correlated. Those scoring high on one test would tend to score high on the others. Spearman arranged a matrix of the correlations between all tests in his battery in a specific way: The first column of the matrix represented the single test that had the highest total correlation with the sum of all the other tests. The second column of the matrix represented the test that had the next highest total correlation with all the other tests, and so on. Spearman observed that, when a matrix of correlations was arranged in descending order of each test's total correlations with the other tests, something quite remarkable happened: A hierarchy existed wherein the correlations between any two tests (columns) formed a constant ratio. As one goes down the columns, even though the individual magnitudes of the correlations in two adjacent columns get smaller and smaller, the ratio between them remains the same. So, if the ratio between correlations in two adjacent columns was 3:2 at the top of the columns, then it would also be in that vicinity at the bottom of the two columns. For example, the two adjacent correlations at the top of the matrix might be .9 and .6, whereas the two at the bottom of the matrix might be .06 and .04, thus preserving the constancy of the 3:2 ratio. So, the ratio of two tests' correlations remained approximately equal even though the magnitudes of the correlations became smaller and smaller toward the bottom of the columns. This hierarchy among the correlations in the columns of the matrix was explained by Spearman as the result of all correlations between different tests being due to the correlation of each individual test with some underlying general factor, which he called g. The test at the top of the column (the one that possessed the highest total correlation with all others) was seen as the most g-loaded or g-saturated test because of its presumed greater emphasis on general intelligence. Thus, the correlations between all tests were viewed as the result of their individual correlations with g. And individuals were viewed as possessing varying amounts of g, leading them to be more or less intelligent.

Spearman's discovery was profound because it implied that some of the differences found among individuals on diverse cognitive tests were the result of a singular aptitude or intelligence, namely g. Soon researchers tried strenuously to prove that the hierarchical nature of a matrix arranged in such a way was an artifact, a necessary result of arranging the correlations in descending order of their total correlations. By the early part of the 20th century, however, the dominant position was that the constant correlation in Spearman's matrix was not an artifact but a genuine empirical finding (Thomson, 1948). The concept of general intelligence was off and running!

In the years since Spearman, g has been derived in many ways, and all of them correlate with each other quite highly. For the past 20 years the most common measure of g has been to view the first principal component from a battery of test scores as the handiest measure of g. Such a first principal component represents the maximum linear variance among the test scores that can be accounted for independently of rotation, and its magnitude reflects the average degree of correlation among the scores. Psychometric researchers argue that the greater the magnitude of g, the more likely it is that a common source was involved in the different test performances. This common source of test variance is seen as a type of primordial mental or biological energy that "flows" into all the different intellectual performances. As already noted, it can be viewed as a cognitive mechanism like attentional energy or metacognitive insight, or it can be viewed biologically as the signal-to-noise ratio in nervous system functioning or the blood glucose level during processing.

The relationship between other measures of general intelligence and g are well known; for example, g is correlated with IQ anywhere from .4 to .9, depending on the characteristics of the sample (e.g., age), the IQ test in question, and the battery of tests used to derive g. Of the 50 or more studies that we have read that report correlations between IQ and g, an approximate average correlation might be in the .70 range. In general, psychometric researchers argue that a test's g-loading is very important for prediction purposes. The higher it is, the better that test will be for predicting both school success and work success. As already seen, some have claimed that g is a better predictor of how well one will do at his or her job than is any other measure, including specific factors like motivation and relevant background experience (Gottfredson, 1986).

Correlates of g.   Although we have been talking about IQ as the best available measure of g, there are many other measures of g beside IQ. For example, SATs, GREs, employment screening tests like subtests of the GATB, and the ASVAB (Armed Services Vocational Aptitude Battery) all contain subtests that are good measures of g, and g derived from them correlates with each other quite highly. In fact, some of them (e.g,. the SATs and the military screening tests) were originally developed as measures of general intelligence, though they were never called by that name (Owen, 1985; Stitch, 1991). The public is largely unaware of this, as are most psychologists. It is probably for political reasons that it is not better known that these tests are, in part, intelligence tests, because one can imagine the morale problems that might ensue if it were known that jobs were assigned according to one's IQ: These are the smart jobs, those are the dumb ones!

If g was a statistical artifact, there would be no need to give it any more attention than we allot to other descriptive statistics. But it is not just a statistical entity that has no bearing on society. It has enormous bearing. Measures of g are correlated with job success, school grades, and microlevel cognitive performances. For example, the speed that one can recognize highly familiar stimuli is predicted by g, as is the speed of doing mental rotations, scanning the contents of long-term memory, and retrieving overlearned lexical tags such as the name of a letter or a word (Ceci, 1990b; Hunt, 1985).

Finally, as if it were not enough that measures of g—most notably IQ—predict a range of real-world attainments as well as microlevel laboratory tasks, there is some evidence that g does this at least to some extent through biologically determined routes, as opposed to primarily through environmental routes. It is beyond the scope of this chapter to provide the evidence for this assertion, but the interested reader can consult Ceci (1990a) for details. Next we briefly provide six pieces of evidence.

First, both IQ and g are highly heritable, with the size of the heritability coefficient depending on factors such as the age of sample, the type of factorial rotation, the types of tests in the battery, and so forth. For the most part, the heritabilities for IQ and g range between .5 and .8, indicating that both g and IQ are transmitted along family lines to a substantial extent.

Second, the g-loading of a given task is correlated with its heritability—the higher its g-loading, the higher the heritability. To many, this relationship between heritability and a test's g-loading is taken to indicate that measures of general intelligence are not merely statistical artifacts but rather valid indices of biological functioning. The more that a test is g-loaded (i.e., at the top of a matrix of correlations), as opposed to being saturated with specific factors, the more it will be heritable.

Third, because racial, social class, and ethnic differences are most pronounced on tests that have both a high heritability and a high g-loading, the inference has been made that such differences on IQ are due to genetic mechanisms that underlie the primary resource pool that underpins g.

Fourth, most of the microlevel cognitive and perceptual tasks that were mentioned before (e.g., the recognition and rotation of familiar stimuli) are also highly heritable, some as high as .7 (Vernon, 1987).

Fifth, the more abstract a test is made, the greater will be its heritability and, hence, the greater its correlation with IQ. Among others, Jensen has viewed intelligence as abstract reasoning (Jensen, 1969).

Sixth, IQ is correlated with real-world successes, such as lifetime earnings and job satisfaction ratings (see Henderson & Ceci, in press).

If the preceding six points are combined into a syllogism, then a reasonable inference might be that IQ is predictive of real-world success because (a) both IQ and real-world success rely on the same underlying general intelligence—g, (b) both IQ and g are determined at least in part by biological factors, and (c) success on real-world endeavors is also, at least in part, biologically determined.

We now turn to a refutation of this syllogism, focusing for our main evidence on an analysis of everyday cognitive performance and its disjunction from non-everyday cognition (i.e., standardized measures of cognitive functioning). We conclude by arguing that intelligence is multifaceted—in contrast with notions of g—and that it is extremely susceptible to environmental or contextual manipulations.

EVERYDAY INTELLIGENCE: CONTEXT AS A CONSTITUENT OF COGNITION

A growing body of research in cognitive development demonstrates that context is not simply an adjunct to cognition, but a constituent of it. Context often determines how a problem will be perceived as well as the strategies a child will deploy to solve it. This much all researchers would accept as it is a form of environmentalism that acknowledges what everyone knows to be true, namely, that aspects of the setting are important in influencing task performance.

But contextual researchers go further than invoking environmentalism in their claims. They argue that cognitive processes are acquired in specific contexts; they cannot be carried out with uniform efficiency in other contexts unless certain developments occur. This can best be seen in a juxtaposition of a traditional model of information processing that shows the basic assumption of transcontextual processing efficiency with a model of context-specific processing. In the traditional model, processes are acquired at various stages of development and, from the moment of their acquisition, they operate transcontextually. For example, if an individual acquires the ability to deduce facts from premises, then he or she can use this skill in the service of drawing deductions irrespective of the context in which the premises and facts occur: Deductions about kinship relations, cooking facts, sports knowledge, and so on would all be made with equal efficiency. In contrast, contextualized models of development argue against this transcontextual assumption. Processes are acquired at various stages, but their use is initially yoked to the specific context in which they were acquired. Thus, the person who has learned to deduce may be able to make deductions in some domains long before he or she can do so in others (Ceci, 1990a). And the same can be said for every other cognitive feat (e.g., metaphorical reasoning, rehearsal, metacognitive insights, etc.). Keil (1984) has shown, for example, that a child can solve certain metaphors long before he or she can solve others, as a result of the fact that knowledge structure in some domains are more developed than in others. The same child who can understand "the thirsty car drank the petrol" may not understand "the hungry reader devoured the book." Ceci and Ruiz (1992, in press) have shown that the same level of multicausal reasoning exhibited in some situations is not exhibited in others, even when the task is structurally identical.

If a 3-year-old is asked how many pieces they would have if an apple is cut in half, she will usually reply 2. If they are asked how many pieces they would have if an orange is cut in half, they would again reply 2. But if they were asked how many pieces they would have if a melon is cut in half, they may reply that it would depend on how large the melon is (Ceci, 1990a)! As humorous as this observation may appear, it does capture the contextual nature of knowledge and processes. If one thought that the 3-year-old in this example possessed a "halving" rule that specified two equal halves for all divided entities, they would be wrong. A child may possess such a rule, but only in certain contexts. And as adults, all of us are a lot less transcontextual than we might think (see Ceci, in press, for examples of domain-specific thinking by adults).

To some, the idea that cognition is inextricably tied to context may seem overly strong. After all, processes involved in such basic activities as reading and arithmetic must operate transcontextually or else there would be enormous problems in our everyday and work lives. And how could context alter the way we read; what does it matter if we read on the beach or in our offices? How could context moderate the reading process? Or the arithmetical process? An examination of these processes reveals the pervasive role that context plays, however. Reading is not reading, is not reading, to paraphrase Gertrude Stein's famous aphorism about roses. To demonstrate this, ask a mechanic to read some manual about diesel engines and try reading it yourself. Then ask the mechanic to read a cognitive psychology text and try reading it yourself. Although the two activities both involve using the same orthography to make sense of the writer's intent, your background context will lead to much greater understanding of the latter material whereas the mechanic's will probably lead to greater understanding of the diesel manual.

As far as arithmetical reasoning goes, Brazilian researchers have shown that children perform much better in some contexts than they do in others, even when the cognitive demands of the two contexts are seemingly identical. For example, Carraher, Carraher, and Schliemann (1985) found that Brazilian street market vendors carry out arithmetical calculations more accurately when such problems are couched in terms of market problems than when they are couched in terms of school problems. Despite some occasional indication in this research that schooling does seem to "free" children from the tyranny of context, overall, it is clear that schooled children are just as liable to reason unevenly across contexts as are unschooled children.

Solutions to a wide variety of arithmetical and logical problems have been shown to be context-specific. Piagetian tasks like conservation of liquid, length, and quantity all have been shown to be extremely susceptible to slight changes in the language of the instructions or in the explicitness of the task demands (e.g., see Roazzi & Bryant, in press, for a review), and solutions to "everyday" kinds of proportional reasoning are also highly context specific (see Schliemann & Carraher, in press, for review). As one example, consider the following results from a study by Schliemann and Nunes (1990). Groups of fisherman were asked to calculate prices and quantities having to do with catching, processing, and selling fish—all of which are things that matter to them. One such problem stated that another fisherman is selling fish at a rate of 75 cruzados for five kilograms. They were asked to calculate how much that fisherman was earning per kilogram. Between 70% and 95% of the fisherman obtained the correct answers to such problems, and there was no correlation between years of formal education (ranging from 0 to 9) and accuracy.

A slightly more difficult type of proportionality problem is worded as follows: "In the south there is a type of shrimp that yields 3 kilograms of shelled (i.e., deveined) shrimp for each 15 kilograms you catch. Now if a customer wants 9 kilograms of shelled shrimp, how much would you have to catch?" On such problems the accuracy rate is around 60%; again, there is no correlation between accuracy and years of formal schooling. Of interest is that even those subjects who attended school long enough to learn the Brazilian method of computing scalar proportions did not use it. The Brazilian method, the so-called Rule of 3, states that you multiply the missing term (?) by the cross-multiplication process. For example,

$$a/b = c/?$$

is solved in Brazilian schools as follows:

$$a \times ? = b \times c; \text{ thus } ? = (b \times c)/a.$$

To see how schooled subjects are not using the knowledge they were taught in school, consider the following problem in which the desired number of kilograms of shelled shrimp is neither a multiple nor a divider of the number given in the problem, making it a harder problem for someone to calculate with a scalar solution (i.e., adding or multiplying) than with the Rule of 3 that they were taught. For example, "How much fish for a customer who wanted 2 kilograms of processed fish when 18 kilograms of unprocessed fish yielded 3 kilograms of processed fish?" One of Schliemann and Nunes' (1990) subjects, a ninth-grade educated fisherman, who had learned the Rule of 3 before he quit school, answered as follows:

> . . . one and a half kilos (processed) would be 9 (unprocessed), it has to be 9, because half of 18 is 9 and half of 3 is one and a half. And a half kilo (processed) is 3 kilos (unprocessed). Then it'd be 9 plus 3 is 12 (unprocessed), the 12 kilos would give the 2 kilos (processed). (p. 263)

Even though this subject had been exposed to proportion algorithms as part of his formal education, he preferred not to use it. Perhaps he did not even know that it was applicable in such a context. One cannot be sure. But it does drive home the risk in presuming that school-taught knowledge is the basis for solving problems in nonschooled contexts.

Does this mean that there are no cognitive processes that are transcontextual, and that none of us is able to solve the same problem in two different contexts? No, we are not making that strong claim here. Some processes do eventually become transcontextual, as a result of their reoccurrence in different contexts. When this happens, the individual must then notice the fact that the same process is available in different contexts (e.g., by analogy); that is, it is important to recognize that the same process that accomplishes some action in one context also accomplishes the same action in a different context. Schliemann and Carraher (in press) noted in their discussion of the Brazilian research on arithmetical reasoning across contexts:

> These findings . . . suggest that proportionality reasoning may develop first in a limited range of contexts and about particular contents. Given the proper conditions, similarities of relations can be detected and transfer and generalization become possible. This recognition may then act as a bridge for transfer of procedures to the unknown contexts. (p. 16)

So, although we do not insist on a strict interpretation of context specificity that would rule out the possibility of transferring a process from one context to another, we do stand by our reading of the cognitive literature, especially when it shows that even well-educated college graduates cannot often perform the same operation in different contexts. Recently, Detterman (in press) eloquently made this point in his analysis of the research on transfer of learning across contexts. Detterman argued that individuals' cognitive processes are tightly tied to the contexts in which they have been acquired, and thus they usually cannot deploy the process to solve an identical problem when it is couched in a different context:

> What is truly amazing about all of these studies is not that they don't really produce transfer across contexts. What is amazing is the extent of similarity it is possible to have between problems without subjects realizing that the situations are identical and require the same process. (p. 14).

WHY COGNITIVE SCIENTISTS DISDAIN CONTEXT

Traditionally, cognitivists have looked upon context as noise, to be gotten rid of by slavishly sanitizing their experiments of all meaning and motivation. When it has proven impossible to purge context from the experiment, researchers have opted to control for contextual factors such as meaningfulness and motivation through statistical partialling. The idea that context should be studied in its own right rather than be partialled out of the experiment seems not to have occurred to most cognitive researchers (Yuille & Wells, 1991).

The reason for short-shrifting context is not hard to find; theorists aim to provide universal accounts of cognition, as opposed to situationally specific accounts (Ceci, Bronfenbrenner, & Baker-Sennett, in press; Weisz, 1978); that is, they hope to show that a variable operates across the idiosyncrasies and vicissitudes of contexts, because to do less would be subject to the criticism that a theory is situationally specific. This is an old idea, especially among developmental psychologists. Weisz (1978) asserted that the ultimate goal of science is to find universal principles that "can be shown to hold across physical and cultural setting, time, or cohort" (p. 2), and many others like Banaji and Crowder (1989), have argued that scientific methods can only succeed if there is a precise technique for translating observations into formalisms such that "the operations of invariant mechanisms can be shown" (p. 1188).

But in their search for universal cognitive mechanisms, researchers have misconstrued an important function of all developmental sciences. A distinctive property of homo sapiens is its ability to adapt to its environment, to respond differentially to different contexts. This insight led Bronfenbrenner (1979) to decry the search for context-invariant mechanisms on the grounds that:

> One can question whether establishing transcontextual validity is . . . the ultimate goal of science. Given the ecologically interactive character of behavior and development in humans, processes that are invariant across contexts are likely to be few in number and fairly close to the physiological level. What behavioral scientists should be seeking, therefore, are not primarily these universals but rather the laws of invariance at the next higher level—principles that describe how processes are mediated by the general properties of settings and of more remote aspects of the ecological environment. (p. 128)

Therefore, when researchers disdain the effort to document contextual influences on mental functioning in favor of searching for cognitive invariances, they are, in effect, calling into question the value of doing research on cognition in real-life settings; if mental functioning is sensitive to its context, this should not be a criticism of the rigor of those seeking to demonstrate this sensitivity (Ceci & Bronfenbrenner, 1991). To ignore context is to ignore the fact that cognition is moderated by it in everyday settings. Increasingly, it has become apparent that cognitive assessments made out of context (e.g., in standardized testing situations) are, at best, only rough approximations of an individual's cognitive ability in everyday settings (e.g., Ceci & Bronfenbrenner, 1985; Ceci & Liker, 1986a, 1986b). Applied cognitive researchers should keep this foremost in their thinking.

CONCLUSIONS

Current research on "cognition-in-context" downplays the usefulness of trying to assess "pure" cognitive-processing efficiency and instead emphasizes the role of context in the assessment of an individual's intellectual potential. Although traditional measures of general intelligence possess good predictive validity in school, job, and training situations, they do not achieve this prediction through a convincing set of demonstrations that the basis for the predictions is cognitive in nature, or that intelligence is a singular resource pool that underpins a significant portion of the prediction. Thus, "prediction" and "explanation" can be fundamentally disjunctive enterprises in science.

Bronfenbrenner's (1979) *person × process × context* approach would seem to have promise for those involved in cognitive assessment. The "person" refers to variables that preexisted and that could influence the operation of the variables of interest (e.g., birthweight may affect brain integrity; genetics may affect activity level, etc.); "process" refers to cognitive activities (e.g., encoding, storing, transforming, etc.); and "context" refers to aspects of the physical, mental, and social setting that could influence the efficiency of "processes." (The mental setting refers to the way that knowledge relevant to a task is represented in long-term memory.) Thus, a *person × process × context* approach leads to a different set of expectations from a traditional assessment. Specifically, it suggests that individual differences observed on a cognitive screening device are tied to a particular constellation of *person × process × context* variables. So, for example, if a test of syllogistic reasoning requires access to a certain domain of knowledge that is not well structured for some persons (i.e., they possess a poor mental context for the deployment of their syllogistic processes), then their poor performance on it would not imply they lacked the relevant syllogistic processes. If another type of material is used that is more elaborately structured in long-term memory, their performance could greatly improve. In short, a *person × process × context* model points to the conclusion that traditional assessment devices achieve their notable predictive validity at a cost: By assuming that an individual is a transcontextual processor without ever testing this assumption by using a diversity of contexts, they may result in needlessly ungenerous estimates of an individual's processing potential in contexts that are well embellished. Even though the traditional tests may predict average worker or student performance under extant conditions, there is no reason to believe that they will do so if the conditions are changed. Thus, prediction may result from a match between the contextual conditions of schools (or jobs) and those of the test. But if we want to know whether a person possesses the capability to process at a certain level of complexity, we ought to inculcate the context, by teaching it. Only then will we be sure that those persons truly lack the necessary processes to perform well.

A related implication of the *person × process × context* approach is that a person who demonstrates a higher level of a cognitive process in one context than in another is assumed to possess the relevant neuroarchitecture to make this process operate at equally high levels of efficiency in all contexts, but only if they could be made equally amenable to the processing requirements. In this sense, the *person* × *process* × *context* approach is akin to an athletic analogy: If an athlete has pole vaulted 18 feet on one occasion, then it is assumed the he or she is capable of pole vaulting that high again, even if on a given day the effort falls short of this mark. The highest score a prospective graduate students scores on the GREs is taken to be an indication of how high they might score, even if on subsequent occasions they fall short of it. (Most graduate admissions know this, and when an applicant has taken the GREs twice, they consider only the higher score.)

Finally, a *process* × *person* × *context* approach to assessment seems particularly important for applied cognitivists because it argues against one of the most common practices in the field, namely, estimating independent effects through the use of statistical covariates. To illustrate this point, consider the task of predicting a job applicant's success at, say, sorting mail by zip code. Suppose that an applied cognitivist responsible for predicting who should be hired for this post knows the following things about applicants: their educational level (a contextual variable) and the type of sorting strategy they prefer to use (a process variable). A common practice among applied psychologists is to estimate the independent effect of strategy type on zipcode sorting by entering educational level as a covariate. Yet, doing this runs a real risk that educational level's effect may be underestimated at one end of the spectrum and overestimated at the other end. The reason this can occur is that multiple regression assumes that these factors influence sorting behavior independently, that is, there is no significant heterogeneity of variance. In this example, the assumption is that the independent variable under consideration (type of strategy preferred) effects the dependent variable (zipcode sorting) identically at every level of educational background. But Bronfenbrenner (1992) has shown that such assumptions are often unsupportable. The result is that multiple regression analysis corrects the relationship between the dependent and independent variables for the *average* relationship between educational level and each of the other variables. When there exist significant departures from the average as a function of the third variable, this ultimately leads to a distortion of the relationship between sorting strategies and zipcode sorting to some unknown degree. And, as Bronfenbrenner (1992) has shown, this leads not just to the possibility but to the likelihood of misinterpretations and faulty predictions. Applied cognitivists ought to be aware of such limitations; a *person* × *process* × *context* approach provides the best solution. It requires the assessment of interactive effects among the relevant variables, thus leading to "ecological niche picking."

Although it is premature to assess the adequacy of this *process* × *person* × *context* view of cognitive assessment, the shortcomings of the traditional "assessment-out-context" approach are apparent. A *process* × *person* × *context* approach, or some comparable means of contextualizing cognitive assessment, holds the promise of discovering specific combinations of variables that are associated with outcomes, uncontaminated by the potentially distorting effects of "averaging" inherent in the mathematics of the statistical control in regression analysis.

ACKNOWLEDGMENTS

Preparation of this chapter was supported by grants from the National Institutes of Health, DHHS #5RO1HD22839 and KO4HD00801, and a Senior Fullbright-Hayes to the first author.

REFERENCES

Banaji, M., & Crowder, R. (1989). The bankruptcy of everyday memory. *American Psychologist, 44*, 1185–1193.

Bronfenbrenner, U. (1992). *The process-person-context model in developmental research: Principles, applications, and implications.* Unpublished manuscript. Ithaca, NY: Cornell University.

Bronfenbrenner, U. (1979). *The ecology of human development.* Cambridge, MA: Harvard University Press.

Carraher, T. N., Carraher, D., & Schliemann, A. D. (1985). Mathematics in the streets and in the schools. *British Journal of Developmental Psychology, 3,* 21–29.

Ceci, S. J. (in press). Now you see it, now you don't: Training for transfer. In H. Rosselli (Ed.), *The Edyth Bush symposium on intelligence.* Tampa, FL: Academic Press.

Ceci, S. J. (1990a). *On intelligence . . . more or less: A bioecological treatise on intellectual development.* Englewood Cliffs, NJ: Prentice Hall.

Ceci, S. J. (1990b). On the relation between microlevel processing efficiency and macrolevel measures of intelligence: Some arguments against current reductionism. *Intelligence, 14,* 141–150.

Ceci, S. J., & Bronfenbrenner, U. (1991). On the demise of everyday memory: The rumors of my death are much exaggerated. *American Psychologist, 46,* 27–31.

Ceci, S. J., & Bronfenbrenner, U. (1985). Don't forget to take the cupcakes out of the oven: Strategic time-monitoring, prospective memory and context. *Child Development, 56,* 175–190.

Ceci, S. J., Bronfenbrenner, U., & Baker-Sennett, J. (in press). Cognition in and out of context: A tale of two paradigms. In M. Rutter, D. Hay, & S. Baron-Cohen (Eds.), *Developmental principles and clinical issues in psychology and psychiatry.* Oxford, England: Blackwell Scientific Publications.

Ceci, S. J., & Liker, J. (1986a). A day at the races: A study of IQ, expertise, and cognitive complexity. *Journal of Experimental Psychology: General, 115,* 255–266.

Ceci, S. J., & Liker, J. (1986b). Academic and nonacademic intelligence: An experimental separation. In R. J. Sternberg & R. Wagner (Eds.), *Practical Intelligence: Origins of competence in the everyday world* (pp. 119–142). New York: Cambridge University Press.

Ceci, S. J., & Ruiz, A. (1992). Cognitive complexity and generality: A case study. In R. Hoffman (Ed.), *The psychology of expertise* (pp. 41–55). New York: Springer-Verlag.

Ceci, S. J., & Ruiz, A. (in press). Transfer, abstractness, and intelligence. In D. Detterman & R. J. Sternberg (Eds.), *Transfer on trial: Intelligence, cognition, and instruction.* Norwood, NJ: Ablex.

Detterman, D. K. (in press). The case for the prosecution: Transfer as an epiphenomenon. In D.

Detterman & R. J. Sternberg (Eds.), *Transfer on trial: Intelligence, cognition, and instruction.* Norwood, NJ: Ablex.

Gottfredson, L. (1986). Societal consequences of the g factor in employment. *Journal of Vocational Behavior, 29,* 379–410.

Henderson, C. R., & Ceci, S. J. (in press). *Is it better to be born rich or smart?: A bioecological analysis of the contributions of IQ and SES to adult income.* Cambridge, MA: MIT Press.

Hunt, E. (1985). Verbal ability. In R. J. Sternberg (Ed.), *Human abilities: An information processing approach* (pp. 42–66). San Francisco: Freeman.

Hunter, J. (1983). *The dimensionality of the GATB and the dominance of general factors over specific factors in the prediction of job performance in the U.S. Employment Service.* (Uses Test Research Report #44). Washington, DC: U.S. Dept. of Labor, Employment, and Training Administration, Division of Counselling and Test Development.

Hunter, J. (1986). Cognitive ability, cognitive aptitudes, job knowledge, and job performance. *Journal of Vocational Behavior, 29,* 340–363.

Hunter, J., & Hunter, R. F. (1984). Validity and utility of alternative predictors of job performance. *Psychological Bulletin, 96,* 72–98.

Hunter, J., & Schmidt, F. (1982). Fitting people to jobs: The impact of personnel selection on national productivity. In M. Dunnette & E. Fleishman (Eds.), *Human performance and productivity* (pp. 21–67). Hillsdale, NJ: Lawrence Erlbaum Associates.

Hunter, J., Schmidt, F., & Rauschenberger, J. (1984). Methodological, statistical, and ethical issues in the study of bias in psychological tests. In C. R. Reynolds & R. T. Brown (Eds.), *Perspectives on bias in mental testing* (pp. 41–97). New York: Älenum.

Jensen, A. R. (1969). How much can we boost IQ and scholastic achievement? *Harvard Educational Review, 39,* 1–123.

Jensen, A. R. (1980). *Bias in mental testing.* New York: Free Press.

Johnson-Laird, P. N. (1983). *Mental models: Toward a cognitive science of language, inference, and consciousness.* Cambridge, MA: Harvard University Press.

Keil, F. (1984). Mechanisms in cognitive development and the structure of knowledge. In R. J. Sternberg (Ed.), *Mechanisms of cognitive development* (pp. 81–100). New York: W. H. Freeman.

Owen, D. (1985). *None of the above: Behind the myth of scholastic aptitude.* Boston: Houghton-Mifflin.

Roazzi, A., & Bryant, P. (in press). Social class, context, and cognitive development. In P. Light & G. Butterworth (Eds.), *Context and cognition: Ways of learning and knowing.* Hemel Hampstead, England: Harvester Wheatsheaf.

Schliemann, A. D., & Carraher, D. W. (in press). Proportional reasoning in and out of school. In P. Light & G. Butterworth (Eds.), *Context and cognition: Ways of learning and knowing.* Hemel Hamstead: Harvester Wheatsheaf.

Schliemann, A. D., & Magalhaes, V. P. (1990). Proportional reasoning: From shops, to kitchens, laboratories, and, hopefully, schools. *Proceedings of the XIV International Conference for the Psychology of Mathematics Education,* Axtepec, Mexico.

Schliemann, A. D., & Nunes, T. (1990). A situated schema of proportionality. *British Journal of Developmental Psychology, 8,* 259–268.

Schooler, C. (1989). Social structural effects and experimental situations: Mutual lessons of cognitive and social science. In K. W. Schaie & C. Schooler (Eds.), *Social structure and aging: Psychological processes* (pp. 121–154). Hillsdale, NJ: Lawrence Erlbaum Associates.

Schafer, E. W. P. (1987). Neural adaptability: A biological determinant of g factor intelligence. *Behavioral and Brain Sciences, 10,* 240–241.

Spearman, C. (1904). General intelligence objectively determined and measured. *American Journal of Psychology, 15,* 206–221.

Sternberg, R. J. (1985). *Beyond IQ: A triarchic framework for intelligence.* New York: Cambridge University Press.

Stitch, T. (1991). Military testing and public policy: Selected studies of lower aptitude personnel. In B. R. Clifford & L. Wing (Eds.), *Test policy in defense: Lessons from the military for education, training, and employment* (pp. 1–76). Boston: Kluwer.

Thomson, G. H. (1948). *The factorial analysis of human ability* (3rd. ed.). Boston: Houghton-Mifflin.

Vernon, P. A. (1987). *Speed of information processing and intelligence.* Norwood, NJ: Ablex.

Weisz, J. (1978). Transcontextual validity in developmental research. *Child Development, 49,* 1–12.

Yuille, J., & Wells, G. (1991). Concerns about the application of research findings. In J. L. Doris (Ed.), *The suggestibility of children's recollections: Implications for their testimony* (pp. 118–128). Washington, DC: American Psychological Association.

8 Medical Cognition: Research and Evaluation

Arthur S. Elstein
University of Illinois at Chicago

Mitchell Rabinowitz
Fordham University

Individuals rarely grow to adulthood and middle age without having some experience related to serious illness. Practically everyone has had some contact with the health-care system and with physicians. As a society, we believe that physicians are educated experts who know what they are doing and upon whose judgment we can rely. They are a highly trained, respected, and well compensated group of professionals. However, as with most professions, physicians vary widely in terms of their skill levels. From the perspective of a medical educator whose goal is to facilitate and assess the medical student's acquisition of skill, it is important to understand what characterizes skilled performance.

The education of physicians is long, elaborate, and expensive, combining didactic instruction, tutorials, seminars, and gradually increasing responsibility for patient care under the supervision of experienced clinicians. This education takes place over many years and in a range of settings. The 4-year curriculum leading to the MD degree in the United States and Canada is generally divided into 2-year components. The first 2 years stress instruction in the conceptual and scientific foundations of medical practice. This component is primarily didactic, lecture-dominated, but with gradually increasing amounts of time devoted to clinical experiences, case-based seminars, and instruction in the fundamentals of taking a medical history and doing a physical examination. In the next 2 years, the student rotates through a variety of clinical settings, concentrating on the major specialties (medicine, surgery, family practice, obstetrics-gynecology, pediatrics, and psychiatry) and taking electives in other medical specialties and subspecialties (e.g., ophthalmology, orthopedic surgery, radiology, nuclear medicine, etc.). A period of 3–7 years of additional training in one of the medical specialties follows. This interval is identified as residency training or postgraduate medical education.

Thus, as students move along the continuum of medical education, their training becomes progressively more specialized and differentiated. The pyramid narrows as one moves to the top of a particular type of expertise.

The structure of medical training makes it convenient to identify and stratify levels of expertise by years of experience and possession of specialty certification. This stratification has become the dominant basis for investigating the characterization of medical competence. Medical students of various years of experience are frequently contrasted with residents or even more experienced physicians (Elstein, Shulman, & Sprafka, 1990). Among those who have completed postgraduate medical education, a distinction is sometimes made between those in academic settings (further stratified by rank) and those in practice. Some researchers have used peer nominations as a means of identifying expert clinicians (Elstein, Shulman, & Sprafka, 1978), but this strategy has been little used in recent years. Although clinicians know which of their colleagues they trust, they appear to know little about their expertise. This is more readily understood if we consider how little a physician's work is publicly viewed. Experienced clinicians may discuss and refer cases to each other but they are rarely observed actually caring for patients.

In this chapter, we describe and contrast two different theoretical approaches that have been used to provide frameworks with which to characterize medical skill. First, the information processing approach that underlies most of the research characterized as "medical problem solving." Second the normative model approach underlying most of the research characterized as "medical decision making." In the remainder of the chapter, we offer an example of research on a treatment decision that compares the decisions of physicians with the recommendations of a normative model.

INFORMATION PROCESSING APPROACH

The information processing approach is based on the metaphor that, like a computer, the mind is a general information processing device. There are two basic premises underlying information processing systems. First, there is some sort of physical symbol (representations) that the system has to work with. Second, is information processing that is based on the notion of symbol manipulation (Newell, 1979; Newell & Simon, 1972). The insight of Newell and Simon (1972) was that the processing of information by people could be conceptualized as the manipulation of symbols (representations) by rules. The consequence of adopting this metaphor for research on the acquisition of skill has been the attempt to specify the "program," the "software," or the rules people at different levels of skill use (consciously or unconsciously) to manipulate representations and to specify the nature of the representation. Thus, this orientation led researchers to take a comparative approach, trying to delineate the processes that differentiate people with differing levels of skill. The behavior of experts is taken as the standard or norm to which learners or less experienced clinicians are compared.

This approach views clinical activity as problem solving involving ill-structured problems (Pople, 1982) with exceptionally large search spaces. (An ill-structured problem is one in which the goal, constraints, and givens are not clearly provided or accepted. Diagnostic problems fit this definition because the goal, a diagnosis, is not provided nor are there well defined limits on what may be done to reach this goal. A medical problem solver could be very efficient in data collection or could wander around considerably.) Medical problem-solving tasks differ from many others used in psychological studies of problem solving where all the elements needed for solution are given at the start and the problem is to find a route to combine or substitute elements or make inferences or moves that can transform the problem as given into the solution (the goal state). Since clinical problems are often initially ill-structured, it is helpful to develop a preliminary problem structure. This structure emphasizes what is judged relevant and needs to be explained. Given some initial data, the problem solver may construct a preliminary representation of diagnostic possibilities or of a single dominant candidate. In either case, the problem representation can guide subsequent data collection. Given the complexity of most clinical problems, it should be apparent that a number of problem representations might be formulated. Examining the differences between the formulations of experts and less experienced physicians has been the goal of many researchers (Barrows, Norman, Neufeld, & Feightner, 1982; Bordage & Lemieux, 1991; Bordage & Zacks, 1984; Evans & Patel, 1989; Feltovich, Johnson, Moller, & Swanson, 1984; Grant & Marsden, 1987).

Research on medical problem solving has also attempted to specify the processes and steps involved in progressing from this initial representation to a diagnosis (Elstein, Shulman, & Sprafka, 1990; Joseph & Patel, 1990; Lesgold, 1987). Data must be collected and interpreted, including items of the medical and personal history of the patient, findings from physical examination, results of laboratory tests or special diagnostic studies. The desired end state must be conceptualized by the problem solver, as it is not given in the problem. Once again, differences in how physicians with differing levels of skill process this information is a central issue in medical problem solving research.

THE NORMATIVE MODEL APPROACH

Research within the normative model approach has taken a different tack. The underlying research question has been, "What should we do next?" The focus is on risky choice and the fundamental metaphor compares clinical practice to a series of lotteries or gambles. The choices of the decision maker, whether among diagnostic tests or between treatment alternatives, are thought of as decisions to participate in one lottery or another. The metaphor emphasizes the uncertain results of clinical interventions rather than the need to determine the causes of the current situation. Probabilities, payoffs, degree of perceived risk, and the decision maker's attitudes toward risks, losses, and gains are central issues in determining preferences. Patients and physicians are trying to achieve several goals, and may want more than is realistically achievable. Since not all goals may be achievable, a trade-off is frequently involved. It is, therefore, important to be as clear as possible about the goals and about their relative importance. Given two or more alternative approaches to a case, the task is to choose the strategy that maximizes benefit and minimizes downside risk. If there are no alternatives, there is no choice. The roots of formal approaches to medical decision making lie in economic theory, whereas those of medical problem solving lie in cognitive psychology and computer science.

Consistent with the lottery metaphor, decision making research regards uncertainty as inevitable. The only question is how to take it into account. No one can guarantee that the hoped-for outcome of an intervention will, indeed, occur. It is advisable to think seriously about undesired outcomes (surgical mortality, complications, and side effects of therapy) as well as the desired improvements and cure. Probabilities are used to represent uncertainty. Biases in probability assessment have been a major theme of behavioral decision research (Elstein, 1988; Kahneman, Slovic, & Tversky, 1982; Ravitch, 1989). Issues of risky choice, inference with imperfect information, values, and trade-offs are all central to decision making research, but are secondary or absent in problem-solving research. On the other hand, issues of knowledge representation and information processing are more prominent in problem-solving research and of less importance in the decision making literature.

In the information processing approach, expert performance is taken as the standard or the norm to which others are compared. In the normative model approach, the behavior of both experts and novices is compared to an idealized model of rationality based on expected utility (EU) theory and decision analysis (Weinstein & Fineberg, 1980; Sox, Blatt, Higgins, & Marton, 1988). Studies in the genre typically focus on any of several issues: revising a diagnostic opinion with imperfect information, or deciding if the benefits of a therapy outweigh the possible risks, or deciding if additional diagnostic tests are needed. Expert-novice differences are not a major theme of this research. In most studies, level of clinical expertise is not systematically varied and across studies, experienced physicians often display the same behavior as beginners. Clinical experience appears to help minimize some of these effects (Christensen, Heckerling, Mackesy, Bernstein, & Elstein, 1991), but others are quite robust.

Prescriptive studies attempt to determine what should be done in a complex clinical situation with competing risks and benefits (Pauker, 1988). Descriptive studies compare the behavior of clinicians in a clinical task with the results of recommendations of a formal model. They examine conflicts or discrepancies between decisions reached by unaided clinical judgment and the choices that would be consistent with expected utility theory. Departures from these normative principles have been demonstrated in practically every phase of the decision process: problem structuring, probability estimation, probability revision, utility assessment, and synthesizing these components to make a decision (Elstein, 1988). In the psychological literature, these discrepancies are identified as "heuristics and biases." Studies of these biases can now be found in the clinical decision making literature as well as in the experimental cognitive literature. Nevertheless, understanding of the conditions that produce these effects is still quite incomplete, so that while a bias can be identified in a data set, it is far more difficult to predict in advance when it will occur.

Conflicts and tension between EU theory and actual decision behavior are a major component of current research on clinical decision making. These situations are interesting for at least two reasons: On the basic research side, psychology has a long history of studying discrepancies between the ways things appear and the way they really are; the work on optical illusions in every elementary textbook exemplifies this tradition and so does work on errors in learning. From a practical standpoint, there has been much concern in the past decade about medical malpractice, ethical dilemmas, spiraling costs of health care, assuring quality, and reviewing use of health services to minimize waste and inefficiencies. Health-service researchers, policy analysts, economists, physicians, and psychologists have all been interested in examining the decisions of clinicians in the light of prescriptive or normative models of choice (Eddy, 1990; Hershey & Baron, 1987; Ritov & Baron, 1990) with a view to understanding why suboptimal behavior occurs and determining what can be done about it. This research leads naturally to considering whether and to what extent everyday clinical decision making would be improved if physicians were to consider the viewpoint and implications of EU theory, even when it is not worthwhile or possible to conduct full-blown decision analyses. One move in this direction is the gradual diffusion of guidelines for managed care and protocols for patient management. A normative model of some kind often lies beneath the surface of these decision supports.

Much of the psychological research on clinical decision making has confirmed the critique of EU theory shared by many psychologists who study decision making: Clinicians often prefer actions that do not maximize expected utility or that violate some principle of the theory (Elstein, 1988; Redelmeier & Tversky, 1990) although the theory itself does not describe clinical decision making. The majority of investigators are not prepared to abandon some variant of utility theory as a normatively correct model of rational choice under risky conditions. In this respect, their position resembles that of scholars of medical ethics: Everyone recognizes that some fraction of the decisions we make in everyday life violate ethical norms we ordinarily endorse. These departures from normatively correct behavior may be regrettable, but are not regarded as supporting a claim that ethical theory should be abandoned as incorrect simply because people do not always obey these principles. Indeed, as Kant (1785/1990) pointed out, if people were not free to disregard these rules and principles, they would have the status of physical laws rather than ethical norms.

There is no comparable normative-descriptive tension in the literature on medical problem solving. Interestingly, formal logic is not accorded the same status in the problem-solving literature as utility theory has in decision making. If people take redundant, inefficient, or illogical steps in solving problems, no one is particularly surprised. No one calls for abandoning logic as a standard simply because people do not use it in everyday inference and reasoning. The implicit stance of the medical problem-solving literature is that, given the complexity of the problem, experts in a domain probably do about as well as can be expected and so their performance can serve as a standard for evaluation and judgment. Decision-making researchers are not nearly so comfortable with this view, perhaps because they are closer to the critical evaluative tradition of health services research.

An Example of Normative-model Research

The question of whether or not to prescribe hormonal replacement therapy for menopausal women is a good example of both the research strategy and the theoretical slant of psychological research on clinical decision making. The decision is a treatment dilemma, not a diagnostic problem, and affects large numbers of women each year.

When a woman enters menopause, the production of estrogen declines and the hot flashes, flushes, and other symptoms of menopause occur. It has been long recognized that replacing this hormone would alleviate these symptoms. Around 1975, however, continued use of replacement estrogen was linked with an increased rate of cancer of the uterine lining (endometrial cancer). Use of the hormone fell, despite subsequent studies criticizing the methodology and findings of these earlier studies. It was then shown that using replacement estrogen had the benefit of decreasing the loss of bone mass and thus reducing the risk of fractures due to osteoporosis. Estrogen also appeared to lower the rate of heart attacks in older women. A combination regimen of estrogen and progestin (another female hormone whose production declines at menopause) was found to lower the rate of endometrial cancer to about the base-rate of untreated women, but the price paid is a possible resumption of menses or erratic episodes of "breakthrough spotting." The stage is now set for a treatment dilemma: Any regimen has both risks and benefits that are deferred 10–20 years into the future, except for symptom relief and postmenopausal spotting. Perhaps because of the complexity of the tradeoffs, hormonal replacement has been controversial among physicians for over a decade. Individual physicians have clear preferences, but there is little consensus among them.

A team of investigators (Elstein, Holzman, Ravitch, Metheny, Holmes, Hoppe, Rothert, & Rovner, 1986) studied this decision problem. Fifty experienced clinicians were individually presented with a set of 12 brief vignettes. Each described a menopausal woman who was not currently on hormonal replacement therapy and who was seeking medical advice about what to do. Each vignette provided a brief summary of pertinent medical history, giving information relating to the level of the patient's risk for osteoporosis and endometrial cancer. The set of cases presented all possible combinations of the two risk factors. The instructions made clear that the women had no strong preferences and would follow the physician's recommendation. Based on the information provided for each case, the clinician had to decide whether or not to prescribe hormonal replacement. They indicated their recommendations by making a mark on a 10 cm line anchored at one end by the phrase "Virtually certain I would not prescribe" and at the other end by "Virtually certain I would prescribe." Marks below 4 cm were interpreted as decisions not to treat, between 4–6 cm as undecided, and above 6 cm as recommendations to treat. After reading the cases and making decisions, a structured interview was conducted to obtain the clinician's estimates of the probabilities of women at various risk levels developing either endometrial cancer or fractures due to osteoporosis, depending on whether or not hormonal replacement therapy was prescribed. The interview was also used to obtain their probabilities and utilities for a hypothetical set of clinical outcomes of both endometrial cancer and hip fracture. These quantitative estimates were entered into the decision tree shown in Fig. 8.1 to arrive at a

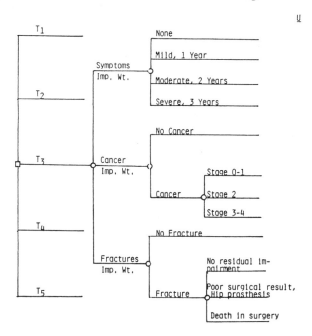

FIG. 8.1. Decision tree for estrogen replacement therapy. T_1 = no treatment; T_2 = estrogen only for up to three years; T_3 = estrogen and progesterone for up to three years; T_4 = estrogen only for five or more years; T_5 = estrogen for five or more years. A complete tree would show branching identical to that displayed for T_3 following each regimen. From Elstein, et al. (1986). Reprinted by permission of *American Journal of Medicine.*

recommended action for each case. The decision tree is a model or representation of the problem that included the risks of cancer and fracture and the benefit of symptom relief. It excluded possible cardiovascular benefits of estrogen replacement and possible effects upon risk for other forms of cancer, notably breast cancer. These outcomes were either unrecognized when the study was done, or else regarded as so unlikely that they could be disregarded for practical purposes. The observed decisions were then compared with those recommended by a decision analytic model that used each physician's subjective probabilities and utilities to arrive at a recommended action for each case.

Although the information provided in these clinical vignettes is sketchy compared to what a physician would know about an actual patient, there were very few "undecided" decisions. Even with relatively little information, these clinicians knew what they would do. There were substantial differences in willingness to treat, but in general the probability of prescribing declined as the cancer risk rose and increased with increasing fracture risk.

The results (summarized in Table 8.1) showed that the decision analysis recommended hormonal replacement far more often than the physicians. They most frequently preferred not to treat, thereby minimizing cancer-associated outcomes at the price of increasing the number of fracture-related outcomes. The decision analysis never recommended this choice. One interpretation of this result is that clinicians felt more responsible for bad outcomes caused by their direct action (cancers associated with hormonal replacement therapy) than for those bad outcomes that "just happen" or that can easily be attributed to other causes (fractures due to osteoporosis that occur spontaneously or because an elderly woman slips on an icy sidewalk). Their behavior could not be attributed to ignorance. The majority knew that an estrogen-progestin combination could reduce cancer risk to about the level of no treatment, but they still avoided this regimen. If the probability estimates and utility assessment can be said to accurately capture their beliefs, then this is an instance of choices that are inconsistent

TABLE 8.1
Cross-Tabulation of Observed Prescribing Decisions
and Recommendations of Decision-Analytic Model.
Data Obtained from 49 Physicians

Observed Decisions	Decision Analysis			
	Treat	Toss-Up	Do Not Treat	Total
Treat	97	105	0	202
Toss-up	23	26	0	49
Do Not Treat	113	224	0	337
Total	233	355	0	588

From Elstein, et al. (1986). Reprinted by permission of *American Journal of Medicine*.

TABLE 8.2
Comparison of Observed Treatment Decisions with Two SEU Models.
Data Obtained from 21 Third-Year Residents

	Decision		
Source	Treat	Toss-Up	Don't Treat
Single-attribute model	58	172	22
Multi-attribute model	20	206	26
Observed decisions	75	32	145

From Evans, D. A. & Patel, V. L. (1989). *Cognitive science in medicine: Biomedical modeling* (p. 34). Cambridge, MA: MIT Press. Copyright 1989 by MIT Press. Reprinted by permission.

with an individual's belief structure, a problem familiar to both social psychologists and ethicists.

Earlier, it was mentioned that years of experience is commonly used as a proxy for expertise in studies of medical decision making. If experience is the criterion and if experts do not do what is expected by theory, what are we to conclude? One interpretation is that the normative theory is incorrect; the experts did the right thing, and the recommendations of the decision analysis are wrong. Another possibility is that experience is a poor indicator of expertise, that experienced physicians may not "keep up" with their field. On this view, the decisions of the subjects of this study might demonstrate that they had learned a now-outmoded decision rule as residents or medical students and that they had failed to keep up with changing opinions in the field.

To test this hypothesis, Elstein, Dod & Holzman (1989) replicated the study (with some slight variations) with 21 third-year residents in three different medical specialties (medicine, family practice, and obstetrics-gynecology) as the subjects. It was thought that if keeping up with the latest academic opinions was the issue, these residents should make very different decisions than the experienced sample. If, on the other hand, the decision was not driven primarily by how current information was understood and processed, the decisions of the two groups should be similar. In fact, their overall decisions were remarkably similar (see Table 8.2). The residents, on the whole, preferred not to prescribe hormonal replacement therapy. These preferences were inconsistent with the recommendations of two normative models that employed their own estimates of the risks and benefits of the two alternatives in slightly different ways (single-attribute and multi-attribute models), while the models agreed 83% of the time. Thus, the reluctance to prescribe cannot be attributed either to lack of clinical experience or to failure to keep up with current academic thinking in the field.

The inconsistencies between the normative model and actual choices show that physicians do not carry out a rapid informal decision analysis in their heads when confronted with treatment dilemmas. In this sense, the critique of EU theory mentioned earlier is confirmed; it does not describe how humans make decisions. Physicians are as highly trained a group of decision makers as this society can produce. They have more hours of practice at their tasks in real world settings (hospitals and clinics) than most groups of troubleshooters and expert analysts. Confronted with a relatively simple decision problem, these experts do not try to do a decision analysis in their heads. Because there are so many patients to see each day and because formal procedures are so labor-intensive, they have instead learned or developed simplifying labor-saving routines that answer specific questions. These routines, which can be conceptualized as production rules or flow charts, are used instead of a more effortful exploration of the cognitive territory (see also Mitchell & Beach, 1990).

But in view of the opinions of most academic physicians—presumably the most expert of all—that hormonal replacement therapy is underutilized, these studies also raise questions about whether we should be at ease about this style of decision making and untroubled by the neglect of SEU-like approaches. Are physicians doing about as well as can be expected, given the complexities of many clinical problems and the abundant uncertainties about the quality of the data and the evaluation of the future that decision analysis entails? Or has evidence been uncovered of systematic, nonrandom deficiencies in decision making that need educational remediation and greater application of formal decision approaches? These questions still engage the attention of the research community.

CONCLUSION

Traditionally, good clinical judgment has been thought to be acquired by a lengthy period of training. Widely used instructional strategies include: observing and imitating the decisions of teachers, supervised practical experience with gradually increased responsibility, review and discussion of difficult cases with mentors, and trial and error. Little theory has been available to guide or modify these practices, which are deeply rooted in clinical experience.

Both the information processing approach and the normative model approach are beginning to influence medical education (Kassirer & Kopelman, 1991; Pauker, 1988; Riegelman, 1991). The information processing work has shown that simply collecting the correct data does not lead to a diagnosis. Diagnostic hypotheses must be activated or retrieved from long-term memory and data must be deliberately related to the hypotheses being considered. Experienced physicians may often omit these steps, for they can quickly recognize a new case as an instance of a familiar category. In these situations, it can be said that pattern recognition replaces more labor-intensive problem solving. But learners cannot use pattern recognition until the patterns have been acquired and so overlearned that they are rapidly and automatically retrieved. For them, and for experienced clinicians confronting a difficult case, a strategy of iterative hypothesis testing will be helpful. The information processing approach reminds the clinician to consider several alternative hypotheses, to ask what data could help to confirm or rule out each, and to deliberately apply the data to the diagnostic hypotheses being evaluated. It thus attempts to guide the process of clinical reasoning to help insure that data are gathered and applied.

The normative model approach highlights difficulties commonly experienced when we try to make decisions in situations with multiple uncertainties. It asks us to become aware of errors that are frequently made as simple problem representations are constructed or rules of procedure are applied. It also offers some strategies for combining probabilities and values in decision making. So far, these analytic tools have been more attractive to policy makers and insurance companies, who necessarily take a societal perspective, than to clinicians who understandably take the perspective of the individual patient. The computational burden of decision analysis is another reason for slow dissemination. This problem is now being addressed by computer programs that crunch the numbers and by computerized decision support systems (expert systems) that offer diagnostic alternatives or suggest useful next steps. In addition to instruction in how to use these aids, educational approaches to medical decision making are beginning to focus on the theory of decision making, on the psychological processes of clinical decision making, and on the role of values (physicians' and patients') in decision making. All these topics are highlighted by the normative model research which thus enters into education, even when decision analysis as a technique is not formally taught.

ACKNOWLEDGMENT

Preparation of this chapter was supported in part by a grant from the National Library of Medicine, RO1-LM-4583.

REFERENCES

Barrows, H. S., Norman, G. R., Neufeld, V. R., & Feightner, J. W. (1982). The clinical reasoning process of randomly selected physicians in general practice. *Clinical and Investigative Medicine, 5*, 49–56.

Bordage, G., & Lemieux, M. (1991). Semantic structures and diagnostic thinking of experts and novices. *Academic Medicine, 66*(9), S70–S72.

Bordage, G., & Zacks, R. (1984). The structure of medical knowledge in the memories of medical students and general practitioners: Categories and prototypes. *Medical Education, 18*, 406–416.

Christensen, C., Heckerling, P. S., Mackesy, M. E., Bernstein, L. M., & Elstein, A. S. (1991). Framing bias among expert and novice physicians. *Academic Medicine, 66*(9), S76–S78.

Eddy, D. M. (1990). Clinical decision making: From theory to practice: The challenge. *Journal of American Medical Association, 263*, 287–290.

Elstein, A. S. (1988). Cognitive processes in clinical inference and decision making. In D. C. Turk & P. Salovey (Eds.), *Reasoning, inference and judgment in clinical psychology* (pp. 17–50). New York: Free Press/Macmillan.

Elstein, A. S., Dod, J. M., & Holzman, G. B. (1989). Estrogen replacement decisions of third-year residents: Clinical intuition and decision analysis. In D. A. Evans and V. L. Patel (Eds.), *Cognitive science in medicine* (pp. 21–52). Cambridge, MA: MIT Press.

Elstein, A. S., Holzman, G. B., Ravitch, M. M., Metheny, W. P., Holmes, M. M., Hoppe, R. B., Rothert, M. L., & Rovner, D. R. (1986). Comparison of physicians' decisions regarding estrogen replacement therapy for menopausal women and decisions derived from a decision analytic model. *American Journal of Medicine, 80,* 246–258.

Elstein, A. S., Shulman, L. S., & Sprafka, S. A. (1978). *Medical problem solving: An analysis of clinical reasoning.* Cambridge, Mass.: Harvard University Press.

Elstein, A. S., Shulman, L. S., & Sprafka, S. A. (1990). Medical problem solving: A ten-year retrospective. *Evaluation and the Health Professions, 13,* 5–36.

Evans, D. A., & Patel, V. L. (Eds.). (1989). *Cognitive science in medicine: Biomedical modeling.* Cambridge, MA: MIT Press.

Feltovich, P. J., Johnson, P. E., Moller, J. H., & Swanson, D. B. (1984). LCS: The role and development of medical knowledge in diagnostic expertise. In W. J. Clancey & E. H. Shortliffe (Eds.), *Readings in medical artificial intelligence: The first decade* (pp. 275–319). Reading, MA: Addison-Wesley.

Grant, J., & Marsden, P. (1987). The structure of memorized knowledge in students and clinicians: An explanation for diagnostic expertise. *Medical Education, 21,* 92–98.

Hershey, J. C., & Baron, J. (1987). Clinical reasoning and cognitive processes. *Medical Decision Making, 7,* 203–211.

Joseph, G. M., & Patel, V. L. (1990). Domain knowledge and hypothesis generation in diagnostic reasoning. *Medical Decision Making, 10,* 31–46.

Kahneman, D., Slovic, P., & Tversky, A. (Eds.). (1982). *Judgment under uncertainty: Heuristics and biases.* New York: Cambridge University Press.

Kant, I. (1990). *Foundations of the Metaphysics of Morals* (L. W. Beck, Trans.). New York: Macmillan. (Original work published 1785)

Kassirer, J. P., & Kopelman, R. I. (1991). *Learning clinical reasoning.* Baltimore, Williams & Wilkins.

Lesgold, A. M. (1987). Problem solving. In R. J. Sternberg & E. E. Smith (Eds.), *The psychology of human thought* (pp. 188–213). New York: Cambridge Univ. Press.

Mitchell, T. R., & Beach, L. R. (1990). ". . . Do I love thee? Let me count. . ." Toward an understanding of intuitive and automatic decision making. *Organizational Behavior and Human Decision Processes, 47,* 1–20.

Newell, A. (1979). One last word. In D. T. Tuma & F. Reif (Eds.), *Problem solving and education: Issues in teaching and research* (pp. 175–189). Hillsdale, NJ: Lawrence Erlbaum Associates.

Newell, A., & Simon, H. A. (1972). *Human problem solving.* Englewood Cliffs, NJ: Prentice-Hall.

Pauker, S. G. (1988). Clinical decision making. In J. B. Wyngaarden & L. H. Smith, Jr., (Eds.), *Cecil textbook of medicine: 18th Ed.* (pp. 74–79). Philadelphia: Saunders.

Pople, H. E. (1982). Heuristic methods for imposing structure on ill-structured problems: The structuring of medical diagnostics. In P. Szolovits (Ed.), *Artificial intelligence in medicine* (pp. 119–190). Boulder: Westview Press.

Ravitch, M. M. (1989). Subjectivity in decision making: Common problems and limitations. *World Journal of Surgery, 13,* 281–286.

Redelmeier, D. A., & Tversky, A. (1990). Discrepancy between medical decisions for individuals and for groups. *New England Journal of Medicine, 322,* 1162–1164.

Riegelman, R. K. (1991). *Minimizing medical mistakes: The art of medical decision making.* Boston: Little, Brown.

Ritov, I., & Baron, J. (1990). Reluctance to vaccinate: Omission bias and ambiguity. *Journal of Behavioral Decision Making, 3,* 263–277.

Sox, H. C., Jr., Blatt, M. A., Higgins, M. C., & Marton, K. I. (1988). *Medical decision making.* Boston: Butterworths.

Weinstein, M. C., Fineberg, H. V., Elstein, A. S., Frazier, H. S., Neuhauser, D., Neutra, R. R., & McNeil, B. J. (1980). *Clinical decision analysis.* Philadelphia: Saunders.

9 Seeing the Invisible: Perceptual–Cognitive Aspects of Expertise

Gary A. Klein
Klein Associates Inc.

Robert R. Hoffman
Adelphi University

"SEEING" AND "SEEING BEYOND"

Novices see only what is there; experts can see what is not there. With experience, a person gains the ability to visualize how a situation developed and to imagine how it is going to turn out. In this chapter we examine how experts can use their knowledge to visualize tasks. Our emphasis is not on rules, or strategies, or size of knowledge base per se, but on the perceptual and cognitive qualities of experience—experts do not seem to perceive the same world that other people do.

Novices see only what is there. As long as people have a general sense of what is going on, they are alert to what is happening in front of them. Chi, Feltovich, and Glaser (1981) found that both expert and novice physics students could identify the critical cues in a physics problem; the advantage that experts had was in perceiving the interactions among the cues. Brezovic, Klein, and Thordsen (1987) studied the decision making of tank platoon leaders and found that during field exercises novices who had just been introduced into the tanks could list as many different cues as the tank instructors. The novices were not overwhelmed with information, and they were reasonably aware of important items of information. Cue acquisition did not appear to be a critical component of expertise. Elstein, Shulman, and Sprafka (1978) found that accuracy of medical diagnoses was minimally related to thoroughness of cue acquisition. For most tasks, higher levels of performance do not necessarily depend on more powerful strategies for acquiring information that is directly perceivable.

Experts can see what is not there. Their experience lets them notice when something is missing. Consider the following example. A new employee in an organization made the observation that projects were usually left for the last moment. She drew this conclusion from watching how several technical reports were completed with considerable strain just before their deadlines. When she shared her observation, however, it was hotly disputed. In fact, the organization had just completed 10 proposals within the past 6 weeks, with such little effort that she had not even known about them. In previous years, proposal writing had been a major burden and so extra care had been taken to prepare in advance. People who had been in the organization for several years could see the difference. The new employee had no way to detect the *absence* of frantic activities. She could notice the times when the system broke down, but not the times when it worked.

What nonobservable events can an expert detect? Only with experience can you visualize how a course of events is likely to unfold, so that you can see the expected outcomes even in the beginning. Only with experience can you form expectancies. Only with experience can you notice when the expectancies are violated, when something that was supposed to happen did not. And only with experience can you acquire the perceptual skills to make fine discriminations.

In the sections of this chapter, we first describe what we mean by "expert performance." Next, we consider traditional theories of expertise that focus on higher order strategies and on the development of a larger knowledge base. Following that is a discussion of perceptual–cognitive aspects of expertise, which leads to a concluding discussion of training issues.

THE DEVELOPMENT OF EXPERTISE

In this chapter, we are interested in perceptual–cognitive phenomena. For example, if a fireground commander is able to judge that a fire is hotter than would be expected, implying the presence of potentially toxic chemicals, we cannot clearly articulate what is being noticed, but we can assert that the color of the fire and the apparent pressure driving the smoke are the perceptual dimensions being used to make the judgment. We want to examine the ability of experts to perceive things that novices and journeymen cannot detect, in order to determine how these "perceptual" abilities can be used to assess proficiency level and to drive training requirements.

We can distinguish among experts, journeymen, and novices. In this chapter, our focus is on the achievement of high levels of proficiency. Swets and Bjork (1990) have asserted that the training of expertise represents a national need. Because of factors such as turnover and technology change, it is essential that we learn how to "bring people up to speed" as rapidly as possible—not just to the level of adequate performance, but to high levels of proficiency. Accordingly, our prime focus is on the difference between competent performers (journeymen) and experts. We are less interested in the transition from novice to journeyman, because the majority of existing training programs are designed to help people achieve mediocre levels of performance. There has been little work in moving people from competent levels of performance to expert performance.

Before going on, we need to be a bit clearer about what we mean by expertise. The achievement of expertise requires a large amount of experience, but simple accumulation of practice is not sufficient. If you endlessly repeat the same exercises, you will not develop very far. In research on firefighters (Klein, Calderwood, & Clinton-Cirocco, 1986), we observed that 10 years with a rural volunteer fire department were not as valuable for skill development as 1 year in a decaying inner city. Although some minimum amount of time is necessary it must be accompanied by a chance to accumulate a varied set of experiences.

When a person attains a high level of proficiency, we expect to see certain characteristics of performance. We expect the person to be able to make judgments and discriminations that are difficult for most other people—the expert's judgments are significantly more accurate and reliable than those of a journeyman. The expert must be able to apply the experience base to a wide range of tasks encountered in the domain, including nonroutine cases that would stymie people who were merely competent. The best experts will set the standards of ideal performance for a domain.

Glaser (1976) has suggested that when people develop expertise the following changes occur:

• Variable awkward performance becomes consistent, accurate, complete, and relatively fast.
• Individual acts and judgments are integrated into overall strategies.
• Perceptual learning occurs so that a focus on isolated variables shifts to perception of complex patterns.
• There is increased self-reliance and ability to form new strategies when required.

It is intriguing to speculate about the way a person develops expertise. Although there are several accounts of this phenomenon (e.g., Glaser, 1976), currently the most widely cited account was provided by Dreyfus and Dreyfus (Dreyfus, 1972; 1986).

Dreyfus and Dreyfus have argued that the achievement of expertise follows a reliable progression of five levels of expertise, ranging from the beginner to the master. Perceptual skills, rather than analytical skills, are assigned a central role in the progression. Table 9.1 presents a description of these five levels of expertise, adapted from Benner (1984).

The five levels of expertise described in Table 9.1 are sometimes hard to apply, for a number of reasons. People rarely perform at the same level on all tasks in a domain. Presumably, someone who is proficient may behave at the level of expert for a few tasks, would perform at the level of proficiency for many

TABLE 9.1
Levels of Expertise

Novice

Beginners have had little experience of the situation in which they are expected to perform. Their initial learning about the situation is in terms of objective attributes—those that are measurable. These are features of the task world that can be recognized without situational experiences. Novices are limited in their understanding to context-free rules that guide action—this means their behavior is limited and inflexible.

Advanced Beginner

They have coped with enough real situations to note (or have pointed out to them) recurring, meaningful situational components. At this level, understanding of aspects of the situation is limited to global characteristics that reflect prior experience in actual situations. Advanced beginners need help setting priorities, because they operate on general guidelines and are only beginning to perceive recurrent, meaningful patterns.

Competent

Performers at a journeyman's level can see their actions in terms of long-range goals or plans. They are consciously aware of formulating, evaluating, and modifying goals-plans. The competent performer is able to generate plans in terms of current and contemplated future aspects that are most important, and those that are not. The competent performer lacks the speed and flexibility that emerges at higher levels of expertise but has a sense of mastery and the ability to cope with and manage a variety of types of situations.

Proficient

Proficient performers perceive situations as wholes, rather than in terms of situational components. Their performance is guided by "maxims." Perception is key. The perspective is NOT thought out but "presents itself" based upon experience. The proficient performer has learned what typical events to expect in a given situation and how plans need to be modified in accord with these events. This also means that she or he can recognize when the expected typical picture does not materialize and can modify plans and goals accordingly. Situational aspects stand out as more or less important in *this* situation.

Expert

Expert performers no longer rely on analytic principles (rules, guidelines, maxims) to connect their understanding of the situation to an appropriate action. The expert, with an enormous background of experience, has an intuitive grasp of each situation and zeros in on the accurate region of the problem without wasteful consideration of a large range of unfruitful, alternative diagnoses and solutions. The performer is no longer aware of features and rules, and his or her performance becomes fluid and flexible and highly proficient.

---

tasks, and would perform at the level of competence for some tasks that were relatively unfamiliar. So it might be a mistake to label a person as *expert* and expect consistent performance at that level. Rather, an expert simply is capable of handling a wider range of tasks nonanalytically, compared to people with less experience. Usually an expert will be proficient at all or most tasks in a domain, but we would not expect equivalent levels of mastery for all subtasks.

A different approach is to model skill development on the cognitive maturation concepts of Piaget, because these are designed to accept variability and fluctuations in performance. The research of Campbell, Brown, and DiBello (1991) on the development of expertise in computer programmers relied heavily on structured interviews with experts and trainees. The subjects were asked "meta-level" questions such as: How do you plan projects? How do you recognize problems? Can you compare how you do things now with how you did things when you were a beginner? Can you tell from a program how expert the programmer was? How did your knowledge of languages help when you learned a new one? The researchers also conducted a longitudinal study, using audiotaped diaries of programmers who were learning Smalltalk, an object-oriented language. The research showed the limitations of trying to distinguish experts from novices without considering intermediate stages of skill development.

Campbell et al. identified a number of developmental milestones in the learning of different program languages. With regard to Smalltalk, the researchers were able to specify seven distinct developmental levels. At each level, performance was distinguishable in operational terms (e.g., specific tasks the person could or could not perform well). This sets the developmental approach of Campbell et al. apart from others (e.g., Dreyfus & Dreyfus, 1986), which distinguish stages solely at a conceptual level, unanchored to empirical markers. The Campbell et al. approach may be a useful strategy for identifying milestones in skill development, and for allowing more useful assessment procedures.

These characteristics help us to tell that a person has acquired expertise, but how are changes brought about? That is the topic of the next three sections.

EXPERTISE AS THE DEVELOPMENT OF HIGHER ORDER STRATEGIES

Many researchers have hoped to find process differences between experts and novices; that is, we would like to show that people jump to new levels of ability because they use different processes, different strategies in solving problems. It would be nice to demonstrate that novices use simple rules, journeymen use more complex rules, and experts use even higher order rules. If we could show that experts use better strategies, then it would be possible to develop tests for such strategies. It might also enable us to teach these strategies. Even better, it might be possible to show that some strategies generalize across domains, in which case we could design generic evaluation and training methods. Because of the high potential payoff for finding strategy differences, a great deal of research has been devoted to this attempt. Much of this work has been done with children, to explain why children are not as competent as adults. Researchers attempted to show that adults were able to call on effective problem-solving strategies that children lacked (e.g., Flavell, 1971; Kail & Hagen, 1977; Ornstein, 1978).

It seemed reasonable to search for strategy differences because the information-processing tradition in cognitive psychology is a framework for understanding thinking in terms of acquiring, and performing operations on, information. It is obvious that experts acquire a more extensive knowledge base, but it also seemed possible that experts have learned different and more powerful operators, better ways of manipulating information.

Chi et al. (1981) studied expert and novice physicists and found that the knowledge bases, rather than the reasoning strategy, accounted for performance differences. Both experts (graduate students—we would call them journeymen) and novices (postintroductory level physics undergraduates) utilized top-down and bottom-up processing. They differed primarily in their "knowledge schemata." Experts possessed a large number of schemata that enabled them to categorize problems according to underlying concepts and laws and then apply well-known basic approaches for solving problems of a given type. In other words, the knowledge base determined the reasoning strategy. There is no evidence that the experts had learned higher order strategies.

We agree with this conclusion that experts do not necessarily use different strategies than novices. We cannot envision training people to become experts by showing them the importance of top-down processing and analysis of deep structure. Hoffman, Burton, Shanteau, and Shadbolt (1991) have also concluded that both experts and novices rely to some extent on top-down and bottom-up reasoning. Both utilize a divide and conquer strategy, and a cycle of forming and testing mental models. Both experts and novices rely on analogies and metaphors. All the various general strategies appear to some extent in almost all forms of reasoning.

EXPERTISE AS A FUNCTION OF KNOWLEDGE BASE

This traditional approach asserts that expertise is a function of the knowledge base itself, and that as people develop richer knowledge bases they are able to represent problems in more powerful ways, and to take more advantage of stronger reasoning strategies. For example, Chi et al. (1981) and Larkin, McDermott, Simon, and Simon (1980) have shown that expert physicists represent problems in a different way from novices. The experts' representations are conceptually richer and more organized than those of the novices. Novices use hastily formed, concrete, superficial problem representations, whereas experts use abstract representations that rely on "deep" knowledge—imaginal and conceptual understanding of functional relations and physical principles that relate concepts (e.g., conservation of energy, laws of mechanics, etc.). Furthermore, experts are better able to gauge the importance of different kinds of information, and the difficulty of problems. They are also more likely to know the conditions that require the use of particular knowledge and procedures (e.g., if there is acceleration, use Newton's second law; Chi, Glaser, & Rees, 1982). Gentner (1988) has also found that experts encode problems using deep structure, whereas novices use surface features.

It is not terribly clear how to operationalize top-down and bottom-up reasoning. What, specifically, counts as an instance of each? Beyond that, we cannot look solely at the nature of the processing (top-down or bottom-up) to directly infer level of expertise. We must consider the knowledge base that is available to the novice, journeyman, and expert. It is often the knowledge base that drives (or limits) the type of processing that is available for use, rather than an individual's choice of processing strategy. Novices may rely more on bottom-up strategies because they lack the knowledge to make a top-down approach work, not because they have not learned the more effective top-down strategy!

The accumulation of information focuses on the knowledge base itself. We have no quarrel with this account—our intent is to try to supplement it by examining the effect of an expanded knowledge base on the perceptual–cognitive aspects of experience. We suggest that the knowledge base and accumulated experiences may change the way people view their worlds.

EXPERTISE AS PERCEPTUAL–COGNITIVE DIFFERENCES

Experts can see things other people cannot. In this section we examine three aspects of expert perception: the ability to see typicality, the ability to see distinctions, and the ability to see antecedents and consequents. We are not asserting that experts use different strategies than journeymen. Clearly, journeymen attempt to judge typicality, to make fine distinctions, and to be sensitive to antecedents and consequents. The problem is that without an adequate knowledge base it is difficult to rely on these sources of power. Gaps in the knowledge base can result in a misleading idea of what is typical, or what is distinct, or what is likely to happen. Sometimes, journeymen will find it safe to use more analytical strategies rather than trust their experience base. It is not that they lack a strategy for using perceptual–cognitive skills. Rather, they have the metacognitive ability to sense when their experience base is not reliable. In most cases, we feel novices, journeymen, and experts each attempt to use perceptual–cognitive skills. They differ in their success, as a function of their experience base.

The Ability to See Typicality

A common example of the ability to judge typicality is the Secretary problem. A new office manager, faced with the need to hire a secretary, may have to conduct many interviews in order to learn the shape of the skill distribution curve, and to tell which job applicants are superior and which are inferior. In contrast, an experienced office manager will already have a sense of the typicality and variability of secretarial skills so that, if an outstanding applicant shows up as the first one interviewed, a job offer can be made immediately without having to conduct additional interviews.

There is no way for a novice to judge what is normal and what is an exception. Consider a study by Chi, Hutchinson, and Robin (1988), in which descriptions of novel dinosaurs were presented to children who were "dinosaur expert" or novices. These novel dinosaurs were designed to be either typical or atypical. The experts, of course, realized immediately that a dinosaur was typical of a class of dinosaurs and were then able to attribute all the relevant features from the family to which the novel "typical" dinosaur belonged. The experts were equally proficient at determining that a novel dinosaur that was not typical did not belong to any of the familiar families. Novices lacked this ability to judge typicality and to use it to infer other characteristics. A journeyman is likely to have a general sense of typicality, but we feel that there is a clear difference between the journeyman and the expert in ability to rapidly "size up" a situation.

Klein et al. (1986) found that expert firefighters could rapidly size up a situation by identifying it as typical, and that this judgment of typicality evoked several important types of knowledge: recognizing plausible goals, recognizing relevant cues, recognizing events that are expected, and recognizing feasible courses of action. These observations were supported by subsequent studies with tank platoon instructors and design engineers (see Klein, 1989, for a summary description of these projects).

Here is another example of how a proficient firefighter used his ability to size up a situation rapidly. He arrived at the scene of a fire in an apartment building and found that the nearby hydrants were not functional, and that the tanker trucks contained the only water available to him. He did not know the exact source of the fire, but he judged that if he did not act immediately the apartment building would be beyond saving. So he ordered his crews to direct all the water on the basement site that appeared to be the most likely source of the fire. He was successful in extinguishing the fire; if he had been wrong, he would have had to watch helplessly while the building burned down. His rapid situation assessment provided him with a goal (hit the fire immediately), a sense of critical information (limited resources and a likely candidate as the site of the fire), expectancies (waiting would just make the fire uncontrollable), and a reasonable course of action (direct the water at the basement where the smoke was thickest and darkest).

The ability to judge typicality enables experts to perform more effectively and efficiently than journeymen. By quickly seeing which goals are feasible, experts can direct their actions and not waste any effort. By recognizing which cues are relevant, experts can avoid information overload. By anticipating what events to expect, experts can rapidly notice if they have misperceived the situation. And by recognizing a typical course of action, experts can respond rapidly. This type of recognitional decision making enables experts to handle complex cases under time-compressed conditions where analytical methods would not be possible.

The ability of experts to size up situations is also seen in the classic research program conducted by de Groot (1946/1965), who showed chess players difficult chess problems. Grandmasters were able to recognize the best move, often as the first one they considered. Moderately skilled players rarely even considered the best move. De Groot carefully reviewed this think-aloud protocol and concluded that grandmasters were able to recognize threats as deviations from a norm. Such recognition was usually part of the initial evaluation, the first perception of a problem. In contrast, players at lower skill levels had to carefully look for the threats. De Groot identified "anticipation of urgency," "anticipation of solvability," and "intuitive faith in a possibility" as aspects of how a grandmaster could size up situations quickly and accurately, whereas players at lower skill levels had to search to analyze the dynamics of a position.

Moreover, according to de Groot, the sense of typicality carries with it a basis for forming expectations—for judging the level of outcome that is possible in a situation. In this way, a strong chess player can consider a move and judge it as favorable or disappointing in terms of what it yields. In contract, a journeyman cannot sense the level of outcome that should be possible and is forced to consider many moves in order to form a yardstick for evaluating any individual move.

The ability to judge typicality should enable people to detect when expectancies are violated (e.g., when expected events did not occur). Recently, Fraser, Smith, and Smith (1990) reviewed the literature on heuristics and decision errors. One of the topics they addressed was the negativity bias—the difficulty people have in using missing information, or events that were supposed to occur but did not. They found some evidence for such a tendency, in studies of inexperienced subjects (although there were still no compelling reasons interpreting them as errors). But a study by Christensen-Szalanski and Bushyhead (1981) found that experienced decision makers—physicians—used the absence of symptoms as efficiently as their presence. This supports our thesis that expertise permits the effective use of invisible cues.

If experts are able to size up situations quickly, we would expect to see evidence for such ability under time pressure. Calderwood, Klein, and Crandall (1988) compared chess masters with Class B players (journeymen). Games were played under regulation time (approximately 150 seconds per move) and blitz conditions (approximately 6 seconds per move). For complex moves, the masters showed little performance degradation with time pressure, whereas the move quality decreased sharply for the Class B players. These data suggest that the journeymen could not rapidly size up a situation the way experts could, and that this ability of experts made them less vulnerable to time compression. Is the ability to play blitz chess well a unique skill, unrelated to general chess ability? No, it seems that blitz chess calls on many of the same skills as regulation chess. Charness (1981) has reported data showing that performance under regulation time is highly correlated ($r = .85$) with performance under blitz conditions, further suggesting that expertise depends on rapid perception–action links.

The use of typicality judgments is important for problem solving as well as decision making. Elstein et al. (1978) studied the way physicians made diagnoses and found that the physicians rarely used a purely inductive method of letting the data drive the inferences. Even though the physicians were trained to reserve judgment rather than contaminate the process, they still could not resist forming early impressions. Elstein et al. referred to this strategy as a hypothetico-deductive method, because the early judgments were hypotheses that helped to direct the subsequent information gathering. Without early hypotheses, the information gathering would have been inefficient and interminable. Weitzenfeld, Klein, Riedl, Freeman, and Musa (1991) observed the same phenomenon in a study of expertise in software troubleshooting. Experts were able to formulate initial hypotheses, or stories of how the problem might have arisen, and could use these hypotheses to direct the search for more evidence. Where do these hypotheses come from? Presumably, they involve the same mechanism of situation assessment as was discussed earlier—using experience to judge typicality.

How does this ability to judge typicality develop? In time, the knowledge base develops, and a person may be able to recognize situations that are similar to previous experiences. It is tempting to infer that experts retrieve specific instances and use these to guide their behavior. Currently, the field of analogical problem solving is receiving a great deal of attention, and it is likely that this research will generate useful findings. However, Klein et al. (1986) tried to identify specific analogues that helped firefighters make difficult decisions. We obtained little evidence for the use of analogical reasoning in this domain. Doubtless there are task conditions in which analogical retrieval plays an important role—low time pressure, and relatively low experience levels—which make individual incidents more informative (see Klein & Calderwood, 1988). And when our experts (average amount of experience was 23 years) did use analogues, the analogues were judged to be very helpful. Nevertheless, we suspect that analogues are more prevalent for journeymen than for novices. When people are able to gain a great deal of experience, particularly direct experience, we hypothesize that individual incidents become less vivid and blend together in memory, enabling the expert to make additional types of judgments—detecting typicality and variability.

Another possible explanation for the ability to judge typicality, besides analogical reasoning, is pattern matching. The hypothesis is that experts are better at pattern matching. Chase and Simon (1973) demonstrated that expert chess players used content knowledge to recognize patterns, rather than their possessing superior factual memory. And Simon and Gilmartin (1973) estimated that chess masters store a large repertoire of between 10,000 to 100,000 patterns.

But the story is not so simple. If expertise were just a matter of pattern matching, why would experts also be better at handling nonroutine events and complex variations? De Groot (1990, personal communication), Holding (1985), and Elstein et al. (1978) have all been very critical of the idea that experts simply possess a large repertoire of specific patterns, enabling them to rapidly match events to prior experiences. We entirely agree with their criticisms. Experts must be recognizing complex invariants nested within complex and often irrelevant data. Pattern matching is perhaps a component of judging typicality (depending on the task), but it is not sufficient—something must provide a basis for inferences. In simple situations pattern matching might be enough, but for complex cases it is difficult to see how pattern matching would allow the expert to derive a sense of the situation ("I should be able to get out of this with only the loss of a pawn") and of promising courses of action ("How can I take advantage of my well-placed knight?").

At present, there is no satisfactory explanation of how experts can quickly size up situations and judge typicality. This ability sets experts apart from novices and from journeymen and represents one way that experts can use their experience to see subtle and critical aspects of a situation.

The Ability to See Distinctions

Experts are particularly better than novices and journeymen in making fine perceptual discriminations. The effects of perceptual learning can be seen in common experience. Consider televised broadcasts of Olympics events such as gymnastics and diving, where expert analysts notice aspects of performance that we novices can detect only when shown the slow-motion replay. Lesgold, Rubinson, Feltovich, Klopfer, and Glaser (1985) have shown the importance of perceptual skills for radiology diagnosis. And Shanteau (1985) has demonstrated perceptual skill differences for experts versus novices and journeymen in a wide variety of fields. Most of Shanteau's early work focused on an expert's "hit rate" within the framework of research on judgment and decision making. Shanteau found that expert judgment can appear unreliable in domains such as psychiatric diagnosis (where there are no correct answers, so feedback is problematic), whereas in domains such as soil and livestock judging, experts can be very reliable (Phelps & Shanteau, 1978). The reader who is interested in additional discussions of perceptual learning and expertise should consult Chi, Glaser, and Farr (1988) and Hoffman, Burton, Shanteau, and Shadbolt (1991).

The Ability to See Antecedents and Consequents

Experts can visualize how a situation developed into its current state, and they can visualize how it will continue to develop. Kahneman and Tversky (1982) have described a simulation heuristic that people use to arrive at judgments, and Klein (1989) has discussed the importance of this heuristic for decision making and problem solving.

Mental simulation is an important source of power. It enables people to judge how a situation may have developed. Pennington and Hastie (in press) have shown that jurors rely on mental simulations to determine whether a given argument appears plausible. Mental simulation also enables decision makers to evaluate a course of action without comparing it to others. By imagining how the course of action will be carried forward, the decision maker can respond to the quality of the end states that are anticipated. De Groot (1946/1965) has used the term *progressive deepening* to describe how chess players follow a sequence of moves. Holding (1985) has reviewed a wide range of studies on chess expertise and notes that experts are able to "look deeper" into a line of play as well as recognize a better set of moves to consider in the first place. In other words, experts start out with an advantage. They can consider a better set of options, but they also use their understanding of the domain to trace these options to a greater depth, searching for pitfalls and for opportunities. Nonexperts perform the same functions, but without the benefit of a large experience base.

We feel that skill at mental simulation sets experts apart from journeymen and novices. In the study of tank platoon leaders discussed earlier (Brezovic et al., 1987), whereas the novices attended to the same range of cues as the experts, the experts were also visualizing where the adversary's tanks were moving, on the other side of hills and behind ridges. The experts were also visualizing the location and progress of sister platoons. The novices showed minimal awareness of any event that was not physically present.

We assert that experts have an important advantage over journeymen in being able to visualize how situations have developed, and how they are going to evolve. This is especially salient in the skills of expert aerial photo interpreters who, from a single photo, can perceive the long processes that led to the formation of the given terrain (Hoffman, 1984). Novices and journeymen have difficulty in seeing anything other than the current state of a situation, and for this reason they are often unclear about the dynamics of a situation. Novices and journeymen also have difficulty in keeping up with situations, because they lack a basis for anticipating changes and generating expectancies. To use an aviation term, they are usually *flying behind the airplane*. It is no wonder that their responses are variable, awkward, and unintegrated.

IMPLICATIONS AND APPLICATIONS OF A
PERCEPTUAL–COGNITIVE VIEW OF EXPERTISE

Theory and application both benefit when they are linked. Without an applied focus, it is easy for theory to lose focus, and to address easy problems rather than hard problems that demand greater complexity. Application without theory can also lose shape and become a disorganized collection of practices. If our perspective on expertise is to develop, it must have value in shaping practice.

Some Implications for Training

How long does it take to become an expert? Simon and Gilmartin (1973) estimated that chess expertise depends on acquiring the knowledge base that allows one to distinguish among approximately 10,000 to 100,000 patterns, and they estimated that this might take up to 10 years. Medical expertise also seems to take about 10 years; and the interpretation of aerial photographs has been estimated to require about 5 years minimum for expertise. In our own work with expert nurses, pilots, and fireground commanders, moderate proficiency (the achievement of journeyman status) seems to take at least 2 years to develop, given continual practice. Many more years are necessary before the person is considered an expert.

There is little reason to believe that we can help people achieve expertise by training them to use the same reasoning strategies as experts. Means, Salas, Crandall, and Jacobs (in press) have reviewed the literature on attempts to teach people generic strategies for decision making and for cognitive development and found no evidence for the effectiveness of such attempts. Means et al. did not find any unambiguous success stories but were able to find many instances of minimal success or outright failure, with one exception: It does seem possible to train people to improve metacognition. Otherwise, it seems fairly clear that there is usually little value in attempting to teach generic reasoning skills.

So how should we approach the job of training people to become experts? If expertise is so dependent on learning to perceive the world differently, then we should look at ways to sharpen perceptual skills, rather than ways to simply add to the experience base. This would enable people to make more rapid and accurate judgments about the nature of the situations they are in.

We can identify at least four strategies for increasing the development of perceptual–cognitive skills: personal experiences, directed experiences, manufactured experiences, and vicarious experiences.

Personal Experiences

The acquisition of personal experiences is straightforward, but inefficient. It is obvious how to gain 10 years of experience—devote 10 years to it. But time-on-the-job is not the key. Rather, the opportunity to be continually challenged seems central.

There is a difference between performing a job automatically and being sensitive to changes in context. There is a difference between performing a job by using standard operating procedures and developing a feel for the situation. Dreyfus and Dreyfus (1986) have argued that an expert learns to give up analytical strategies, including the standard operating procedures that are taught to beginners. In some domains, such as terrain analysis, all cues are always systematically analyzed (Hoffman, 1984). In other domains, the process of explicit analysis can interfere with necessary perceptual learning. Gallwey (1984) has suggested for such domains that someone who insists on analyzing each incident will make less progress and may even be interfering with progress, compared to someone who is learning to rely on perceptual capabilities.

So, the straightforward way to achieve expertise is through direct experience, but this involves more than time-on-the-job. It involves the number, range, and difficulty of challenges faced, and it involves the way a person is able to learn from each incident, along with factors such as degree of engagement with the task.

Directed Experiences

Surveys indicate that over 70% of organizations in the United States use some form of one-on-one instruction to train employees (Lee, 1991). On-the-Job Training (OJT) frequently depends on tutoring from co-workers and supervisors; yet there has been little research on the skills necessary for effective tutoring. Recently, Crandall, Kyne, Militello, and Klein (1991) performed a knowledge elicitation study of master tutors in two domains—critical care nursing and musical instruction. Whereas these domains had different requirements, a list of common skills was compiled: observation of performance, assessment, modelling, guiding motivation and attitudes, relieving anxiety, developing a professional identity.

There appears to be a clear value for organizations to carefully examine their reliance on tutoring, and to adopt measures for more carefully selecting and training tutors. Typically, tutors in the workplace are given no training, and the result may be to reduce the value of OJT. It is the perceptual–cognitive skills of the tutor that the trainee needs to acquire, and these are precisely the skills that are most difficult to communicate. A perceptual–cognitive approach to defining tutor skills and helping tutors learn ways to pass these skills along to trainees could have great value.

It is worth noting that many skills of master tutors are difficult or impossible to incorporate into Intelligent Tutoring Systems (ITSs), thereby setting bounds on the effectiveness of an ITS within a workplace setting.

Here is an example of tutoring expertise, using an incident studied by Crandall et al. (1991):

A music tutor described how she assessed a young woman who was becoming proficient on the viola. The tutor was surprised to find that the student's tone was off. Upon probing, we found that it was not simply that the student was not hitting the notes, since most viola players are off a bit. Rather, what struck the tutor was that the student was not adjusting her fingering. Even for long notes, the student was not sliding her fingers to make corrections. So the critical cue wasn't what the tutor heard, but what she didn't hear. Her expertise enabled her to have a clear expectancy of how a student at this level should be adjusting. The expectancy was so clear that the tutor could immediately notice that the playing was flawed.

This incident demonstrates the use of expertise to form and use expectancies, and to focus on what was not happening as a cue to improving performance.

Manufactured Experiences

It may be inefficient or impractical to rely on personal experiences, and in such cases it may be useful to present simulations. Computer technology is increasingly able to provide low-cost and high-fidelity simulations that, if used properly, can speed the acquisition of expertise.

One great advantage of training simulations is that they allow one to sharpen discriminations. By facing stimulus configurations that are similar, the trainee has to learn how to make finer distinctions. Also, a person can practice with a larger and more varied set of configurations. So, simulations can allow a person to develop situation assessment skills, and to quickly size up a situation (Lintern, 1991).

Such training need not be extremely expensive. To increase the ability to rapidly size up a situation, simple visual displays could be used for presenting task and cue configurations. This would give practice in determining the different aspects of situation assessment—plausible goals, critical cues, expectancies, and courses of action that are likely to succeed.

For instance, if expertise depends on experience with tough cases, we could increase the rate at which tough cases are encountered. Rothkopf (1982) provided an illustrative anecdote. Mechanical looms break down in a number of ways, some of which are rare. It used to take 5 to 7 years to become an expert loom operator because some loom breakdowns occurred only once every 5 to 7 years. To expedite matters, a training loom was constructed that could be deliberately made to show each breakdown type. The time needed to achieve expertise was dramatically reduced.

Vicarious Experiences

A third approach is to use vicarious experiences. For example, stories are accounts of the experiences of others and are often sufficiently vivid to serve as additions to the experience base. Connelly and Clandinin (1990), Howard (1991), and Schank (1990) are only a few researchers who have recently examined storytelling, and Wilensky (1983) has provided a carefully worked-out presentation of issues concerning story grammars.

Klein (1989) has described a strategy that can be used for training—the Critical Decision method. Experts are asked to recount unusual and particularly challenging episodes, or stories, and the interviewer then uses probe questions to investigate what the expert was trying to do, what mistakes would have been made by someone with less ability, and so on. (The initial story account usually glosses over many important details about the role of expertise in the incident.) These accounts are documented in writing and made available as training materials; sometimes a videotape of the interview itself serves as training material.

Essentially, the critical incidents function as stories, and every attempt is made to maintain the account in the respondent's own words. But the respondent may be confused about sequence, so a second sweep is used to pin events to a timeline. Because people often take aspects of expertise for granted, it is necessary to take a third sweep through the incident account, using probes to find out how the situation was perceived, what goals were judged as feasible, and so on. Usually, there will also be a fourth sweep through the account, attempting to identify possible mistakes. These data are appended to the story account. Sometimes it is possible to incorporate these details into the narrative account itself. And sometimes the incident account is diagrammed, and the probe responses are represented as branches from the main theme. Here is an example cited by Crandall and Gamblian (1991), who collected and formatted stories to be used in training nurses working in a neonatal intensive care unit (NICU). The incident was presented by an experienced nurse working in the NICU:

> Recently I had a primary baby, a 28-weeker, who had been born at home. The type of birth meant the baby was open to infection, but he had had an antibiotic series and had stabilized nicely. This was about two weeks after we admitted him: I came on duty and the first thing I thought was—his color's different. It wasn't any dramatic change or anything, not the gross gray-green they get later. More like a shadow across him. It was really subtle. I checked his chart—blood count looking okay, and no change otherwise. Monitors looked okay. He was sleeping so I went ahead with care for the other baby I had that night and got back to him around midnight.
>
> I had found in caring for him that if I spoke quietly as I opened the isolette and then touched him gently that he would rouse, open his eyes and turn his head a bit. I often held his foot, rubbing the sole as he was waking, and he would curl his toes around my finger. This night he had much more trouble rousing. He didn't respond to my touching his feet, and he couldn't seem to get his eyes fully open. He seemed floppy, with less muscle tone than I was used to.
>
> When I went to weigh him, I really began to worry. Many kids hate being weighed, but he liked it. Typically, he would really come to an alert state, opening his eyes wide, moving his legs and feet, and turning his head toward me. I would talk to him, it was a time for interacting with this baby that I looked forward to. This night as I put him on the bedside scale he sneezed a couple of times, turned his head away, and then his whole body went flaccid. It struck me that he was really taxed, and was shutting out. I put him in his isolette and he immediately went into a

sound sleep. I charted all this, and made a mental note to really keep an eye on him. I didn't yet think he was septic, just that something was going on. His O_2 was stable, not increasing, and I had not seen any dramatic color changes. I thought, maybe he's worn out after the evening visit with his folks—I'll see if he recovers.

We drew blood at 4:00. Although he was usually very reactive to the heel prick, this time he roused, fussed briefly, and then went right back to sleep. His blood gasses were not as good, but not remarkably different. He still seemed very lethargic. Towards early morning, he began having some apnea and bradycardia. Again, nothing severe, but a change from earlier in the shift. By the time the day nurse came on, he was looking blue around the mouth. I was relieved that the nurse who took over for me had taken care of him before. She knew him, and I also knew she would relay my concerns to the doctors during rounds. I told her I was really worried about him, that I thought he was getting sick. She took a look at him and said, "Gee, he really does look different." It turned out that he had a massive infection. He was really sick. I think if we had waited even one or two days longer he would have been in a badly deteriorated state, and might not have made it. As it was, he pulled through.

What Can Go Wrong?

One of the difficulties of spotting sepsis very early is that the signs may be extremely subtle. A nurse, even a highly experienced one, may misread the cues or be misled when some cues are present but others are lacking. Sometimes a nurse may think a baby is becoming septic when that's not the case. And sometimes, she may miss those early, subtle cues. What follows are incident accounts that illustrate these situations, along with some ideas about what may have lead the nurse to an erroneous conclusion. We offer them in the spirit in which they were shared with us—that we learn from mistakes, and that even the most skilled, vigilant, and caring nurse misses occasionally. (pp. 10–11)

This is a story about perceptual learning and experience—being able to size up a situation. Crandall and Gamblian (1991) found that stories such as these were evaluated as very helpful for expanding the expertise of experienced nurses who were new on the neonatal intensive care unit, and who needed to come up to speed quickly. They also found that cues embedded within such stories showed high rates of retention weeks after being presented to nursing students.

Chi, Bassok, Lewis, Reimann, and Glaser (1989) studied the use of examples by good and poor college students who had not taken a course in college physics; the task was to solve problems in mechanics. The good students were able to benefit from examples because they were monitoring their understanding of the examples and were actively trying to expand their comprehension of general principles. In contrast, the poor students did not try to generate more global comprehension of examples and did not monitor their own understanding; they relied heavily on examples but were apt to misapply these examples. In other words, poor students may prefer to learn from analogues, but analogical learning is risky because students often do not know what lessons to extract from the analogues.

The use of vicarious experiences treats expertise as a resource. Klein (1992) has suggested that we think about a general discipline of knowledge engineering, akin to petroleum engineering. If knowledge is a resource, we can develop techniques for locating critical knowledge in an organization—identifying the experts. We can develop techniques for eliciting the knowledge, and for processing or codifying it. Finally, we can develop strategies for applying the knowledge, as in training. Knowledge engineering has been discussed in the context of expert systems, and indeed expert systems are a prime example of how to engineer knowledge. But there is no reason why it is necessary to use only expert systems for knowledge engineering. The Critical Decision method is a low-technology strategy that does not depend on computers at all.

Thus far, we have used the Critical Decision method as a knowledge engineering strategy in several different domains. Crandall and Gamblian (1991) used the method to capture and communicate subtle perceptual skills needed by nurses working in a neonatal intensive care unit. Weitzenfeld et al. (1991) used the method to capture important aspects of the expertise of highly skilled computer programmers working for AT&T and developed a training course for improving the troubleshooting and debugging skills of journeyman programmers. Crandall and Klein (1989) used the method to explicate the skills of expert scientists and program managers working at Wright-Patterson Air Force Base, in order to train entry-level scientists and engineers. Projects such as these illustrate how the study of expertise can lead directly to applications for training, particularly to bridge the gap between journeyman and expert levels of performance.

Before turning to a discussion of assessment, we should note that we have not considered those ideas about the training of expertise that can be derived from traditional psychological research on learning (e.g., learning is enhanced by motivation, or by informational feedback; learning is enhanced by an appropriate mix of "part" and "whole" training or massed and distributed practice; temporary memory should not be overloaded, and so on). Our reason for not exploring these ideas is that we find them to be underspecific and therefore of little use when actually applied to a "real-world" domain. For example, to encourage perceptual learning and pattern recognition, one might want to deliberately overload temporary memory, to force the trainee out of an analytical mode. For discussions of training issues from a traditional learning–human factors perspective, see Duncan (1974), Hagman and Rose (1983), and Holding (1987). Also, see Schneider (1985) for a skeptical appraisal of conventional wisdom in this field.

THE ASSESSMENT OF EXPERTISE

One dimension for assessing expertise involves reasoning strategies. If expertise depended on advanced forms of reasoning, it would be clear how to perform assessments. We would ask people to describe the strategy they used in solving a problem, either an actual problem they remembered, or a problem with which they were presented. If there was evidence for the use of more sophisticated strategies, and evidence that these strategies were used skillfully, we could infer that the person showed signs of expertise.

However, as we have argued earlier, there is little evidence that experts use different, let alone more powerful, reasoning strategies than novices, or than journeymen. Experts can draw upon a larger experience base, and this may enable them to use particular strategies, but the strategies themselves do not confer expertise. Nevertheless, it may be possible to examine the strategies people use to take advantage of their declarative knowledge, perceptual–cognitive knowledge, and other aspects of their experience base.

We generally know who the experts are. They notice the subtle but critical cues that others miss. They can reliably make discriminations that are opaque to others. They have clear judgments of the appropriate ways to act in a situation. They can anticipate what is supposed to happen next, and their expectancies are so clear that they quickly notice when they are wrong, so they can rethink their interpretation of what is going on.

We can suggest several ways to distinguish experts from novices and journeymen: performance, content knowledge, and developmental milestones.

Performance

There are clear ways to distinguish expert and journeyman performance. Turning to the suggestions of Glaser (1976), we should be able to distinguish expert performance in terms of variability–consistency, accuracy, completeness, and speed. We would expect expert performance to be smoother, whereas journeymen should exhibit discontinuities in shifting and lurch from one subtask to the next. Even these differences will not always emerge—experts may take longer than journeymen in sizing up a task, and impulsive novices may be very fast. But holding accuracy constant, experts will generally be able to perform more quickly.

A prime example of a performance assessment method is the use of chess ratings, which reliably differentiate between players of different strengths and can be calibrated to predict the proportion of games that will be won by players of unequal strengths. Although this is close to an ideal strategy, in most domains it is not feasible to achieve such precision.

We have speculated that experts are better able to anticipate future events, compared to journeymen. Klein and Peio (1989) employed a prediction paradigm to study this. The application domain was chess. It was argued that strong chess players (i.e., those rated as Class A or as experts) should be able to anticipate the moves in a game played between two experts, whereas mediocre players (rating of 1300 or below) should have much less success in predicting the moves in the same games. The study demonstrated that it was possible to significantly discriminate between experts and novices in terms of their prediction accuracy. This prediction paradigm should be applicable to a variety of domains.

Content Knowledge

There are also ways to distinguish experts and journeymen in terms of their content knowledge. The focus here is on what experts know, rather than on their performance.

Expertise can be assessed in terms of content knowledge, as in tests of declarative knowledge. Expertise can also be studied in terms of the way people see relationships between concepts, especially causal relationships. The work of Schvaneveldt (1991) shows how a simple approach called a conceptual graph can be useful to illustrate how someone understands a domain. Multidimensional scaling techniques were used to generate graphic representations of knowledge structures. This representational format may support methods for distinguishing expert from journeyman conceptual relationships. Multidimensional scaling techniques usually require a great deal of effort to apply, and instructional designers have learned that much of the same benefit can be obtained from informal use of semantic nets (e.g., the concept maps described by McFarren, 1987, and McNeese et al., 1990).

In performing and interpreting research studies, it is important to be sensitive to the dependent variable being used. Even if the design is rigorous, an abstract and tangential measure can mislead us about the phenomenon being studied. For example, Bateson, Alexander, and Murphy (1987) studied expert and novice computer programmers and found that program recall was not as good a test of knowledge as more naturalistic tasks like writing programs or explaining programs. Feltovich, Spiro, and Coulson (1989) said: "Memory for material that has been taught is not the same as learning from instruction" (p. 118).

In this context, we should also mention a project recently completed that used the Critical Decision method for defining the cues used by commercial aviation checkpilots, as they evaluated pilots for certification to fly different aircraft (Kaempf & Klinger, 1992); the goal was to define the cues and to help to standardize the assessment procedures in a way that was sensitive to the perceptual cues relied on by expert evaluators of pilot performance.

Developmental Milestones

Another way to assess expertise is to use progress along skill development milestones. The model presented by Dreyfus and Dreyfus (1986) provides a potential basis for assessing skill. The Piagetian model of Campbell, Brown, and DiBello (1991) may be an even more useful framework for determining a person's progress in mastering a domain.

Our conclusion is that the assessment of expertise can focus on performance, content acquisition, or developmental milestones. Each of these has its own limitations. We have identified a number of dimensions that could be used for assessment and provided some examples of assessments that have been carried out.

CONCLUSIONS

This chapter has examined a view of expertise centered around the idea that experts can see aspects of a situation that are not accessible to people at lower skill levels. Traditional accounts of expertise have tended to emphasize the strategies that experts use, and the knowledge base that experts have compiled. One attractive hypothesis is that expertise is a function of learning more powerful generic strategies and higher order rules (e.g., Flavell, 1971; Kail & Hagen, 1977). Such a view is attractive, because we should be able to identify these strategies and train people to use them. It is usually a good idea to search for generic strategies, because these can be leveraged across many different situations. Unfortunately, this hypothesis has not been a very successful explanation. It does not appear that experience enables people to learn more powerful problem-solving strategies.

A second view of expertise is that the larger knowledge base of experts permits the use of powerful strategies that are also known to journeymen and to novices (Chi et al., 1981). Clearly, experts have acquired more knowledge, so it makes good sense to posit a difference in knowledge base between experts and nonexperts. We have no great quarrel with this approach, but we find it to be somewhat disappointing in terms of what it tells us about the functions of the knowledge base, and in terms of applications to training and to assessment. It emphasizes knowledge rather than the way knowledge is put into action. For these reasons, we feel it may be useful to examine a somewhat different perspective, one that centers around the way that experts perceive tasks and situations:

1. There are several ways that experts can see things that others cannot: Experts can use their knowledge base to recognize typicality, experts can use perceptual learning to make fine discriminations, and experts can use mental simulation to represent antecedents and consequents.

2. Experts can also use their knowledge base to apply higher level rules, such as top-down processing. Such rules are also in the repertoire of novices and journeymen. People at lower skill levels infrequently use higher level strategies because they lack the experience base to make such strategies work.

3. Therefore, trying to train general strategies for thinking like experts may not be worthwhile. Attempts to teach such strategies are not useful in developing expertise, and research does not demonstrate the effectiveness of such attempts.

4. Training can address methods for sharpening perceptual skills and changing the way situations are experienced. There are ways of providing personal experiences, manufactured experiences, and vicarious experiences to accelerate the growth of expertise. We have shown how models of expertise can form the basis of knowledge engineering programs for training specialists in areas as diverse as nursing, computer programming, and research management.

5. It may be useful to develop a discipline of knowledge engineering, to direct us in eliciting and applying expert knowledge.

ACKNOWLEDGMENTS

Support was received for Dr. Klein's work from the U.S. Army Research Institute, Contract MDA903-89-C-0032. The support of Judith Orasanu, Michael Drillings, and Michael Kaplan is gratefully acknowledged. Also appreciated were the comments and reviews from Beth Crandall, Caroline Zsambok, and Michelene Chi.

REFERENCES

Bateson, A. G., Alexander, R. A., & Murphy, M. (1987). Cognitive processing differences between novice and expert computer programmers. *International Journal of Man–Machine Studies, 26,* 649–660.

Benner, P. (1984). *From novice to expert: Excellence and power in clinical nursing practice.* Menlo Park, CA: Addison-Wesley.

Brezovic, C. P., Klein, G. A., & Thordsen, M. (1987). *Decision making in armored platoon command* (KATR-858(b)-87-05F). Yellow Springs, OH: Klein Associates. Prepared under contract MDA903-85-C-0327 for U.S. Army Research Institute, Alexandria, VA.

Calderwood, R., Klein, G. A., & Crandall, B. W. (1988). Time pressure, skill, and move quality in chess. *American Journal of Psychology, 101,* 481–493.

Campbell, R. L., Brown, N. R., & DiBello, L. A. (1991). The programmer's burden: Developing expertise in programming. In R. R. Hoffman (Ed.), *The cognition of experts: Psychological research and empirical AI* (pp. 269–294). New York: Springer-Verlag.

Charness, N. (1981). Search in chess: Age and skill differences. *Journal of Experimental Psychology: Human Learning and Memory, 7,* 467–476.

Chase, W. B., & Simon, H. A. (1973). The mind's eye in chess. In W. G. Chase (Ed.), *Visual information processing* (pp. 215–281). New York: Academic Press.

Chi, M. T. H., Bassok, M., Lewis, M. W., Reimann, P., & Glaser, R. (1989). Self-explanations: How students study and use examples in learning to solve problems. *Cognitive Science, 13,* 145–182.

Chi, M. T. H., Feltovich, P. J., & Glaser, R. (1981). Categorization and representation of physics problems by experts and novices. *Cognitive Science, 5,* 121–152.

Chi, M. T. H., Glaser, R., & Farr, M. J. (1988). *The nature of expertise.* Hillsdale, NJ: Lawrence Erlbaum Associates.

Chi, M. T. H., Glaser, R., & Rees, E. (1982). Expertise in problem solving. In R. J. Sternberg (Ed.), *Advances in the psychology of human intelligence* (pp. 7–25). Hillsdale, NJ: Lawrence Erlbaum Associates.

Chi, M. T. H., Hutchinson, J. E., & Robin, A. F. (1988). *How inferences about domain-related concepts can be constrained by structured knowledge.* Pittsburgh, PA: Learning Research and Development Center, University of Pittsburgh.

Christensen-Szalanski, J. J. J., & Bushyhead, J. B. (1981). Physicians' use of probabilistic information in a real clinical setting. *Journal of Experimental Psychology, 7,* 928–935.

Connelly, F. M., & Clandinin, D. J. (1990). Stories of experience and narrative inquiry. *Educational Researcher, 19*(5), 2–14.

Crandall, B. W., & Gamblian, V. (1991). *Guide to early sepsis assessment in the NICU.* Fairborn, OH: Klein Associates.

Crandall, B., & Klein, G. A. (1989). *Organizational expertise at WRDC: A roadmap to survival and success* (Final Rep. prepared under Contract F33615-88-C-1707 from MacAulay Brown, Inc.). Yellow Springs, OH: Klein Associates.

Crandall, B., Kyne, M., Militello, L., & Klein, G. A. (1991). *Describing expertise in one-on-one instruction* (Final Tech. Rep.). Contract MDA903-91-C-0058, U.S. Army Research Institute, Alexandria, VA.

de Groot, A. D. (1946/1965). *Thought and choice in chess* (1st ed.). New York: Mouton.

Dreyfus, H. L. (1972). *What computers can't do: A critique of artificial reason.* New York: Harper & Row.

Dreyfus, H. L., & Dreyfus, S. E. (1986). *Mind over machine: The power of human intuitive expertise in the era of the computer.* New York: Free Press.

Duncan, K. D. (1974). Analytical techniques in training design. In E. Edwards & F. P. Lees (Eds.), *The human operator in process control* (pp. 283–319). London: Taylor & Francis.

Elstein, A. S., Shulman, L. S., & Sprafka, S. A. (1978). *Medical problem solving: An analysis of clinical reasoning.* Cambridge, MA: Harvard University Press.

Feltovich, P. J., Spiro, R. J., & Coulson, R. L. (1989). The nature of conceptual understanding in biomedicine: The deep structure of complex ideas and the development of misconceptions. In D. A. Evans and V. L. Patel (Eds.), *Cognitive science in medicine: Biomedical modeling* (pp. 113–172). Cambridge, MA: MIT Press.

Flavell, J. H. (1971). What is memory development the development of? *Human Development, 14,* 225–286.

Fraser, J. M., Smith, P. J., & Smith, J. W. (1990). *A catalog of errors.* Columbus, OH: The Ohio State University, Department of Industrial and Systems Engineering.

Gallwey, W. (1984). *Inner game of tennis.* New York: Bantam Books.

Gentner, D. R. (1988). Expertise in typewriting. In M. T. H. Chi, R. Glaser, & M. J. Farr (Eds.), *The nature of expertise* (pp. 1–21). Hillsdale, NJ: Lawrence Erlbaum Associates.

Glaser, R. (1976). Cognition and instructional design. In D. Klahr (Ed.), *Cognition and instruction* (pp. 303–315). Hillsdale, NJ: Lawrence Erlbaum Associates.

Hagman, J. D., & Rose, A. M. (1983). Retention of military tasks: A review. *Human Factors, 25*(2), 199–213.

Hoffman, R. R. (1984). *Methodological preliminaries to the development of an expert system for aerial photo interpretation* (Report ETL-0342). Ft. Belvoir, VA: Engineer Topographic Laboratories, U.S. Army Corps of Engineers.

Hoffman, R. R., Burton, A. M., Shanteau, J., & Shadbolt, N. R. (1991). *Eliciting knowledge from experts: A methodological analysis.* Unpublished manuscript. Garden City, NY: Department of Psychology, Adelphi University.

Holding, D. H. (1985). *The psychology of chess skill.* Hillsdale, NJ: Lawrence Erlbaum Associates.

Holding, D. H. (1987). Concepts of training. In L. G. Salvendy (Ed.), *Handbook of human factors* (pp. 939–962). New York: Wiley.

Howard, G. S. (1991). Culture tales: A narrative approach to thinking, cross-cultural psychology, and psychotherapy. *American Psychologist, 46*(3), 187–197.

Kaempf, G. L., & Klinger, D. W. (1992). *Integrated measurement of crew resource management and technical flying skills.* Final Report under contract DTRS-57-89-D-0086 for the Federal Aviation Administration. Fairborn, OH: Klein Associates Inc.

Kahneman, D., & Tversky, A. (1982). The simulation heuristic. In D. Kahneman, P. Slovic, & A. Tversky (Eds.), *Judgment under uncertainty: Heuristics and biases* (pp. 201–210). Cambridge, MA: Cambridge University Press.

Kail, R. V., & Hagen, J. W. (Eds.). (1977). *Perspectives on the development of memory and cognition.* Hillsdale, NJ: Lawrence Erlbaum Associates.

Klein, G. A. (1989). Recognition-primed decisions. In W. Rouse (Ed.), *Advances in man–machine systems research* (Vol. 5, pp. 47–92). Greenwich, CT: JAI Press.

Klein, G. A. (1992). Using knowledge engineering to preserve corporate memory. In R. R. Hoffman (Ed.), *Psychology of expertise: Cognitive research and empirical AI*. New York: Springer–Verlag.

Klein, G. A., & Calderwood, R. (1988). How do people use analogues to make decisions? *Proceedings of a workshop on case-based reasoning*, 209–223. San Mateo, CA: Morgan Kauffman Publishers.

Klein, G. A., Calderwood, R., & Clinton-Cirocco, A. (1986). Rapid decision making on the fire ground. *Proceedings of the Human Factors Society 30th Annual Meeting, 1*, 576–580. Dayton, OH: Human Factors Society.

Klein, G. A., & Peio, K. J. (1989). The use of a prediction paradigm to evaluate proficient decision making. *American Journal of Psychology, 102*(3), 321–331.

Larkin, J., McDermott, J., Simon, D. P., & Simon, H. A. (1980). Expert and novice performance in solving physics problems. *Science, 208*, 1335–1342.

Lee, C. (1991, October). Who gets trained in what. *Training*. Minneapolis: Lakewood.

Lesgold, A., Rubinson, H., Feltovich, P., Klopfer, D., & Glaser, R. (1985). *Impasses in complex perceptual learning*. University of Pittsburgh, PA: Learning Research and Development Center.

Lintern, G. (1991). An informational perspective on skill transfer for human–machine systems. *Human Factors, 33*, 251–266.

McFarren, M. R. (1987). *Using concept maps to define problems and identify key kernels during the development of a decision support system*. Unpublished master's thesis, Air Force Institute of Technology, Dayton, OH.

McNeese, M. D., Zapf, B. S., Peio, K. J., Snyder, D. E., Duncan, J. C., & McFarren, M. R. (1990). *An advanced knowledge and design acquisition methodology: Application for the pilot's associate* (Final Report AAMRL-TR-90-060). WPAFB, OH: Armstrong Aerospace Medical Research Laboratory.

Means, B., Salas, E., Crandall, B. W., & Jacobs, T. O. (in press). Training decision makers for the real world. In G. A. Klein, J. Orasanu, R. Calderwood, & C. E. Zsambok (Eds.), *Decision making in action: Models and methods*. Norwood, NJ: Ablex.

Orstein, P. A. (Ed.). (1978). *Memory development in children*. Hillsdale, NJ: Lawrence Erlbaum Associates.

Pennington, N., & Hastie, R. (in press). A theory of explanation-based decision making. In G. Klein, J. Orasanu, R. Calderwood, & C. E. Zsambok (Eds.), *Decision-making in action: Models and methods*. Norwood, NJ: Ablex.

Phelps, R. H., & Shanteau, J. (1978). Livestock judges: How much information can an expert use? *Organizational Behavior and Human Performance, 21*, 109–219.

Rothkopf, E. (1982, October). *Basic research and applied psychology: The quest for symbiosis*. Paper presented at the First Annual Adelphia University Conference on Applied Experimental Psychology, Adelphi University, Garden City, NY.

Schank, R. C. (1990). *Tell me a story*. New York: Scribner.

Schneider, W. (1985). Training high-performance skills: Fallacies and guidelines. *Human Factors, 273*, 285–300.

Schvaneveldt, R. W. (Ed.). (1991). *Pathfinder associative networks*. Norwood, NJ: Ablex.

Shanteau, J. (1985). Psychological characteristics of expert decision makers. *Applied Experimental Psychology Series, 85*(2). Kansas State University, Manhattan, KS.

Simon, H. A., & Gilmartin, K. (1973). A simulation of memory for chess positions. *Cognitive Psychology, 5*, 29–46.

Swets, J. A., & Bjork, R. A. (1990). Enhancing human performance: An evaluation of "New Age" techniques considered by the U.S. Army. *Psychological Science, 1*, 85–96.

Weitzenfeld, J. S., Klein, G. A., Riedl, T. R., Freeman, J. T., & Musa, J. (1991, October). Knowledge elicitation for software engineering expertise. *Proceedings of the Fifth SEI Conference on Software Engineering Education*, Pittsburgh, PA.

Wilensky, R. (1983). *Planning and understanding: A computational approach to human reasoning*. Reading, MA: Addison-Wesley.

Author Index

Note: Italicized page numbers refer to bibliography pages.

Subject Index